# FOR DUTY AND HONOR

# FOR DUTY AND HONOR

## Tennessee's Mexican War Experience

# TIMOTHY D. JOHNSON

## The University of Tennessee Press

Frontispiece: Courtesy of David Wright.

**Search Tennessee's Mexican War rosters at:** utpress.org/downloads

Library of Congress Cataloging-in-Publication Data

Names: Johnson, Timothy D., 1957- author.

Title: For duty and honor : Tennessee's Mexican War experience /
    Timothy D. Johnson.

Description: First edition. | Knoxville : The University of Tennessee Press,
    [2018] | Includes bibliographical references and index. |

Identifiers: LCCN 2018019675 (print) | LCCN 2018019967 (ebook) |
    ISBN 9781621904397 (kindle) | ISBN 9781621904380 |
    ISBN 9781621904380 (hardcover)

Subjects: LCSH: Mexican War, 1846-1848—Tennessee. | Tennessee—History,
    Military—19th century. | Soldiers—Tennessee—History—19th century.

Classification: LCC E409.5.T4 (ebook) | LCC E409.5.T4 J65 2018 (print) |
    DDC 973.6/2—dc23

LC record available at https://lccn.loc.gov/2018019675

Designed and composed
by Nathan W. Moehlmann,
Goosepen Studio & Press

# CONTENTS

# ILLUSTRATIONS

# ACKNOWLEDGMENTS

As is always the case, writing a book for an academic press requires the assistance of a lot of people. Research for such a study takes one to far-flung, unexpected places—and I mean that in both a geographic and mental sense. And writing is an exercise best done in quiet solitude and with time granted by a reduced teaching load. Then, at the end of several years of labor, there must be an editor at a press who sees value in the project and who offers to consider it for publication. At the outset, I acknowledge and extend my gratitude to two institutions for supporting this work, and for providing the circumstances necessary to bring this book to fruition. Lipscomb University has always provided me with necessary resources to allow me to travel to repositories, and in recent years, I have benefitted from reduced classroom duties, giving me broader opportunities to press forward with this project. I especially wish to thank Provost Craig Bledsoe, along with Norma Burgess, Dean of the College of Liberal Arts, and Sciences and Howard Miller, Chair of the Department of History, Politics and Philosophy at Lipscomb for their ongoing support. As is always the case, the staff at Lipscomb's Beaman Library (especially Eunice Wells) went over and beyond the call of duty to provide cheerful assistance. The other institution to which I am indebted is the University of Tennessee Press. Scot Danforth, Director of the Press, has had a keen interest in this project since I first mentioned it to him several years ago, and he was eager to receive the finished manuscript for consideration. I have worked with the staff at UT Press before, knew the quality of their work, and was pleased that the press embraced this project.

Others have provided various forms of support, and I acknowledge their gracious assistance. One of my students, Sterling Bishir, entered all of the names of the Tennessee volunteers by company and regiment onto a spreadsheet, which was a valuable addition to my research. Al Austelle at Lipscomb University is always willing and able to assist me when I have technology questions. Jennifer Pepper made it possible for me to have a picture of William Walton with her excellent pencil sketch. I am grateful to the following people at the Tennessee State Library and Archives: Myers Brown, Tom Kanon, Darla Brock, and Megan Spainhour. From the Tennessee State Museum, I appreciate the aid of Richard White, Robert DeHart, and Debbie Shaw. In rendering unique help in my research efforts, I thank John O'Brien of the Pratt Museum at Fort Campbell, Trevor Plante at the National Archives, Bruce Winders at the Alamo, Congresswoman Diane Black, and also Beth Weaver (MD) who shared her medical expertise. I especially acknowledge Jon Atkins of Berry College, whose insights helped guide me through Tennessee's political history and Annalisa Zox-Weaver who helped me improve the quality of the narrative. Several friends, like Lowell Hagewood and Guy Swanson, shared their past research and offered helpful counsel. Still others provided me with their knowledge, insights, family papers, and pictures, and I gratefully acknowledge their help: Carole Bucy, Frank and Johnnie Curry, Sheri Eubanks, Jamie Johnson, Kristi Jones, Wayne King, Nathan Knight, Robin Montgomery, Charles Richards, Tom Seals, Kenneth Thomson, Ahmed Valtier, Mary Ann Short Warren, and Rick Warwick. Also, my thanks go to John Holtzapple and Thomas Price at the James K. Polk Home in Columbia.

Two people warrant special recognition. Derek Frisby is a friend and fellow historian who teaches at Middle Tennessee State University. We have worked together for several years on the "Battle of Monterrey Skeletal Remains Project," and in our collaboration, he provided valuable insight into my efforts to reconstruct the events that unfolded at Monterrey on September 21, 1846. Derek is a tireless and meticulous researcher. He is also a talented cartographer, and I thank him for applying his expertise in creating the maps in this book. Also, I owe my thanks to David Wright, an accomplished artist from Gallatin, Tennessee. One of David's paintings depicts Tennessee volunteers marching off to war in 1846 with Gallatin's Mexican War Monument and an American Flag in the background. When I saw it in his studio, I asked if I could use the image for the cover of this book, and he graciously consented.

Finally, I must extend thanks to the growing Johnson clan. I am grateful for my family's interest in my work and for the inspiration they provide. So, my thanks go to Jayne, Garrett, Griffin, Angi, Graham, Lindsey, and also to my mother, Bea. I also wish to remember my father, Hollis Johnson, and my father-in-law, Harold Pierce, both of whom passed away within a month of each other while my work on this book was in progress. On a lighter note, granddaughters Amelia and Maddie Blake have discovered my study and have a great fascination with books (and the keys on my laptop). So now a shelf in one of my bookcases is dedicated to their interests, which Amelia says is "perfect."

I have striven to make this a story worth reading, and also one that is fair and accurate. For any of my shortcomings in accomplishing this task, I apologize and take full responsibility.

TIM JOHNSON
*Lipscomb University*
*Nashville, TN*

# PROLOGUE

The discovery of skeletal remains in Monterrey, Mexico, several years ago was a significant event. Because of artifacts found with the bones, local authorities quickly concluded that they must have been U.S. soldiers killed at the Battle of Monterrey in 1846 during the Mexican-American War. The location of the burial sites, close to a fort that had been attacked by the First Tennessee Regiment, led to a hypothesis that some of the remains might belong to Tennessee volunteers. Thus, began an effort, spearheaded by Captain Jim Page, army historian at Fort Campbell, to bring the remains back to the United States. This story is shared in greater detail in the Epilogue, but I relate this much here to give the reader a sense of when and how I first became interested in Tennesseans and their role in the war. I heard Captain Page speak on the subject in Nashville in 2011, and found the story of the bones intriguing. I had spent considerable time researching and writing about the Mexican-American War, but my past work had not dealt specifically with Tennessee's involvement in the conflict, and frankly, I knew very little about my home state's role in the war. I began to dig deeper into the lives of the Tennesseans who had volunteered to go to Mexico in 1846 and 1847, and soon decided that there was a larger story worth telling to a broader audience. That was the beginning of my resolve to write this book.

Americans, in general, know very little about the war with Mexico, despite its significance to the history of the United States. The two-year conflict required the collaboration of a small regular army with a mass influx of volunteers to achieve the nation's objectives. It was America's first expeditionary war, its first experience with large scale guerrilla operations, and its first time to engage in urban combat. When it ended with the Treaty of Guadalupe Hidalgo in 1848, it had changed the country significantly. The Mexican-American War is important to American history for two reasons. First because it expanded the nation's western border to the Pacific Ocean, thus bringing to fruition manifest destiny's dream of territorial control over the entire continent. Second, it accelerated the coming of the Civil War, while serving as a training ground for the generation of young officers who later led Union and Confederate armies. But the Mexican War is one of the forgotten conflicts in American history for the same two reasons: the territorial conquest is seen as an unjust land grab and therefore unworthy of commemoration, and the war that it helped foster just fifteen years later was so large that it relegated the earlier, smaller conflict to the shadows of history.

Historians have worked to bring the Mexican War out of the shadows by producing a growing list of worthy titles, but few of them are studies of particular battles or units. Christopher Dishman's book on the Battle of Monterrey and Richard Bruce Winders's study of the First and Second Mississippi Volunteer Regiments are rare examples. Nor have there been studies conducted of particular states and their role in the conflict, with Randy Hackenburg's book on Pennsylvanians being a notable exception. Tennessee has never been the focus of a Mexican-American War study, despite the state's significant role in the conflict. Even general Tennessee state histories provide only cursory overviews. For example, Robert Corlew's well-circulated and oft-read history of Tennessee includes less than a page on the Mexican War. Paul H. Bergeron, Stephen V. Ash, and Jeanette Keith are co-authors of *Tennesseans and Their History*, a general survey that contains but a couple of passing references to the war.[1] With over five thousand Tennesseans volunteering to fight in Mexico and with a native son as commander-in-chief, there is justification to think of the conflict as a major chapter in the state's history. This study endeavors to tell the story of Tennessee's Mexican War experience.

Why fight a war with Mexico? Politicians North and South often viewed the desire to expand slavery as a driving force behind the war, and abolitionists were convinced that the conflict was being waged in a quest for new slave territories. No one can doubt that the slavery issue played a role in the desire to push the nation's borders west. Even President James K. Polk's expansionist policies were motivated, at least in part, by his financial investments in land and slaves. Tennessee's political and economic hierarchy supported the war, but the extent to which slavery served as their primary motivation deserves scrutiny. At the time of the war and in the years immediately following, about a third of Tennessee households owned nearly three-fourths of the land property. However, only 2 percent of households met the definition of planter (twenty or more slaves). During the decade of the 1840s, the percentage of slave-owning state legislators dropped from 79 percent to 65 percent. This suggests that slavery's influence on policymakers in Tennessee might have actually declined during the period.[2]

However, breaking the state down into its three sections, or as Tennesseans call them, the three grand divisions (west, middle, and east), a different perspective emerges that indicates at least a possible correlation between support for slavery and support for the war. According to 1841 numbers, no legislators from East Tennessee owned slaves, thirty-three legislators from Middle Tennessee were slave owners, and from West Tennessee thirteen legislators owned slaves.[3] When one compares these numbers to the state's volunteer companies by section at the outset of the war, one finds the following. Three regiments of volunteers were mustered into service in May and June 1846 (two infantry and one mounted). Those regiments contained a total of thirty companies: six from West Tennessee, sixteen from Middle Tennessee, and eight from East Tennessee. That more Tennesseans volunteered from the section with the most slaveholding legislators suggests a possible link between support for the war and support for slavery, but East Tennessee, with eight volunteer companies and zero slave-owning legislators, makes such a connection problematic.

So, while the connection between slave interests and the war were certainly demonstrable, it should not be over-estimated in assessing why the average Tennessean volunteered to fight. Indeed, one would be hard pressed to find references to slavery in the correspondence of the state's volunteers. Some may have volunteered out of economic self-interest.

In the past, veterans had received land bounties and pensions for their service, and such prospects may have been an incentive for lower classes. However, what one finds repeatedly in letters and diaries are references to terms like duty, honor, and glory. Because historians have generally argued that the conflict was a dishonorable land grab, it seems incongruent that Tennesseans often cited honor as a primary motivation for volunteering to fight. But that was not an unusual factor when one recalls that they lived in an honor-driven culture when a man's good name counted for everything and when reputations were determined by one's willingness to fight for a cause. Honor and virtue were common traits of manliness in the early republic. While these characteristics were generally acquired through public perception and "resided largely in the life of the mind," they often were demonstrated in deadly contests of masculinity.[4] This study argues that Tennesseans were less motivated by slavery and policy decisions in Washington and more concerned with community expectations and personal responsibility, that is to say, honor.

Moreover, it was not just personal but also state and national honor that elicited a sense of obligation or duty. Today it is common to say that a soldier died "in the line of duty," but the phrase as used in the nineteenth century was "in the line of his duty." Modern usage has dropped the possessive pronoun "his," thus rendering the meaning of duty as something more generic and impersonal; but, a century-and-a-half ago, duty was a binding obligation deeply felt by every individual. Convinced in their belief that the Rio Grande was the legitimate Texas border, Tennesseans rushed to defend the country's honor when its territorial integrity was violated–they did so out of duty. It was, after all, a time when people believed in the sanctity of borders. Such motivations to fight in 1846 were felt across the country, but they were particularly acute in Southern states like Tennessee. In his 1982 book *Southern Honor*, Bertram Wyatt-Brown reminds readers that honor was at the center of the South's moral code.[5]

Another factor compounded the ramifications of doing one's duty, and it had to do with battlefield success or failure. The concept of honor was intensified by the fact that in the nineteenth century, volunteer companies were raised in local communities. Sometimes they were simply local militia companies that had been organized on paper for years, and the members of such units were neighbors, friends, and former schoolmates. In cases when it was necessary to raise a company from scratch, local men from a town or from several communities generally clustered in the same county would show up at the designated location to enlist. So, for example, a Lawrence County company would be made up of approximately a hundred young men mostly from Lawrenceburg but also from surrounding towns in the county; a Madison County company would be comprised of men from the town of Jackson and surrounding areas, and so on. Ten companies then came together to form a regiment of approximately a thousand men. That meant that towns and counties took particular pride in their units and monitored the news to discover how their boys had performed in combat. That in turn put added pressure on the soldiers who knew that their conduct would not go unnoticed. Their actions on the battlefield would be a great source of satisfaction or disappointment, pride or embarrassment to family and friends back home, and success or failure could have an impact on postwar relationships, opportunities, and careers.

In his recent study of Mississippians, noted Mexican War scholar Richard Bruce Winders deftly describes what motivated the typical 1846 volunteer. "The quest for personal, state, and national glory was a powerful motive in the Mexican War. The possibility of achieving it was thought worth the risk of one's life." In comparing the wartime and postwar experiences of those regiments, Winders demonstrates that the level of success experienced in combat correlated to postwar attitudes. "Attaining glory made for reputation, honor, and a bright future. The lack of it left a soldier with his hope for fame unfilled–a peasant among heroes."[6] What Winders described in Mississippi also applied in Tennessee.

Honor may have motivated Tennesseans more than others because in its brief history as a state, honor had been a characteristic trait. Tennessee was only fifty years old in 1846 and was still in the process of becoming. In 1809, Andrew Jackson, James Robertson, and other prominent Tennesseans asserted a willingness to "risk our lives and fortunes to support the cause of our country," in the event of a war with England.[7] A few years later, many of them proved true to their word by volunteering to fight against the Creek Indians and, more notably, the British. The same sentiments were prevalent three-and-a-half decades later. A young state that was searching for an identity in 1812 had found it by 1846. In addition to fighting for their country's honor, Tennesseans in 1846 felt compelled to volunteer in order to uphold their state's honor. "I fear not that our Tennesseans will nobly sustain the character won for us by Jackson & his men during the last war," wrote politician and Creek War veteran Cave Johnson.[8]

Their fathers' generation had rallied to the flag under Jackson, winning for Tennessee the sobriquet "the volunteer state." Thirty-four years later, the sons felt an obligation to maintain that reputation by once again demonstrating that Tennesseans were courageous, patriotic, and ready to risk their lives for a cause. As historian Tom Kanon explains in his study, *Tennesseans at War 1812–1815*, it was the revolutionary spirit of '76 that animated Tennesseans in 1812. In like manner, it was, to a degree, the spirit of 1812 that animated Tennesseans in 1846. "We had all heard and read of such days in history," wrote John McClanahan, a Mexican War volunteer from Jackson, Tennessee, "and thirsted for an opportunity to show that the iron hearted fortitude and indomitable courage of our ancestors had not degenerated in their sons." In an 1847 article entitled "The Volunteer State," *The National Union*, the Democratic Party's flagship paper in Washington, gushed that the "proud name which Tennessee earned in the last war is being gloriously sustained in this" one. Thus, the state's famous moniker "volunteer state" that originated with Jackson in the War of 1812 was reinforced and solidified during the Mexican-American War. As the Prussian-born Nashville architect and Mexican War veteran Adolphus Heiman wrote in 1858, "Tennessee deserves the name of the 'Volunteer State.'"[9]

The volunteers were Tennesseans first, but they were also Americans with a sense of obligation to country. Their willingness to sacrifice for the advancement of the nation's destiny is clearly articulated by McClanahan, who served in the Second Tennessee Volunteer Regiment. After complaining in a letter home about the pay that volunteers received, he went on to assure his family that he and his comrades answered their country's call gladly despite pecuniary concerns. "I am proud to say that all our volunteers perform all their duties and undergo all their hardships with no less cheerfulness. They are determined to have no duty to their country unperformed, though they should be paid up wholly and solely in *patriotism*." He went on to assure his family that "A place in the hearts of his countrymen is the soldier's reward. We expected little else when we left home, and if we secure it, we shall return happy and amply paid." Historian Bertram Wyatt-Brown aptly sums up the multiple levels and manifestations of honor that were at the core of the South's system of ethics. They included "inner feelings of self-worth, . . . public repute, valor for family and country, and conformity to community wishes."[10]

By volunteering to fight in Mexico, many Americans believed they were advancing the country's destiny through territorial expansion. The lust for land guided goals and ambitions in the nineteenth century. Land acquisition was not just a way of measuring wealth, it was the vehicle by which republican principles would spread across the entire continent. If the War of 1812 had firmly established a permanent foundation of republican principles for the young nation, the acquisition of western land was intended to build on that foundation and expand republicanism for future generations. For Tennesseans, Andrew Jackson had been the key figure in 1812–1814, and the next generation would see its territorial dreams realized by another of its native sons, James K. Polk. Indeed, it seemed that Old Hickory had passed the torch to his protégé, Young Hickory.[11]

Glory and adventure were also reasons why Americans volunteered to fight in Mexico, and those reasons held true for Tennesseans as well.[12] For a young man from modest economic origins, battlefield glory was a viable way to offset the lack of property and power. Whether men were rich or poor, war provided the opportunity to prove their courage and manliness in a victorious struggle, and then return home to family, friends, and sweethearts as a hero. Such accolades could pave the way for all kinds of advancements. Three of Tennessee's Mexican War veterans became governors: William Trousdale, William B. Campbell, and William B. Bate. They were inaugurated in 1847, 1849, and 1883, respectively, with the third one, Bate, benefitting more from his status as a Confederate general in the Civil War. Numerous other veterans were elected to a host of state and local political offices.

No doubt many other reasons compelled approximately 5,400 Tennessee volunteers to go to Mexico: one being the lingering animosity over the Alamo and the fate of one of Tennessee's favorite sons, David Crockett. It was not just revenge for Crockett's death, but revenge for a series of perceived Mexican atrocities. And perhaps there was present in the thoughts of some Tennesseans a bit of that mind set described by W. J. Cash in his classic study of the southerner that "nothing living could cross him and get away with it." Moreover, many people still felt an affinity to former Tennessean and loyal Jackson lieutenant Sam Houston, a veteran of the Battle of Horseshoe Bend, who later sealed Texas independence at the Battle of San Jacinto, and subsequently served as President of the Republic of Texas.[13]

Tennessee's Mexican War experience is largely a military story, but not exclusively. Five regiments of infantry and one of mounted troops served in the war, but only two, the First and Second Tennessee, saw significant combat. Much of this book will focus on those two regiments and their primary combat roles at Monterrey, Veracruz, and Cerro Gordo, but it will examine more than just the battlefield experiences of Tennesseans. It will treat the disparate results of those two regiments' military experience and their return home. The First Tennessee, which made a daring, bloody, and successful charge at Monterrey enjoyed a brighter postwar experience than the Second Tennessee, which made a daring, bloody but unsuccessful charge at Cerro Gordo. The postwar careers of the two regimental commanders, William Campbell and William Haskell provide a window through which one sees the importance of martial success and its impact on honor, acceptance by society, and a sense of self-worth.

Gideon Pillow also played an important role in Tennessee's Mexican War experience. A friend of the president, he was able to escape the consequences of mediocre leadership and even received promotion after his dismal showing at the Battle of Cerro Gordo. Before the war even had ended, Pillow went after his detractors with a vengeance and was able to salvage enough of his reputation to still be regarded as worthy of a general's commission at the start of the Civil War. Pillow's story is a sterling example that even in the mid-nineteenth century, who one knew was as important as what one knew.

The most prominent character during the conflict was President Polk, from Columbia, Tennessean. So, politics, state and presidential, along with anti-war sentiments, constitute other facets of the story that are worthy of examination. Many of the state's loyal Jacksonian Democrats revolted in the mid-1830s to form a highly competitive Whig Party in Tennessee. Their revolt came as a result of Andrew Jackson's heavy-handed approach to the exercise of executive power, and a decade later, the state remained divided over Polk's aggressive war policies. A few historians have written about state politics during this period, most notably Jonathan Atkins and Paul Bergeron, and this study relies on their work, especially Atkins's.[14] Thus, the reader will find that the opening chapter attempts to trace the rough and tumble of Tennessee politics and the development of Polk the politician in the years prior to the war. An anti-war movement also arose in 1846–1847. In Tennessee, as elsewhere, it manifested primarily through Polk's political opponents. However, some people were motivated by moral concerns over pacifism, most notably in the religious community. Such sentiments were present in Polk's home state, and is treated in chapter 8.

Despite being consistently ranked by historians in the upper echelon of important presidents, Polk remains relatively unknown to the general public. The *Baltimore Sun* predicted that Polk's accomplishments would cause his administration to be "recorded as one of the most brilliant in the annals of the nation." But such was not the case. One of his early biographers surmised that Polk lacked the personal characteristics to attract admiring followers, and it is true, he did not have charm or affability nor was he given to compromise. Personally, he was dour, humorless, and puritanical. Professionally, he was a fastidious leader. Politically he was autocratic and Machiavellian. In sum, he accomplished great things but was an unlikeable person. Add to that Polk's leadership over a morally questionable war that intensified the country's sectional problems, and the result is a presidential administration more often pilloried than praised. A modern biographer states it well: "Probably no other president presents such a chasm between actual accomplishment and popular recognition."[15]

Before becoming president, Polk had built his resume in the divisive political arena created by Jackson. Like Jackson before him, Polk had come to Middle Tennessee from the Carolinas, and his family settled in Columbia fifty miles south of Nashville. He returned to his native state to attend the University of North Carolina, and after graduation in 1818, the twenty-three year old began his study of law in Nashville under the brilliant attorney Felix Grundy. Polk was elected to the state legislature in 1823, married Sarah Childress, daughter of a prominent Murfreesboro planter, in 1824, and was elected to the first of seven terms in the United States House of Representatives in 1825. During his fourteen-year tenure in the House, including four as Speaker, he was a staunch Jacksonian Democrat; so loyal to Old Hickory that he earned his nickname Young Hickory. When Jackson's use of executive power led to a political revolt in his home state, Polk returned to Tennessee in an effort to shore up the party, and in the process, he won a hard-fought gubernatorial race. By the time Young Hickory ran for president, he was already experienced in waging partisan battles.

Jackson and Polk were Tennessee's most visible political figures in the 1830s and 1840s, and their strong personalities had political ramifications not only across the state but in national politics as well. The term "strong personality" is not meant to imply extroverted or affable, for, as stated earlier, Polk was neither. Rather, it refers to determination, exertion of power, and the ability to get things done. In the twenty years from Old Hickory's inauguration to the end of Young Hickory's presidency, Tennessee went from a backwater western state that was not much more than a footnote in national politics to an emerging state with an influential position on the country's political landscape. Add Felix Grundy to the mix, and you have what one study refers to as a "Democratic Triumvirate . . . who had together brought the backwoods democracy of Tennessee to prominence in national affairs."[16]

During this same two-decade prelude to the Mexican War, Tennesseans were conspicuously involved in Texas history. Prior to its revolution, when Texas was still part of Mexico, President Jackson attempted to acquire the area. He believed that Texas was originally a part of the Louisiana Purchase in 1803, but that John Quincy Adams had negotiated it away in the Adams-Onís Treaty in 1819. As president, he instructed his Minister to Mexico, Anthony Butler, to negotiate the cession of Texas to the United States. Butler, however, lacked finesse and in time pursued a bribery scheme when certain Mexican officials informed him that a half million dollars well-placed in the hands of the right people would further the transfer of Texas into American hands. Jackson rejected the questionable method and recalled Minister Butler.[17]

Meanwhile, numerous prominent Tennesseans played an important role in the settlement of Texas. James Robertson, founder of Nashville, had relatives involved in efforts to colonize this sparsely settled region of northern Mexico. His sons, Peyton, John, and William, grandson James and nephew, Sterling, were among seventy Tennessee investors who founded a land company called the Texas Association. It secured a land grant in 1825 in present-day Milam County, northeast of Austin, and for the next decade the company promoted settlement in the area. The Texas Association met with limited success, its efforts being particularly hampered when one of its land agents, Nashvillian Hosea H. League, was implicated as an accessory to murder in 1830. Over the years, the land grant given to the Texas Association was known by various names, including the Robertson Colony and eventually Nashville on the Brazos.

Sam Houston also invested in the Texas Association and later found his way to Texas after resigning the governorship of Tennessee. His role in helping Texas win its independence in 1836 is well-known. David Crockett was another prominent Tennessean who ended up in Texas. After losing his Congressional seat in a close race in 1835, he wrote, "As my country no longer requires my services, I have made up my mind to go to Texas." Or, according to other sources, his words to a Memphis crowd were, "You may all go to hell, and I will go to Texas!" A few months after his arrival, he and more than thirty other Tennesseans died at the Alamo. A relative of Sarah Childress Polk and editor of Nashville's first daily newspaper, George Childress, went to Texas in 1836, and soon after he wrote the Texas Declaration of Independence. It was republican idealism that fueled much of the influx of American immigrants who ventured to Texas in the 1830s.[18]

Annexing Texas was a popular idea with many people but also a politically perilous one. Slavery and the abolitionists made the addition of any new territory a controversy, so Jackson did not actively pursue it before leaving office. His successor, Martin Van Buren, also treaded lightly on the annexation issue. With the passage of several years, the national mood changed, and the expansionist impulse superseded abolitionists' arguments. President John Tyler succeeded in getting an annexation resolution passed just before he left office in 1845, and after Polk's inauguration a few days later, the new administration completed the process of bringing Texas into the Union. Because of Tennessee's contributions to the early history of Texas, many people view the two states as more or less joined at the hip. So deep and rich is the legacy of the Tennessee-Texas connection that, in 2014, a local historian in Houston wrote an opinion piece for a Texas newspaper entitled, "Tennessee, Mother State of Texas."[19]

Thus, in 1846, many Tennessee families had already invested time, money, and energy in Texas, and defending its border seemed imperative to securing the safe entry of Texas into the Union. But even before the war began, the Tennessean in the White House was looking beyond Texas, all the way to California as a way of solidifying America's destiny as a continental power. From the rural crossroads communities of Tennessee all the way to Pennsylvania Avenue, Tennesseans of various stripes and economic origins eagerly did their part to advance their country's cause. This account describes and analyzes the role that Tennesseans played in the Mexican War and their efforts to maintain the memory of that war in the decades that followed.

*Chapter One*

# BACKGROUND: POLITICS AND TEXAS

Political competition in Tennessee in the 1830s and 1840s was, in many respects, a microcosm of national politics. At the center of both the formation of the Democratic Party and the development of the second party system was Tennessean Andrew Jackson, who was still remembered as the hero of New Orleans. He became president, promising to clean out aristocratic elitism and give average Americans a voice in Washington. His mission was consistent with republican principles, and evidence that his message resonated with average Americans was clear from the 1828 election results. Nationally, Jackson won 56 percent of the popular vote and carried every Southern and western state, to the dismay and consternation of the East Coast establishment.

Republicanism—that is, limited constitutional government—was the cornerstone belief of the Founders and was still the prevalent ideology across the country when Jackson became president. The young nation still firmly adhered to this belief and was committed to the idea that the people should rule, not be ruled. Pervasive government, special privilege, and executive power have no place in a republic because, as nineteenth-century Americans knew, the level of freedom that individuals enjoy is in inverse ratio to the size of government.[1] These were the principles that swept the Tennessean into office in 1828. Jackson was the very embodiment of the common man, and his mission was to purge the government of the corruption and special interest that had contaminated the Founders' original intent. Jackson's political movement helped to make the notion of "democracy"—once a dirty word—acceptable because it carried with it the idea of returning government to the people.

Four years later, he carried two-thirds of the states, winning 54 percent of the popular vote in a decisive reelection. In 1832, Jackson was still the favorite son in his home state, where he received over 95 percent of the vote in twenty-six of Tennessee's sixty-two counties, and citizens in eight counties voted unanimously for him. However, within two years, both he and his party were losing their grip on state politics. After 1832, Jackson, his policies, and his party began to fall out of favor, and the state did not go for another Democratic presidential candidate until 1856.[2]

The root cause of this dissatisfaction was excessive executive power. The revolt that resulted from Jackson's use of executive power most noticeably manifested in several episodes, but for Tennesseans there were two troubling examples. The first was Jackson's veto of a bill to recharter the national bank because of his belief that it was a special interest that benefitted the aristocratic class. Including his use of the pocket veto, the bank recharter bill was the fourth time Jackson had used the power of the veto. Most Tennesseans had taken a moderate position on the Nullification Crisis by siding with Jackson against South Carolina radicals, but in the matter of the bank recharter, views varied. Some, like John Bell and Ephraim H. Foster, favored the monetary stability represented by the bank. When Old Hickory turned to fellow Tennessean James K. Polk of the House Ways and Means Committee for support, the congressman authored a Congressional report charging the bank with fiscal mismanagement. Polk also asserted that the bank's Nashville branch followed unsound and risky practices. In response, pro-bank business leaders in Tennessee spoke out against the administration's fiscal policy. Hundreds came together in Nashville in April 1833 to protest Polk's bank report.[3]

Some might have been willing to go along with the president's veto of the recharter bill, but when he decided to "kill the bank" by forcing the Treasury Department to remove government deposits, his stern and unyielding action took on a vindictive air of recklessness. The manner in which he went about it appeared as ominous as the act itself. Going against a house resolution, Jackson instructed Treasury Secretary William Duane to remove federal deposits from the bank. When Duane voiced his opposition to the directive—along with his refusal to resign in September 1833—the president dismissed him and appointed a new cabinet official, Roger B. Taney, who carried out his order. But some questioned whether Jackson could fire a member of his cabinet without Senate approval since his appointment had required that body's consent. No president had ever tried to remove a member of his cabinet, so the question of constitutionality had never come up. Jackson, however, believing that he was perfectly within his rights as chief executive officer, did not seek approval before acting. Thus, he had used questionable means to accomplish a questionable end and, in doing so, had assumed unprecedented presidential power. Jackson's heavy-handed approach to dealing with policy differences had become an unwelcome exercise of executive power that was anything but republican.[4]

Nationally, the Bank War, as historians call it, served as the immediate impetus for Jackson's political enemies—Henry Clay, Daniel Webster, and others—to mobilize their efforts into the formation of an opposition party. Having already dubbed the president "King Andrew" because of his authoritarian ways, they called their new party "the Whigs" after the party in England that had historically opposed monarchy, and Whigs intended to benefit from his abuse of power. Even fellow Democrats opposed the president on the issue of removing the deposits—for example, John C. Calhoun, who likened Jackson to Julius Caesar, who raided the Roman treasury.[5] In Tennessee, Jackson's unyielding economic policy and his one-sided political patronage caused formerly loyal Democrats to condemn his dictatorial methods. Party fidelity eroded quickly in Jackson's home state.

The second factor that led to a robust Whig Party in Tennessee revolved around the Democratic nominee for president in 1836. When Jackson backed New Yorker Martin Van Buren over fellow Tennessean Hugh Lawson White, low rumblings of dissatisfaction erupted into a major political revolt against what was perceived as arbitrary and capricious displays of executive power. John Bell, Balie Peyton, Ephraim Foster, Newton Cannon, John Williams, and other prominent Tennesseans led the opposition. They concluded that Jackson had become the embodiment of anti-republicanism by threatening the purity of the federal government through the concentration of power in the executive branch.[6] One Tennessee legislator, Andrew Buchanan from Warren County, gave voice to such fears. "The encroachments of despotism are slow and . . . small, until at length the arm of power is so strong that the people can no longer withstand it." Despotism is an incremental process whose gradualism is often unnoticed until it is too late. "The despot does not usurp at once all the powers which he ultimately claims. He establishes his precedents by degrees." Buchanan continues, "He does not directly tell the people, I intend . . . to put men in office according to my sovereign will and pleasure, . . . he very politely offers to save the people the trouble."[7]

Personal relationships also played an important role in Tennessee politics in the 1830s. While most leading politicians who helped build the opposition party in Tennessee did so to preserve republican principles, some of them were perhaps persuaded to do so because of previous disagreements with Jackson. Newton Cannon first incurred Jackson's wrath in 1812, when, as a juror, he voted to acquit a man who was on trial for murdering a friend of Jackson. In 1835, Cannon was elected governor by defeating Old Hickory's choice, William Carroll. David Crockett, who had once fought alongside the president, had run afoul of Jackson before going to Texas. As a member of the state legislature in 1823, Crockett refused to vote for Jackson for senator, and as a United States Congressman in 1830 he voted against the Indian Removal Act. Moreover, they were on opposite sides in a longtime policy dispute over the disposition of land in West Tennessee. (Crockett did not want to uproot poor farmers who had squatted on the land but could not afford to buy it, whereas Jackson and Polk favored the proceeds going to an education fund. Crockett feared that land speculators and wealthy Jackson campaign supporters would control the proceeds to promote their own interests in West Tennessee.[8]) The consequence of their numerous disagreements on policy issues was that Crockett drifted toward the Whig

Party or, more accurately, Whig Party leadership increasingly saw him as a foil to Jackson. So, Jackson lent his support in Crockett's defeat for reelection. John Williams, brother-in-law of Hugh Lawson White, crossed swords with Jackson in 1814 over supplies for a new militia unit, and a few years later was critical of Jackson during the First Seminole War.[9]

Balie Peyton, a two-term Tennessee Congressman (1833–1837) from Sumner County, was first elected as a Jacksonian. He was an accomplished orator and, like Jackson, he loved horse racing. However, he broke with Old Hickory in 1836 over removal of the federal deposits, tariffs, and the president's spoils system. Peyton was one of several prominent Tennesseans who decided early on to endorse White as the Democratic nominee in 1836, and Jackson's rejection of White was another factor in Peyton's shift in allegiance.[10]

And then there was John Bell from Davidson County, who had once been a staunch supporter of Jackson but who became the central figure in Tennessee's Whig Party. The friction in their relationship was obvious during Bell's competition with Polk for Speaker of the House in 1834. Although the president did not actively support either, he was known to quietly favor Polk, but Bell won in a protracted battle that required ten ballots. As Speaker, Bell made gestures of friendship toward Jackson's men, and even paid the president a visit, accompanied by Balie Peyton, to assure him that he would support the president's policies. However, Bell's great sin was that he was pro-bank (his brother was director of the Nashville branch), and furthermore, he ignored the administration's warning that he change his position. The break was irreparable when Bell refused to support Jackson's hand-picked successor, Martin Van Buren. In May 1835, Bell gave a two-hour speech in Nashville, where he forcefully endorsed White for president. The rousing speech portrayed White as the true friend of the people, and his vehement oration helped ignite an all-out revolt against the Democratic Party in Tennessee. Jackson and Polk denounced Bell as a traitor.[11]

At times, Tennessee's political battles were played out on a national stage. In 1835, Polk again challenged Bell for the speakership, and this time, with Jackson's open support, he won. Bell's attempt to regain the speakership in 1837 failed. Sides had been chosen and enemies made. The

Polk-Bell speakership battle revealed just how deeply divided Jackson's disciples had become, especially in the home state of all three men.[12]

Some of the same issues that played a salient role in the development of the Whig Party in Tennessee—especially Old Hickory's use of executive power—had also fueled the opposition party on a national scale. Thus, Andrew Jackson was the key figure in the development of both parties. Like a nucleus at the center of an atom, with its positive and negative charges constantly orbiting around it, the Tennessean was at the center of the country's swirling political world. Some were attracted to him, others repelled by him. Regardless, it was Jackson around whom political issues revolved.

Hugh Lawson White, the man upon whom much of the 1836 controversy centered, warrants brief attention. Honest and intelligent, White, a Knoxville native, had succeeded Jackson as United States Senator, having been elected unanimously by the state legislature. He was a strict constructionist, opposed to internal improvements, and anti-bank, making him quite harmonious with his friend Jackson. Indeed, he was elected senator as a staunch Jacksonian Democrat. However, White, like so many other Tennesseans, parted ways with Jackson over executive power. Stung by Jackson's refusal to endorse his candidacy, he too joined the revolt and stayed in the race. White portrayed himself as the true defender of republican values and suggested that the aging Jackson had fallen under the spell of the Little Magician from New York. White was a popular candidate in Tennessee, which he won handily, and even carried Jackson's Hermitage precinct by a three-to-one margin, giving Old Hickory an embarrassing poke in the eye. However, White did not show well in other regions as the anti-Van Buren/Jackson vote split three ways among White, William Henry Harrison, and Daniel Webster. Van Buren might have succeeded in winning the successorship to King Andrew, but the 1836 election gave birth to a strong opposition party nationally and a highly competitive two-party system in Tennessee.[13]

From the mid-1830s to the mid-1850s, the state was evenly split between Democrat and Whig. After the anti-Jackson revolt, what had been a solidly Democrat state became an evenly matched, hotly contested state with Whigs often carrying the majority. When Newton Cannon, the state's first Whig governor, comfortably won reelection in 1837 with 61 percent of the vote, it seemed that the new opposition party held a decided advantage. With the Whigs surging, Tennessee Democrats turned to Polk as their nominee for governor in 1839. Polk agreed to step down as Speaker of the House and return home to oppose Cannon for a couple of reasons. First, lending his name to the gubernatorial race might blunt the Whig momentum. In addition, the economic downturn known as the Panic of 1837 had presumably resulted from Jackson's financial policies and consequently had given strength to the Whigs nationally, which provided Polk's second motivation to leave Congress. With growing uncertainty that the Democrats could maintain a majority and Polk his speakership, bowing out of the office gracefully seemed a better political move than waiting for the possibility of being ousted.[14]

The election results were favorable for Democrats in both the executive and legislative branches. Polk enthusiastically took on Cannon by portraying the Democrats as the real defenders of republican virtues. Aggressive electioneering gave Polk a narrow win, with 51 percent of the vote. The rapid defection to the Whig Party in Tennessee seemed stymied for the time being, but Polk's slim victory (2,500 votes) was achieved because he carried Middle Tennessee by a large enough margin to overcome Cannon, who carried the eastern and western counties of the state. The 1839 election ushered in twenty years of ebb and flow between the two parties wherein Whigs and Democrats traded the governor's chair almost every election and the winner never received more than 52 percent of the vote.[15] In addition to the governor's office, Democrats gained control of both houses of the state legislature. Both of Tennessee's sitting senators, Ephraim Foster and Hugh White, were Whigs. At that time, senators were chosen by the state legislatures and when the new Democratic majority in Nashville instructed its senators to vote in favor of President Van Buren's policies, Foster and White both resigned rather that submit. Both were replaced by Democrats.[16]

Polk clearly had emerged as heir to Jackson's political leadership, thus earning his nickname "Young Hickory." As Speaker of the House, he had served Jackson well and earned national recognition and, as governor of the state, he was not only the most important Democrat in Tennessee but he seemingly had rescued the state party from being overcome by the Whigs. Looking ahead to presidential politics, some Democrats were beginning to mention Polk for second place on the party's 1840 ticket, a development that the Tennessean would have eagerly welcomed if it had worked out. Young Hickory was optimistic and not opposed to being considered for the vice presidency.

However, the image of Polk halting the ascendancy of the Whigs in Tennessee turned out to be a mirage. Persistent economic woes in the state as well as throughout the country likely served as a drag that stymied Polk's efforts to restore the party. Nationally, the Democrats suffered their first presidential defeat when William Henry Harrison defeated Van Buren. And the Democrats were so divided on whom to choose as vice president that Van Buren ended up without a running mate. Closer to home, Harrison carried the state by over twelve thousand votes, thus demonstrating that all was certainly not well in Tennessee's Democratic Party. Moreover, Polk lost his bid for reelection in 1841 to Whig James C. Jones, and he lost again when he tried to unseat Jones in 1843. The 1840s turned out to be a Whig decade in Tennessee political history, much to the chagrin of the Jackson segment. Of the eight statewide elections in the decade, Whigs won six, while voter turnout consistently exceeded 80 percent. During this period, the state developed one of the most acrimonious political party competitions in the nation, and the intensity of the battles has been called "partisan fury."[17]

Polk was particularly stung by the loss of the governorship. At the dawn of the 1840s, despair forced Polk to ask himself what this meant for his party and what it meant for his political future. His loss and then victory over John Bell for Speaker of the House, his victory then loss of the governorship, and his failure to make it onto the Van Buren ticket in 1840 were all valuable political lessons. He attributed Whig victories to better organization and harder work. Four years later, Polk would enter the presidency accustomed to acrimony and partisanship.[18] Tight races and political losses had certainly schooled Polk in the harsh realities of politics, and taking into account his political past may help explain how he became such a sternly uncompromising president. On the political battlefield, Polk became determined to destroy Whig opposition in a way that would insure Democrat ascendancy. However, in the early 1840s, few people saw a Polk presidency on the horizon.

Perhaps the most valuable lesson Polk learned while in Congress may have come as a result of watching the way Jackson handled foreign policy disputes. Cases involving France and Mexico present two examples, and both had to do with the failure to pay American claims. In 1831, France had agreed to pay claims dating back to the Napoleonic Wars, but three years passed and it failed to honor the agreement. President Jackson sent an angry message to Congress and, after a heated diplomatic exchange, both countries withdrew their ministers amid talk of war. Cooler heads prevailed, and the French Chamber of Deputies agreed to pay the claims. The other example came late in Jackson's presidency and involved Mexican foot-dragging in the repayment of debts. Again, Jackson acted sternly, railing at Congress that Mexico's actions were adequate justification for war. The issue was not settled before Jackson left office, but in both cases nationalists like Polk saw that the best way to get results was with strong talk and direct confrontation.[19]

What Tennesseans could see in the early 1840s was a collision course with Mexico over Texas's southern border. It was a problem that had been brewing since the mid-1830s, when American immigrants to Texas had prominently participated in the uprising against Mexican rule. The Texas Revolution had ended with Antonio López de Santa Anna's sound defeat at San Jacinto, after which, Sam Houston forced him to sign the Treaty of Velasco, granting independence to the former Mexican state. However, the Mexican government never recognized the validity of the treaty because Santa Anna was a prisoner and thus had signed the treaty under duress. Furthermore, it was not just the legitimacy of Texas independence that Mexico City refused to recognize, it was also the border that the Republic of Texas claimed. The new Lone Star Republic claimed the Rio Grande as its southern boundary, while Mexicans argued that the traditional (and correct) boundary had always been the Nueces River, which flowed into the Gulf of Mexico at Corpus Christi a hundred miles farther north. In the decade following the Texas Revolution, Texans and

Mexicans endured an uneasy and sometimes volatile relationship with Mexican officials, always holding on to the hope of bringing its wayward state back under its control.

In this environment, clashes along the border were common. Jabez Dean arrived in Nashville on March 23, 1842, carrying copies of Galveston newspapers that detailed the disturbing news of a Mexican invasion of Texas earlier that month. Dean was employed as an agent for the Nashville Texas Emigrant Society, an organization that had evolved from the Texas Association, which had been promoting the migration of Tennesseans to Texas since the mid-1820s. Soon after Mexican independence, seventy investors in Nashville received a large land grant in the upper Brazos Valley in what was essentially a land speculating scheme. Among the stockholders were numerous descendants of Nashville's founder James Robertson, as well as Sam Houston and the nephew of Judge John Overton. The enterprise promoted emigration to Texas both before and after the Texas Revolution. Over the years, the settlement was known variously as the Nashville Colony, Nashville on the Brazos, and finally the Robertson Colony, named for one of the company's founders Sterling C. Robertson.[20]

One of the greatest fears among Mexican officials was that the United States would subsume the Republic of Texas through annexation before Mexico could reassert its authority. That fear made the subjugation of Texas imperative, but factors in Mexico prevented it from acting promptly and decisively. Clashes between political factions, federalists and centralists, and a French attack on Mexico in 1838, provided serious distractions from Mexico's plans of reconquest in the late 1830s. However, latent tension between Texas and Mexico erupted in full force in 1841, when Texas tried to make good on its territorial claim over its western neighbor, New Mexico, by sending an expedition of 320 soldiers to Sante Fe. Mexican troops captured the force and marched the men to Mexico City as prisoners. Several months later, in February 1842, President Santa Anna, intending to teach Texas a lesson, sent a Mexican force across the Rio Grande, where it occupied San Antonio for several days.[21] This was the "invasion" that Jabez Dean hurried to Nashville to report.

The Mexican incursion posed a threat not just to the profits of land speculators but also to the sovereignty and security of Texas itself. It was, of course, Texas sovereignty that Santa Anna intended to threaten. In response, President Sam Houston declared that any American who wanted to immigrate to Texas must bring a good musket, powder, and a hundred rounds of ammunition and submit to six months of service in the Texas militia upon arrival. Meanwhile, Tennesseans feared that Mexico's incursion was but a preliminary step to taking back its lost territory. At about the same time, the Tennessee General Assembly unanimously passed a resolution calling on federal officials in Washington to "use every exertion in their power" to bring Texas into the Union. For Southern Democrats, annexation was necessary for the future of slavery, for the security of republican government and for the safeguarding of American borders. Annexation talks were already underway between Texas and the United States, but the path was curvy and filled with potholes, and it would take three more years.[22]

British policy was also a source of concern. Today attitudes are tempered by the history of the twentieth century when the United States and England stood together as allies, especially in two world wars. However, in the 1840s, Americans remembered the Revolution and the War of 1812, along with impressment and British violations of U.S. maritime rights. American trade in Latin American countries was economic competition that the British resented, and the British had constructed a foreign policy designed to block U.S. expansion (territorial and economic) in Texas, Mexico, and elsewhere. Thus, Americans saw England as a potential threat and its actions as a cause to enforce the Monroe Doctrine. They had stood up to the haughty British before and, if necessary, they would do so again.[23]

In 1843, Americans were looking ahead to the presidential race the following year. Four years after losing the presidency to William Henry Harrison, Martin Van Buren launched a political comeback and, with Andrew Jackson's backing, he appeared to be the Democrat frontrunner. Whigs chided Van Buren for his attempted political reincarnation. Joseph Peyton, a Whig congressman from Tennessee and brother of Balie Peyton, made a speech in early 1844 denouncing Van Buren and his effort to use Jackson to resuscitate his career. In his "mistletoe speech," Jo Peyton called Van Buren a "political parasite" who, like mistletoe, owed "its very existence, to the tall trunk of an aged hickory; but so soon as it was attempted to transplant it and force it to live upon its own . . . it shrunk, and withered, and died." Now the only way to revive it "is to call to its aid the strength and support and sustenance of the same old hickory."[24]

Tennessee Democrats were divided over who should be the party's 1844 nominee. While Polk and others were on board with Van Buren, others favored Lewis Cass from Michigan. Some Tennesseans, like Alfred O. P. Nicholson, supported Cass as a way of opposing Polk's leadership as party boss in the state. Defeating Polk's choice for the nomination would have helped Nicholson supplant Polk as party leader in Tennessee.[25] However, Van Buren dealt himself a fatal blow in April when he came out against the annexation of Texas, a development that changed the dynamics and the outcome of the Democrats' Convention. John Tyler, who assumed the presidency upon Harrison's death, had been trying—unsuccessfully—to bring Texas into the Union, but abolitionists, who feared that territorial expansion also meant slavery expansion, were staunch opponents. Their fervent resistance to the expansion of slavery went hand-in-hand with resistance to territorial expansion, and it was this thorny political briar patch that Van Buren hoped to avoid when he took his anti-annexation stand. Not only that, he also wanted to avoid the threat of a diplomatic break with England that might result. It was a major political miscalculation.

Manifest Destiny, the belief that it was America's providential destiny to push its border farther west, had taken hold of the country. Many Americans, especially Southerners, were caught up in the enticement of land and the prospect of controlling the entire continent. In Tennessee, pro-annexation Democrats were so upset with Van Buren's position that they met at the Nashville courthouse on successive Saturdays, May 18 and 25, to listen, as persuasive orators called for immediate annexation. At a similar meeting in South Carolina, speakers called for a Nashville convention to convene in August to push for annexation. Some advocates felt so strongly about the issue that they wanted to make "Texas or disunion" a political issue in the South. However, numerous concerned Tennesseans did not want their state used as a meeting place for architects of such extremism, and they worked to disavow such designs.[26]

Andrew Jackson, cognizant of the severity of Van Buren's self-inflicted wound, called Polk to the Hermitage for a visit. The party needed a pro-expansionist candidate who would seek immediate annexation, counseled Jackson, and it needed a westerner with political experience who could unify the party. Polk still supported Van Buren, but he also favored annexation, making him potentially acceptable to both factions of the party. The ex-president considered Polk just the man to carry the party banner.[27] Tennessee was still more western than Southern, and its own history of statehood was a reminder of the adventurous spirit that resulted in that western push. So, with Jackson's blessing, Polk associates began to work behind the scenes to position Polk as the only logical choice in 1844. The old hickory tree, to use Jo Peyton's metaphor, rejected the mistletoe's attempts to reattach to its trunk, and two weeks later at the Democrat Convention, Van Buren's candidacy withered and died.

Van Buren remained the Democrat frontrunner when delegates convened in Baltimore, despite his pronouncement against annexation. In fact, he had a majority but lacked the required two-thirds. However, Lewis Cass supporters went to work to sabotage the Little Magician's chances, and Tennessee's delegates, fearing that a Van Buren candidacy presaged a defeat in the general election, were willing accomplices. After numerous ballots, the Van Buren vote total dwindled until Cass surpassed him, but neither candidate could gain a majority. The Van Burenites were furious over the political maneuvering orchestrated by Cass supporters, who were derisively called "Jack Casses." Entering the convention, Polk was the favorite choice for the vice-presidency, but his Tennessee friends, primarily Gideon Pillow, had been maneuvering behind the scenes for days to raise his stock. Eventually, Polk emerged as a compromise candidate. Since he had not been party to the cabal to unseat Van Buren, he was still in the good graces of that wing of the party, which now saw a Polk candidacy as a way of stopping the Cass momentum. Polk's political experience, his ties to Old Hickory and, most importantly, his favorable position on expansion, put him in good standing with Democrats nationwide. As the balloting continued, Cass and Van Buren supporters remained stalwarts until the building momentum of the Polk compromise candidacy became more than any of the other camps could stop. Eventually all parties caved and voted for Polk, giving him the nomination unanimously and giving the party the semblance of unity that it lacked just a few days earlier. Now the party had someone to rally around. "I never saw such enthusiasm, such *exultation*, such *shouting for joy*," exclaimed a happy and successful Gideon Pillow.[28]

Ironically, the Whig candidate in 1844, Henry Clay, had also renounced Texas annexation at about the same time as Van Buren. He feared the prospects of a war over Texas and went so far as to assert, "Annexation and war with Mexico are identical." Like Van Buren, Clay's intended purpose was to take that political hot potato off the table. Opposing annexation was a position more palpable to the Whigs but, as it turned out, not to the voting public, which had a growing appetite for land. Rarely have politicians more completely misread public sentiment than did Van Buren and Clay in 1844. Rejecting Texas cost Van Buren his party's nomination, but it would cost Clay the presidency. Realizing that their candidate's opposition to annexation was a losing position, Tennessee Whigs gave only tepid support to Clay's position. Some tried to explain that Clay would pursue annexation when it could be accomplished in good faith with Mexico. For the most part, they simply tried to remain silent on the issue.[29] While some Tennessee Whigs agreed with Clay's stand, most party members supported expansionist policies.

Polk's nomination transformed the 1844 election. He did not shy away from expansionist issues and indeed had been nominated in large measure because he supported annexation. As historian Merrill Peterson put it, "Magically, Texas lifted him to the presidential nomination." The one topic that both Van Buren and Clay had sought to brush aside became the central issue of the campaign, and it served Polk well. Clay began to come around to public sentiment, and he tried to backtrack on the issue, but it was too late.[30]

Democrats tried a variety of approaches to entice voters. Expecting Polk's expansionist stand to be a winning position, they went further by arguing that new western land would ease the anxiety over slavery by providing an overflow region, a safety valve of sorts, for the South's dense slave population. In other words, they argued that territorial expansion would cause slavery tension to dissipate through dispersion. They also employed a populist twist by asserting that Texas would provide land opportunity and economic relief for struggling, small farmers thereby offering a degree of economic equality. Furthermore, Democrats argued that territorial expansion meant extending freedom and republican institutions.[31]

Even though women could not vote, they played a surprising role in the campaign as both parties tried to mobilize that segment of the population. Four years earlier at a Whig rally, women wore sashes that read "Whig husbands or none." This time, Democrats tried to involve women by inviting them to participate in a big rally in Nashville and encouraging them to sew the image of the "Lone Star" on flags to symbolize the party's commitment to Texas annexation. Whigs countered by also securing large-scale female participation in a rally and festival at which women carried Clay banners and filled a twenty-six-carriage processional, one carriage for each state in the Union. The heavy involvement by Whig ladies caused one angry Democrat to condemn the Whig women for being politically partisan while good Democrat women stayed at home "attending to their domestic duties."[32]

Despite winning the presidency in a close election, Polk could not muster enough support to carry his home state. Clay won a majority of the 120,000 votes cast in Tennessee by fewer than three hundred, which was not a surprise considering that Tennesseans had rejected Polk in the last two gubernatorial elections in favor of the Whig candidate. The campaign was fierce and hard fought. Polk's old political rival a decade earlier, Balie Peyton, was so harsh in his criticism that rumors surfaced in the form of a letter to the New York *Evening Post* that Peyton was "conspiring against the life and character of Polk."[33]

Clearly, Polk had not restored Democrat dominance to Tennessee. He had, however, rejuvenated the state party and, nationally, some viewed him as a Democrat savior. Various factions had rallied around Polk and came to view him as a unifier, and Old Hickory's death just weeks after Polk's inauguration seemed to legitimize the latter's position as party leader. Young Hickory was the new face of the Democratic Party, and a stern face it was. Like Jackson, it could be intimidating to be in the presence of Polk and look into his "penetrating eyes," as one historian described them. Polk's political rise had been full of partisan campaigns and close elections. The "violence of party feeling," as Polk once characterized it, had forced people to draw lines and choose sides.[34] During the past decade, he had waged political battles with Whigs for the Speakership (three times), governor of Tennessee (three times), and now president—each time with Andrew Jackson's blessing. He had lost as many races as he had won and in the process learned the number one rule that in politics there are no rules. Now others sought Polk's blessing—he was the party leader, and the position gave him a sense of stewardship. He was the caretaker who had to solidify the party's standing, the guardian who had to protect what Jackson had left him. This perhaps contributed to his intense desire to give his party every edge possible and keep it strong through executive authority. As president, Polk would play the role of partisan very well.

The new president made his expansionist intentions clear in his inaugural address. However, in the final days of the outgoing administration, John Tyler had accomplished annexation by joint resolution of Congress. It was Congressman Milton Brown from Jackson, Tennessee, who introduced the resolution into the House of Representatives, so as Polk entered office, Texas was already a *fait accompli*. But Texas was not all that was on Polk's mind. As promised in his campaign, Polk made it clear that he would settle the Oregon question, and he served notice to England that he wanted the question answered. Remembering Andrew Jackson's stern example in foreign policy, Polk did not blink when he stared John Bull in the eye. Whigs were divided: many of them opposed territorial expansion and all of them, still stunned by Clay's defeat, wanted to block the Democrat program.[35]

When President Tyler succeeded in pushing an annexation resolution through Congress in 1845, Mexico's border dispute with Texas became a border dispute with the United States. Incoming President Polk's determination to defend the Rio Grande boundary claim led to an escalating series of events that focused renewed attention on the border issue with both countries determined to defend their land claims. What had for years been a Mexico/Texas controversy now became a Mexico/United States controversy, and Polk's unyielding determination set the two countries on a collision course that resulted in war.

The series of events that led to the war have been covered in detail elsewhere, but a few pertinent facts warrant summary here. Having broken off diplomatic relations after annexation, the Mexican government, headed by José Joaquín Herrera, responded positively to the Polk administration's willingness to negotiate a settlement. But while Herrera expected to begin the talks with U.S. indemnification for Texas, Polk considered that to be a settled fact and intended for the talks to concentrate on the border question. Fueled by rumors of British interest in California, Polk also instructed his representative, Louisiana expansionist John Slidell, to secretly explore the possibility of purchasing the land extending from Texas to the Pacific, with California being of paramount interest.[36]

Unfortunately, the talks never materialized. Slidell's diplomatic title, along with the object of his mission, made it impossible for the Herrera government to negotiate without losing credibility with the Mexican congress and people. For refusing to meet with Slidell, Polk ordered an army under Zachary Taylor to advance into the disputed territory and take a position on the bank of the Rio Grande. What Washington considered a show of force to gain negotiating leverage, Mexico City interpreted as a provocation that violated its territorial integrity. Taylor's advanced position prodded Mexican troops into crossing the Rio Grande to protect their country's land claim and, on April 25, 1846, they attacked an American patrol from Taylor's army.

The fact that both country's forces were operating in disputed territory mattered not to Polk, who, anticipating an attack on Taylor's force, had already begun to prepare a war message. The news of the attack gave the president cause for action. He delivered a war message to Congress in which he stated that Mexico had "invaded our territory and shed American blood on the American soil." Indeed, he asserted that a state of war already existed by an act of Mexican aggression. This attack was but the latest in a list of "injuries" and "insults" perpetrated by Mexico,

Polk continued, and now war existed solely because of the actions of Mexico itself. Despite the fact that Polk had acted provocatively, from the president's perspective, Mexico had been the instigator and honor required an appropriate response. Perhaps Polk also held to Andrew Jackson's personal motto, "Death Before Dishonor."[37]

When war came in May 1846, Tennesseans already had a long-standing interest and involvement in the region and were eager to defend the southern boundary. Once annexation occurred, a threat to Texas was de facto a threat to the United States. Mexico's actions posed a threat to American sovereignty, and what is more it was a challenge to American honor.

Polk's war message carried by a wide margin, owing in part to the fact that Democrats allowed hardly any time for debate and also to the clever wording of the message. It started by asserting that Mexico's attack meant that a state of war already existed, and thus Polk was calling on Congress to provide recruits and funding. It was a twist that put the Whigs over a barrel. To vote against this would have the appearance of not supporting the troops. Even with a comfortable vote tally, 174 to fourteen in the House and forty to two in the Senate, opponents were loud and mostly Whig. Many Americans suspected that Polk had provoked the clash along the Rio Grande as a means of instigating a war of territorial acquisition with California being the ultimate prize. Those who voted against war were mostly northeastern Whigs whose primary fear was that slavery expansion would go hand-in-hand with land expansion. However, Southern Whigs who wanted to oppose Polk's policies worried about speaking out against the war for fear of being labeled unpatriotic.

But war-making power was exclusively the authority of Congress, and some Tennessee Whigs spoke out regardless of labels. Polk, they argued, had unlawfully sent American troops into disputed territory north of the Rio Grande. His actions were not only unconstitutional but also immoral. The war, they charged, had been "unconstitutionally commenced by a president who was bent on territorial aggrandizement." Meredith P. Gentry from Franklin was the leader of the Tennessee Whigs in the House of Representatives, and he pointed out that the Rio Grande had never been the settled boundary of southern Texas. He called Polk's position "an artful perversion of truth." Congressmen Edwin H. Ewing of Nashville and Milton Brown from Jackson called Polk's actions unconstitutional, pointing out that the resolution annexing Texas in 1845 had left the settlement of the border issue to the United States government, not to presidential fiat. One Tennessee Whig argued that Polk's artful wording clouded the issue over whether Congress was actually voting on whether a state of war already existed. This subtlety allowed Polk to declare not only where the legitimate boundary was but also the existence of a state of war without Congressional approval.[38] Now Young Hickory's methods were the heavy-handed ones, reminiscent of the executive style of Andrew Jackson.

Even some professional soldiers, usually the last who want to go to war, expressed misgivings about the conflict. Captain Robert E. Lee, an 1829 graduate of West Point, expressed his moral dilemma in a May 1846 letter to his wife. "I fear the country is already disgraced for its puerile conduct." Lee thought that Polk had been provocative and underhanded in maneuvering the Mexicans into attacking U.S. forces on the Rio Grande. "I wish I was better satisfied as to the justice of our cause." Years later, Ulysses S. Grant succinctly characterized the war as "unjust."[39]

Despite the criticism, the Democratic press supported the president. The *Nashville Union* even attempted to shift culpability of starting the war to Taylor, saying that it was his idea to move his army to the Rio Grande. Regardless of one's position on the origins of the war, events along the Rio Grande in spring 1846 were pivotal for Tennesseans. The *Nashville Whig* newspaper had condemned the pro-annexationists, and had earlier warned that to annex Texas while it was at war with Mexico was tantamount to an act of war by the United States on Mexico. However, after Taylor was attacked on the border, the paper said that it was a matter of honor that Americans not allow Mexican attacks to go without response. "Let Mexico, therefore, be summarily and thoroughly thrashed!" A warlike response would be giving Mexico what it deserved. In general, and regardless of party, many Tennesseans were jubilant about volunteering to fight.[40]

*Chapter Two*

# TENNESSEE VOLUNTEERS

Based on newspaper reporting in the state, as far as Tennesseans knew, President Polk had sent Zachary Taylor's army to the Rio Grande merely to prevent an invasion from Mexico. When the news arrived that Taylor's army had been attacked, a wave of "indignation" swept across the state because Mexico had violated the country's territorial integrity. "Our soil had been invaded and American blood had been spilled . . . by an aggressor, who had so long refused to mete out to us even-handed justice." Mexico had "taken advantage of our spirit of forbearance," wrote John Blount Robertson from Nashville.[1]

Few Tennesseans doubted the veracity of Polk's words that American blood had been shed on American soil. "Patriotic enthusiasm pervaded all ranks of our people," remembered William Bowen Campbell, who accurately summed up how the majority of Tennesseans felt in 1846, when he stated that "Patriotism required a quick & ready obedience, no matter by what means the conflict between the two nations had been caused."[2] The war permeated all thought and discussion across the state. Those most eager to fight seemingly did not question the policies that brought about the clash and simply considered it their patriotic duty to turn out. The rightness of the cause, the morality of the war, one's party affiliation, none of it mattered to most Tennesseans. All that mattered to the patriot was the knowledge that his country was at war—and that fact alone placed on him the obligation to serve. "Justice, pride and patriotism, all demanded that we should promptly inflict upon our perfidious enemy" the penalty for its actions.[3]

Rather than consider the decision for war as sudden and unreasonable, many Tennesseans thought that it was overdue and justifiable. Forbearance had finally given way to "just retribution which had been so long slumbering 'neath the hand of mercy.'" One local newspaper in Lincoln County denied that Americans were rushing to war. "A Christian people will use all honorable means to avoid" war, it proclaimed. But the attack on U.S. forces along the Rio Grande was foolishly perpetrated by a "misguided people" hungry for war. Mexican aggression was the universal understanding of the war's origins. The same paper a few days later published a poem that contained the following lines: "Rise! Patriot, rise! March to your country's call, For her resolve to conquer or to fall. Let Tennessee's flag in pride and triumph wave, Where valor soon will dig her foes a grave."[4]

Without waiting for the official call for volunteers, communities across the state sprang into action. A militia company in Nashville calling themselves the Nashville Blues, sent Governor Aaron V. Brown a message on Saturday, May 9, informing him that the unit had already met and was ready to offer its services. Furthermore, because of "the distinguished patriotism that has always characterized *Tennesseans*," and because the Nashville Blues was such a "long standing" company and ready to serve, it appealed to the governor that it be "allowed the privilege of manifesting that spirit. . . . [illegible] that would properly represent the state's reputation."[5] Seventy miles south of Nashville, Lawrence County residents gathered at the Lawrenceburg courthouse to listen to patriotic speeches about Mexico's violation of U.S. sovereignty. Citizens in Wilson County (Lebanon) and Sumner County (Gallatin) as well as residents from across the state were already coming together to form volunteer companies.[6]

The martial ardor among Wilson County residents intensified when former governor James C. Jones asserted that he would personally lead a company of volunteers in Mexico. In response, an elderly man named Bradley, who had fought with Jackson during the Creek War, stepped forward and said that although he was now too old and decrepit to fight, he had two sons. Bradley made what was intended as a chivalrous offer. According to a newspaper account, he said that although he was unable to support himself and he depended on his boys "to sustain me in my old age, yet I wish you to put them both down on your list—they must go with you." Bradley had acted heroically at the Battle of Tallushatchee in November 1813, reportedly leading his regiment in a charge after all of the officers had been incapacitated. Perhaps Bradley wanted to relive the glory of his youth vicariously through his sons.[7] Nowhere was the attitude of Tennesseans better articulated than in a letter written by George W. White of Manchester, Tennessee, to Major-General Thomas H. Bradley of the state militia. "[O]ur people have fallen by the hands of Mexicans," he wrote. "Volunteers have been called out; our country is invaded, and we *must* meet the crisis like men, like Tennesseeans, Americans, like our fathers did in other days."[8]

West Tennesseans were also eager to serve. In Memphis, a town on the Mississippi River with a population of 3,500, young men began to organize companies and practice drilling in early May. Morgan B. Cook raised a company called the Gaines Guards, and a man named E. F. Ruth used the sheriff's office on Main Street to enroll men into a company called the Memphis Rifle Guards. A veteran of the Texas Revolution named William N. Porter organized a company of mounted troops called the Eagle Guards, and still more volunteers came forward. Local residents persuaded former mayor J. J. Finley to form a company, and a recruiting office was set up in the offices of the *Daily Eagle* newspaper for that purpose. A company called the Shelby Highlanders resulted from the effort. The Jackson Greens, comprised predominantly of Irishmen, was organized by a Captain Dunn. Cook and Ruth camped their men on Hernando Road just outside of Memphis on Levi Lorance's property, and they dubbed the camp Anderson Barracks after Nathaniel Anderson, a prominent citizen whose three sons had enlisted. City residents brought food and supplies to the camp. Meanwhile, Memphians were growing restless and wanted Governor Brown to make the call for troops official.[9]

Residents all across the state were already preparing for service, but the governor waited for mobilization orders from Washington before issuing an official call for troops. On May 13, the same day that Congress voted to declare war, Governor Brown took action in an attempt to catch up with his citizens. He issued "Order No. 1," which specified how companies were to be organized—one captain, one first lieutenant, one second lieutenant, four sergeants, four corporals, and fifty privates. He also instructed all the state's militia companies to collect supplies and be ready to mobilize. To assist financially in the effort, the Union and Planter's Bank offered a loan of $100,000.[10]

When the call from Washington came for volunteers on May 24, Tennessee was already a step ahead. The War Department requested three thousand men from Tennessee to fill two regiments of infantry and one of cavalry. Governor Brown began the mobilization process by dividing the state into four organizational sections with a militia general supervising the call up of troops in each. To facilitate equitable opportunities across the state, a prescribed number of companies were to be mustered in from each region. West Tennessee, under the oversight of General Hays and headquartered in Memphis, was to accept six companies. Two regions in Middle Tennessee, one under Major General William B. Campbell headquartered at Nashville and the other under Major General Thomas H. Bradley headquartered at Jackson, were responsible for eight and nine companies, respectively. And in East Tennessee, Major General William Brazelton at Knoxville, was to accept seven companies. Tennessee mustered in the prescribed number of companies by region, ten of cavalry and twenty infantry, in less than two weeks. Thirty companies comprised of just under three thousand volunteers were accepted into a twelve-month commitment, but thousands more were turned away. In Lebanon, the call for volunteers came with a twist of irony—it was published in the *Lebanon Banner of Peace and Cumberland and Presbyterian Advocate*.[11]

So many Tennesseans wanted to serve that state officials resorted to a lottery to determine who would have the "privilege" of being inducted. Disappointed volunteers who were not chosen offered up to $250 for a chance to go to Mexico. However, none would "yield that privilege to others," and it became impossible "even to *purchase* a place in the ranks." Such a situation was "indeed, a strange spectacle to behold men thus wrestling for a post so fraught with danger, suffering and death: yet, Tennessee presented even such a picture," remembered a Nashville volunteer. Another, from near Memphis, wrote that it was not a matter of "Who will go?" but "Who will remain?"[12] Two of the companies already raised in Memphis, the Shelby Highlanders and Jackson Greens were turned away. However, the Highlanders, who had invested considerable money in uniforms and equipment, refused to disband. They remained organized in the hope that they would be needed later and, in the meantime, offered their services to march in parades and participate in other patriotic gatherings.[13] Selecting which companies would go sometimes came down to politics.

Politics infused other aspects of the volunteer units as well. In Lawrence County, political differences rooted in the 1844 presidential election had caused the local militia company to split into two units. Democrats who supported Polk assumed the name Lawrenceburg Blues, while Whigs who had favored Henry Clay for president called themselves the Clay Guards. After the declaration of war, however, patriotism trumped partisanship and the two consolidated into one company, adopting the name Lawrenceburg Blues before heading for Nashville to report for duty. Politics were also a pervasive part of officer selection in volunteer units wherein the men elected their officers at the company (lieutenants and captains) and regimental (majors and colonels) levels. Being elected an officer often resulted more from prominence in the community than from proven competence in a military setting, and local prominence came from wealth, influence and political connections. So, a company commander might not be the man with the most ability but the candidate who served the best liquor in election day. And volunteers from a free society were sometimes loath to submit to the rigorous discipline of men who were friends back home, even though combat success might depend on it.[14]

The three regiments that formed in the 1846 surge of volunteers were just the beginning. The following year, as the war dragged on unexpectedly long, Tennesseans filled the ranks of three more regiments designated the Third, Fourth, and Fifth Tennessee Infantry. Although none of those units arrived in Mexico in time to participate in the major battles, they illustrate a relatively sustained measure of support for the war throughout its duration. But it would become evident later that the level of success for the original three regiments had a geographic impact on where future support for the war remained strongest. That a total of 5,392 Tennesseans answered their country's call during the course of the war was a great source of pride in the state. "No state can boast a more valiant and patriotic population than Tennessee, the home and burial place of the immortal Jackson," said a New Orleans newspaper.[15] When Tennessee needs her sons to come forward, declared *The National Union*, they respond in a "swelling tide of patriotism." The "VOLUNTEER STATE . . . [is always] ready to vindicate the country's rights." A Knoxville newspaper editor proudly asserted that General Taylor was merely waiting for the Tennessee boys to arrive so he could begin his triumphant march to Mexico City.[16]

Nashville was the designated rendezvous point for the 1,070 members of twelve Middle Tennessee companies. Nine of the companies appear to have been previously existing militia units from the following counties: Davidson (2), Dickson, Hickman, Lawrence, Marshall, Smith, and Sumner (2). Then the ranks of three more companies were filled by ballots from Bedford, Lincoln, and Warren Counties. Among those turned away was an entire company from Marshall County calling itself the Cornersville Rifles.[17] (When officially mustered into service in early June, those previously existing militia units became volunteer companies in the U.S. Army.) These companies came together to form the First Tennessee Volunteer Infantry Regiment. Its organization and company commanders are listed below.

### First Tennessee Volunteers
#### (Col. William B. Campbell, Lt. Col. Samuel R. Anderson)

| | |
|---|---|
| Company A—Centreville, Hickman County | (Capt. John W. Whitfield) |
| Company B—Lewisburg, Marshall County | (Capt. Harris Mauldin) |
| Company C—Dixon Springs, Dickson County | (Capt. L. P. McMurry) |
| Company D—McMinnville, Warren County | (Capt. Adrian Northcutt) |
| Company E—Nashville, Davidson County | (Capt. Benjamin F. Cheatham) |
| Company F—Hartsville, Sumner County | (Capt. Robert A. Bennett) |
| Company G—Fayetteville, Lincoln County | (Capt. Pryor Buchanan) |

Company H—Carthage, Smith County          (Capt. William B. Walton)

Company I—Gallatin, Sumner County          (Capt. William M. Blackmore)

Company K—Shelbyville, Bedford County          (Capt. Edmund Frierson)

Company L—Nashville, Davidson County          (Capt. Robert C. Foster III)

Company M—Lawrenceburg, Lawrence County  (Capt. William B. Allen)[18]

Members of the First Tennessee chose William Bowen Campbell to command the regiment as colonel. Campbell was a native Tennessean and an attorney who had been elected to the state legislature in 1835. The following year, he resigned in order to serve as captain of a company in the Seminole War. After a year in Florida, he was elected as a Whig to the first of three terms in the U. S. House of Representatives, before returning to Middle Tennessee (1843) to practice law, where he also accepted an appointment as major general in the state militia. At age thirty-nine, Campbell's military experience, leadership skills and political connections made him an excellent choice as regimental commander. As his adjutant, Campbell appointed Adolphus Heiman, an immigrant from Prussia who had only been in Nashville for a few years in 1846. Already an architect of note before the war, he would become Nashville's best-known architect in the 1850s, designing some of the city's most impressive buildings in Greek Revival style.[19]

Campbell's experience notwithstanding, he was reluctant to leave home. He held moderate political views and had broken with the Democrats for the same reason as so many others: a departure from republicanism and the trend toward centralized federal power. Although a strict constructionist, he had not supported nullification, which he deemed extreme. He supported the war with Mexico but seemed not to share the same level of martial spirit as his fellow Tennesseans. His greatest hesitation, however, was leaving his wife, who was not in good health and who was disappointed with his decision to leave home for a year. But Campbell was patriotic and as a prominent member of the community he felt obligated to duty. In a letter to his cousin David Campbell, former governor of Virginia, he wrote, "I could not get out of this business with honor."[20]

A history of Hickman County reveals bits and pieces about some of the young men who volunteered for service in Company A. John C. Ward was related to Colonel Campbell, and after his Mexican War service he was a physician in Centerville for fifty years. Numerous members of the Totty family volunteered for service in Company A, including the six-foot-tall, two-hundred-pound Lewis P. Totty who had previously served in the state militia. The Totty's Bend area of Hickman County bears the family name. Another member of the company was Zebulon Hassell, whose son would later marry Lewis Totty's daughter. Dr. Daniel McPhail was a surgeon in the regiment and also the brother-in-law of Captain John Whitfield, the company commander. Joseph Weems came from a prosperous family that owned eight hundred acres and fifty slaves. After settling in the area, his father, William Loche Weems, purchased land near a mineral waters spring. Mineral water was thought to have great medicinal benefits, curing everything from skin rashes to digestive ailments, and one could supposedly profit from either drinking or bathing in it. Weems called the springs "Bon Aqua," meaning "good water," built cabins, and marketed the springs as a health resort, and over the years visitors traveled long distances to enjoy the resort.[21] These and countless other blood connections made it difficult to shirk one's duty without losing face in the family as well as the community.

For John Blount Robertson of Davidson County, the decision to volunteer was more about adventure. He admitted to having "a strange hankering to see a battle" and relished the challenge to "test my powers of endurance in the trials incident to a campaign." Robertson knew that a soldier's life was filled with danger and hardship, but those concerns were not great enough to dampen the romantic adventure that he associated with military service. Plus, he admitted that he wanted to see Mexico. The excitement of such an undertaking, Robertson concluded, provided "an opportunity to gratify at once my patriotism and my curiosity. The temptation was too strong to resist."[22]

Still others volunteered for altogether different reasons. Twenty-one-year-old James W. Wynne, who went by the name Bolivar, was from a prominent slave-owning family in Sumner County. His father, Alfred R. Wynne, was the owner of Wynnewood Inn, a resort built at another mineral spring, this one in Castalian Springs. Bolivar, had spent much of 1843 and 1844 in Missouri, where he fathered a child with a woman named Julia. Soon afterward, in January 1845, Bolivar left Missouri, briefly visited his family at Castalian Springs, then traveled to New Orleans and Texas before returning home in time to enlist in a company of volunteers being raised to go to Mexico. There were rumors that Bolivar's travels were an attempt to evade his fatherly responsibilities, but such was obviously not the case, for he and Julia married at some point, and spent their post–Mexican War years in Texas. Younger brother, Robert Bruce Wynne, age nineteen, also volunteered, and despite his youth, he already had developed a fondness for liquor. Before leaving home, he admitted that he had engaged in much foolish frivolity, and from the content of later letters, it appears that drinking was a primary source of his dissipation. However, he tried to assure his father that he had reformed his behavior. Alfred Wynne probably took consolation in the fact that his wayward sons would be under the command of Alfred's business partner Samuel R. Anderson.[23]

The Middle Tennessee companies quickly converged on Nashville and joined the two Davidson County companies that were camped at the horse racing track two miles south of the city. The regiment would be officially mustered into service in the first week of June 1846, but meanwhile other communities in other parts of the state were keeping pace with their own organizing efforts.

East and West Tennessee were equally represented in the makeup of the Second Tennessee Volunteer Infantry Regiment, with four companies coming from each region. Each company's location of origin and its company commanders are listed below.

### SECOND TENNESSEE VOLUNTEERS
### (COL. WILLIAM T. HASKELL, LT. COL. DAVID H. CUMMINGS)

Company A—Knoxville, Knox County     (Capt. George W. McCown)

Company B—Huntingdon, Carroll County     (Capt. Henry F. Murray)

Company C—Knoxville, Knox County     (Capt. John L. Kirkpatrick)

| | |
|---|---|
| Company D—Memphis, Shelby County | (Capt. E. F. Ruth) |
| Company E—Memphis, Shelby County | (Capt. Morgan Cook) |
| Company F—Jackson, Madison County | (Capt. Timothy P. Jones) |
| Company G—Chattanooga, Hamilton County | (Capt. William I. Standifer) |
| Company H—Athens, McMinn County | (Capt. John D. Lowry)[24] |

Authorities designated Memphis as the rendezvous point for the companies formed in West Tennessee—B, D, E, F. Members of Company B called themselves the Carroll Guards. Initially they were uncertain if their company was needed, but upon receiving confirmation of their selection, they hurriedly gathered their supplies and left Huntingdon on June 4. Their march to Memphis took several days. On day two, they reached Jackson, where they received an enthusiastic welcome from the locals, who had prepared dozens of tubs of an alcoholic drink called "mint sling." The volunteers eagerly accepted the hospitality and imbibed freely. By one account, each "soldier drank to the top of his bent, and the result was that a number of them were soon placed *hors du combat*," a French term referring to a soldier who is no longer capable of performing his duty. Private Ivory Kent was among the worst offenders, for he was still so inebriated the next morning that he had to be placed in a wagon to start that day's march.[25]

This was apparently not an isolated event for Kent. He was Canadian by birth and a "journeyman hatter," but he was probably best known as a perpetual drifter. Later in the day, as the column approached the town of Denmark, Captain Henry Murray, company commander, ordered Lieutenant Isaac Hawkins to stay with Kent as they passed through the town to prevent him from drinking. Hawkins had little trouble with him until they reached the far end of town where, as they passed a saloon, Kent bolted for the door and entered the establishment. He already had a glass of whiskey in his hand when Hawkins reached him and ordered him not to drink it. Kent "swore a terrible oath that all hell could not prevent his drinking," and as he raised the whiskey to his lips, Hawkins reached out and upset the glass, spilling most of its contents on the floor. Kent set the glass down and drew a knife from his belt. He was the "perfect impersonation of fury," with his teeth tightly clinched and his fiery eyes staring at the lieutenant. Hawkins stared back, preparing to defend himself as the room fell silent. Tense seconds passed, and then perhaps thinking about the repercussions that would accompany his actions, Kent re-sheathed the knife, picked up the glass, and downed the remaining amber liquid; then, without a word, Kent went back out into the street and resumed the march with the rest of the company.[26]

For their regimental commander, the men of the Second Tennessee chose William T. Haskell, an attorney from Jackson. He was born in Murfreesboro in 1818 and graduated from the University of Nashville before fighting in the Seminole War. His family moved to West Tennessee when he was young, and his father, Joshua, became a circuit judge. In physical appearance, William was tall and somewhat pale, but he was always immaculately dressed and well-versed about a wide variety of topics. Haskell was "astonishingly brilliant and eloquent," thought an acquaintance, R. A. Young, and "he talked well on every subject." He also served in the state legislature as a Whig and was known for writing poems and songs and for oratorical skills that rivaled Daniel Webster's. Although he was only twenty-seven when the war started, Haskell was well-respected and deemed competent to command the regiment as colonel. "He is active and energetic and will no doubt pay all proper attention to his regiment," thought Sergeant John McClanahan, a fellow Jackson native.[27]

It took longer for the Second Tennessee to get organized because half of its companies had to travel all the way across the state, which in some cases was a three hundred–mile journey. As the companies converged on Memphis, the locals became increasingly frustrated in the last week of May. Volunteers from other states were already steaming down the Mississippi River, usually stopping at Memphis on their way. Earlier in the month, the West Tennessee volunteers thought they were ahead of the game, but here they were standing on the bank of the river watching as boys from other states passed by on their way to war, and as of yet no Tennessee units had left the state. Most people blamed the governor for waiting too long to issue orders. When Missouri and Kentucky volunteers stopped over in Memphis, the locals shared with them their anger over not being called to action sooner. Intended to be a good-natured poke, as the Missouri troops were pushing away from the dock to continue their journey, their band played a song called "Oh, Take Your Time Miss Lucy." Supposedly, the jab was aimed at Governor Brown and not Tennesseans in general, but the sting was no less sharp.[28]

While the two infantry regiments converged on Nashville and Memphis to await steamboat transports to New Orleans, the First Tennessee Mounted Regiment had a longer and more arduous journey. Its companies hailed from throughout the state, each making its way to Memphis, where it would await orders to continue by land through Arkansas and Texas, thence to the Rio Grande. Similar tales of over-indulgence like the one involving Private Kent emerged regarding some of the Knoxville volunteers. The Knox County company was hardly away from home when it began to imbibe in hard drink—"Rye-O" they called it. The company commander, Captain William Caswell, had to keep a watchful eye over some of them, like James Brazelton who, Caswell informed his wife by letter, would probably be the source of much trouble.[29]

The mounted troops would take a back seat to the two infantry regiments, which figured prominently in three battles from the fall of 1846 to the spring of 1847. Because they did not travel by water, it took them considerably longer to reach Mexico, and their war experience would be a disappointment. To avoid confusion in referring to the First Tennessee Infantry Regiment and the First Tennessee Mounted Regiment, henceforth this account will refer to the latter as the Tennessee Mounted Regiment or simply the Mounted Regiment when dealing with the horse soldiers. Jonas E. Thomas from Columbia commanded the regiment, and it was comprised of companies as listed below.

### MOUNTED REGIMENT OF VOLUNTEERS
### (COL. JONAS E. THOMAS, LT. COL. ROBERT D. ALLISON)

| | |
|---|---|
| Company A—Hickory, Fayette County | (Capt. Joseph S. Lenow) |
| Company B—Statesville, Cannon County | (Capt. J. H. Marshall) |
| Company C—Columbia, Lewis/Maury County | (Capt. A. G. Cooper) |

| | |
|---|---|
| Company D—Big Spring, Meigs County | (Capt. L. D. Newman) |
| Company E—Cornersville, Marshall County | (Capt. Milton A. Haynes) |
| Company F—Tazewell, Claiborne County | (Capt. N. A. Evans) |
| Company G—Memphis, Shelby County | (Capt. William N. Porter) |
| Company H—Washington, Rhea County | (Capt. James Gillespie) |
| Company I—Alexandria, Dekalb County | (Capt. John F. Goodner) |
| Company K—Knoxville, Knox County | (Capt. William Caswell)[30] |

While the First Tennessee waited to depart Nashville, William Campbell wrote to his Virginia relative, David Campbell. David was not only a former governor, but also a veteran of the War of 1812 and William trusted his council. William's conscientiousness caused him concern about his responsibilities as regimental commander and his duties as a high-ranking officer. On the eve of his departure for the seat of war, the gravity of the situation caused him to reach out for advice. "I shall expect to hear from you often," William wrote, "particularly on the subject of my duties as Col., the etiquette, etc., of the army."[31]

The regiment departed from Nashville a few companies at a time on June 4, 5, and 6, and each day a crowd of well-wishers gathered at the wharf to see the men off. The Young Men's Bible Society of Nashville gave each volunteer a New Testament before he left the city, and on the fifth, the Nashville Female Academy hosted a flag ceremony for the soldiers, which Campbell and numerous members of the regiment attended. The girls of the senior class had commissioned a regimental flag, which they presented to the unit. It had an azure blue field trimmed with bright orange fringe. In the center of the flag was the image of an eagle, and in its talons the inscription, "First Regiment Tennessee Volunteers." Above the eagle were the words, "E Pluribus Unum" and below it the motto, "Weeping in solitude for the fallen brave is better than the presence of men too timid to strike for their country." Academy Headmaster C. D. Elliott addressed the crowd with a speech that "was fraught with patriotic and soul-stirring sentiment." He told the gathering about how the flag's motto was derived. Some days earlier, he said, he had asked the students if they would rather be in the company of those who volunteer "to fight the battles of their country" or those who were "too timid to go?" The unanimous response was, those who fight. After Elliott's speech, Zachary Taylor's niece, Irene Taylor, presented the silk flag to Colonel Campbell, who made some remarks before turning the standard over to the color bearer of Nashville's Company L.[32]

The design of the flag, indeed the entire ceremony, is instructive in its symbolism and in what it revealed about honor and community expectations. For a bunch of twenty-something-year-old young men to gather at the academy in the presence of a host of teenage girls merely served to reinforce the volunteers' determination to show their valor. John Robertson recalled the scene: "It was a proud day for Tennessee! Here were her fairest daughters assembled in all the purity of maidenhood, to express in the strongest, yet most delicate manner, that deep sense which they entertained for the justice of our cause, and to signify their high esteem of that patriotism that had clothed us in the costume of war." They had come in their virtue, Robertson continued, to honor the valor that the volunteers were demonstrating with their willingness to fight for home and country. "Even the fairest portion of Heaven's creation," Campbell later recalled, "shook off their fears & lauded the prompt offering of the 1st Reg." As in "ancient Sparta," the girls "had come to send their friends and brothers forth to battle, with the promise of praise to the brave and threats of infamy for him who faltered." The motto embroidered on the flag drove that last point home by issuing a not-so-subtle warning for the boys not to dishonor their people by shrinking from their duty.[33]

The two Nashville companies commanded by Benjamin Franklin Cheatham and Robert C. Foster III were among the units that departed Nashville on June 5, as was William M. Blackmore's Sumner County boys. A crowd of hundreds from Nashville and surrounding communities gathered at the wharf on the east side of town to see them off. Mothers and fathers, sisters and sweethearts, friends and the curious came for hugs and handshakes before the troops boarded the steamer *Conner*. In the crowd, too, were veterans of Horseshoe Bend and New Orleans. Now in their fifties and sixties, they looked at the young volunteers with pride but with the unspoken expectation that their legacy of battlefield victory would be upheld by the younger generation. Their presence there could not help but conjure images of Old Hickory himself, who had died exactly one year earlier, on June 8. The young volunteers understood the symbolism as well as the obligation represented by the presence of the previous generation of volunteers. According to John Robertson, "it stimulated our hearts to keep pace with our increasing sense of responsibility, and we were not loth to emulate the deeds of our fathers." The task of upholding the state's honor and reputation had fallen to them, and they felt it. When all was ready, the *Conner* pushed away as a cannon fired a salute. Loved ones cheered and waved, and many a young volunteer, attempting to muster a soldier's stern resolve, felt the embarrassment of a tear roll down his cheek.[34]

Filled with pride and courage, the Tennesseans began their trek down the Cumberland River, leaving in increments over a two-day period. For several miles, hundreds more well-wishers lined the riverbank, waving as the steamer passed. Heading downstream from Nashville meant going north to Clarksville and on through Kentucky to the Ohio River. The same path, but in the opposite direction, would be the invasion route of a Union army just fifteen years later. At Paducah, Kentucky, their voyage took them west to the Mississippi River, and from there, down to New Orleans and the beyond to the Gulf of Mexico. A Tennessean traveling the same route with another volunteer unit the following year wrote home with a description that likely expressed the same sentiments in June 1846. When our ship entered "the mighty Mississippi I was truly astonished at the magnificence of the scene. Like a genuine Green horn, fresh from the mountains of East Tennessee, I gazed upon the scene with wonder." On June 8 and 9, the steamers made a brief stop at Memphis, where West Tennessee troops were still gathering—and waiting. It was a disconcerting encounter for the Memphians, who had watched with disappointment a week-and-a-half earlier as volunteers from other states passed by on their way to Mexico. Now disappointment turned to dismay when they saw that Middle Tennesseans also were going to beat them to the theater of war. The Memphis volunteers were the closest to transportation access, indeed they were closest to the war, and had been organized and ready to go for weeks, yet all they could do was stand on the cliffs overlooking the river and watch as Middle Tennessee volunteers passed by. Their misfortune at the outset was perhaps an omen of things to come.[35]

The four Memphis companies had been ready to go since late May, and similar to their Middle Tennessee counterparts, they had participated in flag ceremonies in preparation for their departure. The companies had gathered at the Gayoso House, a new luxury hotel in downtown Memphis, where the companies received their flags. Two of the units had flags presented by the ladies of Memphis. A third presentation was made to the Gaines Guards by Sarah Anderson, the daughter of Nathaniel Anderson and sister of the three company members. The flag she presented had been hand painted by Captain Joseph P. Keyser who refused pay for his work. Unfortunately, there was no description of the image.[36] Again, the presence of females at such events was intended to boost the men's incentive to be courageous and make the home folks proud.

Another memorable flag ceremony occurred in Jackson to honor the Madison County volunteers. William Haskell, not yet elected regimental commander, had recruited and was the leader of this company. A gifted orator, he had used his eloquent tongue to convince many Jacksonians to enlist by promising that the war would be an opportunity for revenge against Mexico for killing Americans. In fact, his motives were personal, for his brother Charles had been killed in the Goliad, Texas, massacre in 1836.[37] The company's moniker became, fittingly enough, the Avengers. On June 2, local residents came to the courthouse, where Haskell's nineteen-year-old sister Caroline addressed the crowd on behalf of the ladies of Jackson. Her speech offered little indication of the flag's design except that it was emblazoned with an eagle, "the majestic emblem of your country's glory," and in it she challenged the volunteers with the common refrain of honor. "Avengers! Look upon that Banner! There is no stain upon its silken folds—no spot to dim the brightness of its sheen," she exhorted. Then she continued by admonishing them to be sure that "when you return with it, no stain of dishonor shall attach to it." Miss Haskell also invoked the heroism of "your fathers," whose memory should "not be tarnished by their sons." And like William, she still felt the sting of the loss of her brother who died at the hands of

Mexican troops a decade earlier, and also like William, she saw this war as vengeance. "[T]here is blood upon the walls of the Alamo still crying up to heaven," she reminded the crowd, "and scattered ashes on the plains of Goliad, uncoffined and unrevenged! Avengers! Take this Banner!"[38]

Lieutenant Wiley Hale, a friend of the Haskell family, promised not to betray the trust of the community then accepted the flag on behalf of the company. Hale was actually more than just a family friend; he was considered a protégé of William Haskell who, upon being elected commander of the Second Tennessee, would appoint Hale his adjutant. Haskell had high hopes for Hale after the war and kept the young subaltern by his side in Mexico. In addition, according to local legend, Hale intended to receive the hand of Miss Caroline Haskell in marriage when he returned, which is likely the reason he was chosen to receive the flag from her at the ceremony.[39]

The "Avengers" left Jackson on June 3, but pulling the disparate companies of the Second Tennessee together in Memphis was hampered by distance and geography. For example, one of its companies (G) was from Chattanooga in Hamilton County, and it did not muster into service until June 18. The company elected as its captain William I. Standifer, a Whig and recent member of the state legislature. In 1862, Standifer helped capture James Andrews, the leader of Andrews's Raid, otherwise known as the Civil War's Great Locomotive Chase. Also in the company were the prominent landowner Private Washington Pryor as well as Private John T. Read, whose father was an officer in Andrew Jackson's army at New Orleans. Read became a physician and later served as a surgeon in the Confederate army. In 1872, he opened the historic Read House Hotel. By the time the Hamilton County company was organized and ready to march, its sister units in the Second Tennessee were already departing Memphis, heading for Mexico.[40]

The Mounted Regiment came from all over the state, and the companies from East Tennessee spent most of June traveling to their rendezvous point at Memphis. They were to travel to Mexico with a regiment of volunteer cavalry from Kentucky, and while the Tennesseans camped outside of Memphis on the east side of the Mississippi River, the Kentuckians camped within sight but on the west side of the river in Arkansas. Before leaving Memphis, the regiment elected as its colonel Jonas E. Thomas from Columbia, who won out over Milton A. Haynes by a vote of 659 to 197. Captain Haynes, commander of Company E from Marshall County, was ranked eighteenth in the 1838 class at West Point, and was a veteran of the Seminole War in Florida. After his one-year volunteer service in Mexico, he practiced law then became lieutenant colonel of artillery in the Confederate army during the Civil War. Another company commander in the Mounted Regiment, who later fought for the Confederacy, was John F. Goodner of DeKalb County's Company I. He later served in the Seventh Tennessee Infantry, which was engaged in the Peninsula Campaign and at Fredericksburg before Goodner's resignation from Confederate service in spring 1863.[41] The Mounted Regiment had a much longer, slower journey to Mexico, and consequently played no role in the war until 1847.

A host of new volunteer regiments meant the creation of new generalships to command thousands of additional troops. These are the circumstances that brought Gideon J. Pillow back into public attention in the summer of 1846. After helping his friend and fellow Columbia resident become president two years earlier, Pillow sought payback. He first wanted a judgeship and in a letter to Polk asserted, "I could become eminent upon the bench," but the president tactfully brushed away that request.[42] In addition to being a capable attorney, Pillow was a wealthy planter with extensive land and slave property in Tennessee, Arkansas, and Mississippi. His farming techniques utilized the latest advances, he was a strong advocate of crop diversification, and he also raised prize cattle. He would become famous, or more accurately, infamous, after the Mexican War while serving as a Confederate general. His untimely departure from his army prior to its surrender at Fort Donelson in 1862 permanently damaged his reputation. Pillow was not only politically connected in the state, but also ambitious, arrogant, and at times naive. His connections would serve him well; his vanity and naïveté would not.

When the war came in May 1846, Pillow wanted Polk to appoint him a brigadier general. Unlike lower-grade officers, who were elected to their posts in volunteer units, generals received their commissions only through presidential appointment, and Pillow, after all, had been a major general in the state militia. Tennessee's Governor Brown endorsed the idea, and his recommendation carried the weight of personal relationship. Brown had been Polk's law partner, and he too had worked to get Polk elected in 1844. Additionally, Brown had married Pillow's sister, Cynthia, in 1845, so the three men constituted a strong triumvirate interlocked by politics, profession, and family. The president consented to this request and immediately sent Pillow's nomination to the U.S. Senate for confirmation as brigadier general. From Polk's perspective, sending such a close friend and ally to Mexico to serve in the army would give him eyes and ears on the ground.[43]

Pillow's commission was dated July 6, and when the news reached him one week later, he left his Columbia plantation in the hands of his brother and set out immediately for Memphis, where volunteer companies continued to rendezvous. His orders instructed him to take command of the two infantry regiments and the mounted regiment, which together would constitute a brigade in Major General William O. Butler's volunteer division in Zachary Taylor's army. Pillow's appointment was purely political. Polk overlooked qualified and worthy candidates in appointing generals to the army largely because the present makeup of the regular army officer corps was heavily Whig in composition, and the president, who had fought difficult battles in both national and state politics, viewed the army that he was sending to Mexico through a political lens. From Polk's perspective, an adequate share of army leadership, as well as the adulation that would accompany victory, should go to Democrats.[44]

Nationally, Whigs were surprised at Pillow's appointment and thought it betrayed rank partisanship. In Memphis, there was disappointment because locals believed that Levin H. Coe, the competent and talented Inspector General of the state militia, should have received the post. Coe was a local favorite and an influential Democratic politician who had served in the Tennessee State Legislature, including being voted Speaker of the House. His name had even surfaced as a gubernatorial candidate. He had played a major role in seeing to the supply needs of the West Tennessee companies in Memphis and expected that Polk would appoint him general. Those who knew Coe were angry that he had been "cheated" in the appointment process, and the *Memphis Eagle* stated that in selecting Pillow, the president could not have made a "more unfit, unmerited, or unpopular appointment." Perhaps as a face-saving measure, Polk offered Coe a commission as major in the Quartermaster Department of Taylor's army, but Coe declined. Later, in 1850, when Coe was attorney general in Memphis, he was shot in the back during a gunfight in the city streets over bank fraud accusations. He died a few weeks later at the age of forty-four.[45]

A considerable number of Tennesseans thought William Campbell, a Seminole War veteran and militia general, would be tapped by Polk for a generalship despite his prominence as a Whig. That he was overlooked in favor of Pillow, angered Colonel Campbell's uncle David. In a pointed letter to his nephew in July, David wrote: "A personal disrespect has been offered to you by the president in appointing Pillow over you." Lamenting the infusion of politics into the war, David continued: "I see now that this Mexican war is to sink down into a miserable party affair. You whigs will compose a large portion of the rank & file, but you are to be kept there. There will be no rising among the whig volunteers you may be assured." He insisted that he knew Pillow's character, referring to him as a "low demagogue" whose only qualification for command was "party servility," and he warned, "You are in continual danger if you have over you an unprincipled General Officer."[46]

In the colonel's correspondence, it is clear that he understood the politics of the army's makeup. Campbell had asserted before leaving Nashville that politics had been involved in the selection of the companies for mobilization. It was the "old political companies," he called them, that Governor Brown had admitted into the service. Campbell was well-aware that Democrats outnumbered Whigs by two hundred in his regiment, and yet he still won the balloting for colonel by 169 votes. Soon after reaching Brazos, Campbell concluded that half of the companies in his regiment were commanded by incompetent officers who showed little promise in overseeing their men. He was determined to bring them around, but "Politics is somewhat in my way as all my field officers are Democrats and are somewhat jealous of any character I may acquire and therefore do not second my exertions to institute rigid discipline."

Campbell's subordinates assumed that he too was driven by political motives, but he believed that in time he could convince them that they were mistaken. Either way, the experience convinced Campbell that "I shall never again have a desire to ingage in any political contest or to seek office. When I return home I will lead a private life."[47]

Pillow arrived in Memphis on July 18, more than a month after the First Tennessee had departed, but while other volunteer companies from Tennessee, Kentucky, and elsewhere gathered to await transports. At about the same time Pillow arrived, so too did the company of mounted troops from Knoxville, commanded by Pillow's old friend William Caswell. Pillow referred to him as "an old college mate . . . who I used to love very much." Caswell was a fellow lawyer and his friendship with Pillow trumped the fact that he was a Whig, for Pillow asked Caswell to join his staff as aide-de-camp. Not wishing to leave the Knoxville Dragoons, the captain at first demurred, but friends urged him to reconsider. He accepted the offer, left his company, and joined General Pillow at the Commercial Hotel, from whence he wrote his wife telling her that his personal comfort would improve because of his new station; "I shall be in clover."[48]

Pillow was only in Memphis a few days but long enough to conclude that, despite his controversial appointment, the boys in his new command accepted him. His warm reception convinced him that "I shall have no difficulty in making my Troops all like me." It was an inaccurate conclusion. Nevertheless, he left Memphis on the steamer *Champion* with two servants, Alfred and Ben, and his new aide-de-camp, arriving at New Orleans a few days later. He and Caswell stayed at the St. Charles Hotel along with other generals headed for the seat of war: James Shields, John A. Quitman, and John E. Wool. While there, Caswell assisted Pillow in purchasing supplies to properly outfit Pillow and his headquarters tent in Mexico: mess chest and boxes ($36), cots ($7), collar and cuffs for Pillow's coat ($10), silver serving pieces, and so forth. While in the Creole City, they ate well and drank the best wines, and because Caswell was short of cash, Pillow paid for everything. Pillow took in the sights of the city, and before leaving he made sure to visit Congo Square to "watch the Negroes dancing."[49]

*Chapter Three*

# FROM TENNESSEE
# TO THE RIO GRANDE

By steamboat the trip from Nashville to New Orleans took nine days, and the boys of the First Tennessee arrived there in mid-June. When they disembarked in New Orleans, they marched through the streets to the St. Charles Hotel, and crowds cheered them, perhaps remembering the last time Tennessee volunteers came to their city. After a brief interlude, they loaded on the steamer again and went two miles out of town to their camp site. Bivouacking away from the sins of the city was intended to encourage order and discipline. In the few days that they remained there, several at a time were permitted to go into the city for a visit, however, the Tennesseans were inventive in finding ways to avoid the guards and slip out of camp to explore the Creole City. Those caught—and it was more than a few—were placed in the guard house.[1]

From New Orleans, William Campbell wrote to uncle David to report his arrival near the gulf. There was "but little sickness amongst the men," and not only did they feel good but they looked good as well. "My Regiment is said here to be the finest looking Regt. that has passed here en route to Genl. Taylor," Campbell wrote with pride. Captain Robert Foster informed his mother in a letter that he paraded his Nashville company through the streets of New Orleans, and not only did a crowd follow them but also the following day local newspapers called it "the finest and best drilled company of Volunteers that ever paraded through the streets of N.O." The most important praise from Foster's perspective, however, came from the men of the ranks, who were of "standing and respectability" and who came forward, "crowding me with compliments." That, Foster understood, would bode well for his post-war pursuits. Campbell was also pleased with the compliments offered to the Tennesseans, but he added, "I hope they will give a good account of themselves on the Rio Grande." He predicted that if there is a battle to come, the Mexicans would put up a good fight. Private Bruce Wynne of Sumner County wrote home to his father, Alfred, that all the boys are healthy and that they are "eager to give the Mexicans a chance to see some of the Old Tennessean."[2]

Such letters from New Orleans would be the last time that members of the regiment would be able to report that everyone was healthy. The Mexican War experience serves as a reminder that, prior to the twentieth century, more soldiers died of disease that of combat. Once they arrived on the Rio Grande, illness began to take its toll. Dysentery and measles as well as tropical diseases like yellow fever proved deadly for the volunteers. During the war, three men would die of such maladies for every one killed in combat, and the Tennesseans were destined to do their share of suffering.

On June 17, the First Tennessee loaded on three sailing vessels, *Charlotte*, *Chapin*, and *Orleans*, for the voyage across the Gulf of Mexico. By mid-day of June 18, they had exited the mouth of the Mississippi and were in open water, where they would spend the next few days. Initially the bobbing and swaying of the ships produced nausea in almost every man, rendering the crowded ships a "disgusting scene." When they hit the gulf all were vomiting, reported Daniel King in a letter to his wife, Sarah. I "never experenced the like as to mi part I only pucked six days and nite." He continued his letter, describing the lost contents of his stomach, and probably using more descriptive details than his wife wanted to read. Eventually, the seasickness subsided for most of the men and they began to take note of the beauty around them. Porpoises and flying fish were an entertaining novelty. At night, John Robertson would crawl out on the jibboom, the wooden pole that extends beyond the front of a sailing vessel to support the rigging, and from his perch there, he watched the bow of the ship cut through the waves. As the water rolled to either side of the ship, it glowed with a phosphorescent blue-green lumination that fascinated Robertson.[3]

When they arrived at their destination, Brazos Island near the mouth of the Rio Grande, a major storm created such turbulent waves that the men could not off-load for several days. Finally, on June 30, the discouraged and contentious Tennesseans staggered ashore and joined the swelling number of volunteer units arriving in Mexico. The encampment was a hundred yards from shore, and there were long lines of tents that accommodated other volunteers from Alabama, Kentucky, Missouri, Maryland, and elsewhere. Here, the Tennessee boys got their first look at Mexicans who were working for the quartermaster department unloading supplies. Their leather breeches and wide-brim hats drew considerable attention from the curious Americans. There were already more than two thousand volunteers camped in the vicinity, with Texans, Louisianans, and others having already moved inland with the regulars. In fact, the "whole border of the Rio Grande is swarming with volunteers," reported one Kentuckian.[4]

Unfortunately, the growing number of troops around the Rio Grande contributed to a logistical logjam that beset Taylor's command. At the outbreak of hostilities in April, his army had numbered about four thousand, but in mid-summer it was in the process of swelling to over ten thousand. The general's plan was to move his troops inland by steamboat as far as Camargo and then turn south to advance on the city of Monterrey. It was about 125 miles to Camargo as the crow flies but significantly farther when following the serpentine path of the Rio Grande. The army's primary problem was a lack of wagons to carry its supplies once it broke away from water transportation. With no prospects of getting more wagons, Taylor began to purchase pack-mules, which were plentiful in the area.[5]

In the weeks since leaving home, officers drilled the men whenever possible in an effort to turn the raw recruits into a respectable fighting force. Boredom and drilling seemed to be the order of each day along with the futile effort to keep the blowing sand out of their clothes, knapsacks, bed rolls, and other supplies. Volunteers were notoriously undisciplined and often resisted the loss of freedom that the regimented life of a soldier represented. Some of the units were shaping up more quickly than others. Nimrod D. Smith of Gallatin asserted that "it would only require a half observer here to see that Sumner is the Star County of the Volunteer State." An Alabamian recorded in his journal while on Brazos Island that, among all the volunteer units, the Tennesseans "are admirably well drilled and I think the most warlike people now mustered into service."[6]

Brazos was not a healthy place. To get drinking water, the soldiers dug large holes in the sand, then placed bottomless barrels in the holes to allow the brackish ocean water to leach up through the sand and fill them. It was a little salty but the best tasting water they had had since leaving New Orleans. They assumed that the sand was sufficient to filter out impurities, but that was an inaccurate and unfortunate assumption. Some of the men began to suffer from diarrhea immediately. The regimental commander quickly noted the inadequate provisions and insufficient transport. While Washington officials had been calling for volunteers, thought Campbell, they should have been giving more attention to supplying the men once they arrived in Mexico.[7]

On Saturday, July 4, ships in the Gulf fired salutes in celebration of the nation's birthday, and next day many of the Tennesseans attended a memorable worship service, which, as one soldier remembered, was "the last Sabbath we kept" until their twelve-month service expired. Two days later, just over a week after they had arrived on the island, several companies received orders to leave Brazos and begin their move up the Rio Grande. Depending on the availability of transports, the Tennesseans, along with volunteers from other states, started snaking their way up the river in intervals.[8]

Their first sight of the Rio Grande left some of the volunteers disappointed. Having imagined a wide, powerful river perhaps akin to the Cumberland or Tennessee Rivers back home, they were surprised to find a relatively narrow stream. "There are no trees upon its bank," wrote Wiley Hale, except for "low undergrowth called in this country 'Musquite Chapparral' which is so thick as scarcely to be penetrable by a man on horse back." However, the landscape did not disappoint. They noted the beauty of their surroundings as they pushed upriver by steamboat following the river's winding path. The cultivated fields along the river bank indicated the richness of the soil that needed only "Yankee enterprise," thought Robertson, to give the region the "full development" warranted by its potential.[9]

Twenty-five miles inland, they made camp at a place called Lomita, a small hilltop village next to the river. It was comprised of only a handful of adobe huts, but soon after the troops arrived, Mexicans began to appear in camp to sell bread, tortillas, melons, and milk. The prices were sometimes high but hungry soldiers were willing to pay. Colorful wild flowers decorated the landscape around Lomita as well as a variety of cacti including a night-blooming species. The daily temperatures sometimes topped a hundred degrees, but they were still close enough to the coast to catch an occasional breeze that kept the heat from being stifling. Flies and mosquitoes, however, were constant annoyances, but worse than anything was the measles that had broken out among the men. Lomita was the collection point for the Tennessee regiments as well as for other units. Several companies of the Second Tennessee had caught up, but it would be another month before its remaining East Tennessee companies arrived.[10]

Having been gone only two months, some of the men already missed home and anticipated their return. Bruce Wynne from Castalian Springs was one of them. In addition to his older brother, Bolivar, who volunteered with him, Bruce had five younger brothers and five sisters. In a letter home, he mentioned his siblings by name and said that he thought of them often, and in his imagination, he could see them playing in the yard. He encouraged the entire family to think about him while he was away. Bruce also missed the family slaves. "I wish to be remembered to all of our Negroes who I have much regard for. I often fancy they hold a conversation about us while they take their meals out in the field." He also requested that his father give his regards "to all of my friends without distinction of sex and to all my relations." Eagerly awaiting his welcome return home, he expected family and friends back in Tennessee to show "that love and respect which is only due to a soldier—to a volunteer and an honorable man."[11]

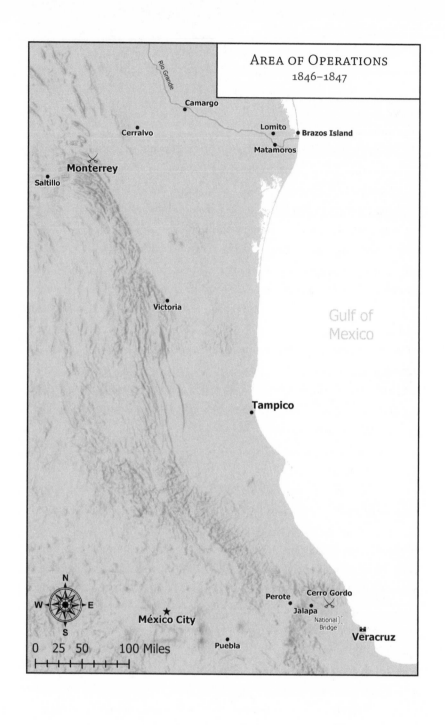

AREA OF OPERATIONS
1846–1847

Rio Grande

Camargo

Cerralvo

Lomito

Brazos Island

Matamoros

Monterrey

Saltillo

Victoria

Gulf of
Mexico

Tampico

N
W — E
S

México City

Perote

Cerro Gordo

Jalapa

National
Bridge

Veracruz

Puebla

0   25  50        100 Miles

Lomita was also the place where sickness really began to take its toll on the men. Many of them had suffered from dysentery since Brazos Island, and a growing number of measles debilitated others. In July and August, death and disease became the army's paramount problem, and the First Tennessee was not exempt from the syndrome. Those who were too ill to be of further service but were deemed capable of traveling received a surgeon's certificate and were sent back home. In early July, seven Tennesseans were sent home, but one, John Clymer, died on the way. Twenty more sick arrived back in Nashville on October 1 and three days later another two hundred. Writing from Lomita in mid-August, one soldier reported that "measles has been the most fatal disease we have had."[12] In their first five weeks at that site, seventeen First Tennessee volunteers died. In addition, Dr. Daniel McPhail, a regimental surgeon from Williamson County, had been left behind at Matamoros because of illness, and he too had died. It was also at Lomita that Captain A. S. Alexander, commander of the Lawrence County company, resigned for undisclosed reasons. Local lore suggests that he might have had a drinking problem, but a contemporary published account suggested that political differences within the company compelled his resignation. The company elected William B. Allen to take his place.[13]

Some soldiers, however, tried to paint a rosier picture than actually existed in their letters home in order to save their family from unnecessary worry. John McClanahan feared that the returning sick were spreading "exaggerated accounts of our condition" to folks back home. Well aware of "the tender sensibilities of woman's, and particularly of a parent's, heart, I have carefully avoided writing home any gloomy accounts of our hardships and privations," he wrote. Any man who wishes to exhibit "the character and reputation of a soldier" ought not share such depressing information with loved ones. So, McClanahan enjoined his family not to be troubled by the stories told by the poor boys who had been sent back home. "I wish to caution you against the dolorous tales which any of them may tell." Some of the healthy Tennesseans were even light-hearted, like Sergeant Fleming Willis from Jackson, who sent word back home that he intended to marry when he returned, and he wanted the damsels with whom he was acquainted to decide which of them will marry him. However, Willis's good-natured intentions would not be realized, for he was destined to die in the battle of Cerro Gordo six months later.[14]

Members of the First Tennessee had also had sufficient time to form opinions about their officers. Colonel Campbell was liked and respected, but the men's favorite seemed to be the regiment's second in command, Lieutenant Colonel Samuel R. Anderson. The son of a Revolutionary War officer and born in Virginia, the forty-two-year-old Anderson grew up and was educated in Middle Tennessee. As a prominent businessman, he had the kind of social standing in his community that often served as a prerequisite for election as an officer in a volunteer unit. In Mexico, he was even-tempered and fair in his treatment. A Sumner County soldier said that Anderson "is pleasing the men well." Indeed, the soldier went on to assert that Anderson is probably "the most popular man in the Regiment—and without disrespect to Col. Campbell I think he deserves it."[15] This soldier's characterization of a superior officer is interesting but consistent with the nature of volunteer units wherein privates vote on their officers, who in turn should strive to please the men and not the other way around.

Other Tennesseans were already serving in army units in Mexico before the three Tennessee regiments even left the United States. One was William B. Bate from Sumner County who had left home as a teenager in about 1845 and secured a job on the steamboat *Saladin* which traveled back and forth from Nashville to New Orleans. Following the initial Mexican attack on the Rio Grande in April, General Taylor immediately called for four regiments of Louisiana volunteers to augment his army. The request was for a ninety-day commitment and volunteers received a twenty-five-dollar enlistment bonus, an enticing opportunity for the nineteen-year-old Bate, who happened to be in New Orleans when he heard of Taylor's call. He immediately volunteered.[16]

These early recruits had joined Taylor's army in northern Mexico, but in late July their three-month enlistments expired before they had an opportunity to fight. Many of them were angry at being sent back home without seeing combat, robbed of their chance for glory and adventure. Louisiana newspapers railed against the injustice. There is no record of how Bate felt about his misadventure, but his unit was on its way back to the coast when he ran into some old Tennessee friends near Lomita. He was able to visit for a few days, but on July 30 a Sumner County acquaintance in the First Tennessee penned a letter home stating that "our friend Billy Bate leaves in a day or two for home." Billy Bate indeed went home to Tennessee, but a year later he returned to Mexico as a lieutenant in the Third Tennessee Volunteer Regiment. The Third Tennessee got to Mexico in late 1847, after the major battles had been fought and when occupation duties were all that remained. Thus, Bate was too early and too late to make his mark in Mexico, but he would make an indelible mark a decade-and-a-half later on numerous battlefields, and again years later in state politics.[17]

Balie Peyton was also in New Orleans when war broke out. The former Tennessee congressman and cofounder of the state Whig Party who had worked hard but unsuccessfully to defeat Polk in 1844 had moved to Louisiana several years earlier for financial opportunities and to develop his law practice. He had been named a U.S. Attorney in Louisiana, and from New Orleans, Peyton continued to maintain contact with Tennessee politicians. When hostilities began, Brigadier General Edmund Pendleton Gaines, the commander of the Western Military Division, tried to facilitate a rapid buildup of forces on the border by authorizing the recruitment of six-month volunteers. Peyton, whose wife had died the previous year, sent his children to live with family in Gallatin and volunteered his services. By the end of May, Peyton had helped raise an entire regiment and had been named colonel of the unit. In all, four thousand Louisianans answered Gaines's call. Recounting the story of Peyton's quick action, a Tennessee newspaper dubbed him "that gallant Peyton." Soon after arriving on the Rio Grande with his Louisiana troops, Peyton received the pleasant news that his friend William Campbell and a regiment of Tennessee boys had arrived at Brazos Island, and he sent a message to Campbell asking that he come to Peyton's camp for a visit.[18]

Soon, however, Peyton received unpleasant news. Gaines had acted without authority in calling for volunteers, and as soon as War Department officials in Washington learned of his actions, they sent a testy message to the general. The illegally organized Louisiana units had to disband. They were given the option of either going back home or re-enlisting under government sanction for a twelve-month term of service. Angry and disappointed, none of them re-enlisted and all returned to New Orleans, where they were officially discharged in August. Back in Tennessee, the Nashville *Republican Banner* reported the episode with disdain. "Thus are the interests of the country sacrificed—the spirit of the volunteers crushed; and all to serve the dishonest purposes of party." The paper's editor believed that Peyton's opposition to Polk in 1844 was the real reason for the rejection of his troops. It was "shameful partisanship," wrote the editor. But actually, Peyton did not accompany his regiment back to New Orleans. Perhaps to have the last word with the president, he went to Zachary Taylor's headquarters and served as a volunteer aide-de-camp. He was still a volunteer staff officer and with the army a few weeks later at the Battle of Monterrey.[19]

One more Tennessean who was not among the three original volunteer regiments warrants mention. It was Thomas Claiborne Jr., who owed his officer's commission to his personal friendship with the president. Claiborne's father, Major Thomas Claiborne, fought in Jackson's army in the Creek War, before serving a term in Congress, and later befriending his Nashville neighbor James K. Polk. Polk had taken a liking to the major's son Thomas, and in 1841 he asked the eighteen-year-old lad to accompany him on the gubernatorial campaign trail. Thomas came to regard Polk as a "great and good man," and after predicting that Polk would be elected president one day, he said, "I want you to remember me."[20] Polk did.

After his inauguration, Polk sent for young Thomas, requesting that he come to Washington. The president evidently intended to be Thomas Claiborne's political mentor. He appointed Claiborne to a position in the Treasury Department, but he told the young Tennessean that he mainly wanted him "near the seat of government, to have you meet the prominent men of affairs, and also to have you observe men of force who from time to time visit here." In Treasury, Claiborne worked under the oversight of Ransom H. Gillette. Claiborne remembered that Gillette did a lot of talking and very little working, but he boasted that he did not worry about job security, because as a "protégé of the President it was not thought to dismiss me."[21]

At the onset of war, the government sought to expand the army through two avenues. One was to call for volunteers and assigned quotas from the various states—the means by which the First and Second Tennessee and the Mounted Regiment had come into the service. The other was to fund the organization of additional regular army units. One such regiment that fell under the regular army denomination was a new Mounted Rifle Regiment in which Claiborne succeeded, with Polk's help, in securing a commission as second lieutenant. It was a low-ranking commission, but the president promised, "I will see to your promotion." Claiborne's superior was Thomas Ewell from Jackson, Tennessee, who recruited in his hometown for regular army service in the summer and fall of 1846. His recruiting slogan was "last and only chance to get into the war." Claiborne went on to serve honorably in Mexico, and later had a robust career in the Confederate cavalry. However, Lieutenant Ewell was killed the following year at the Battle of Cerro Gordo.[22]

Trailing Campbell's First Tennessee was Haskell's Second Tennessee, which began leaving the state on June 10. However, its companies left Memphis piecemeal, leaving it quite strung out and playing catchup. About the time the Memphis companies reached Vicksburg, Sergeant Ruffin C. Sneed and Private Columbus R. Miller of Company E, the Gaines Guards, got into an argument, which was the prelude to a fight in which Miller shot and killed Sneed. A native of north Alabama, Sneed had become a respected member of the Memphis community. He was buried in Natchez, and Miller was handed over to military authorities when they reached New Orleans.[23]

The Second Tennessee began to reach Lomita in late July and continued to arrive through the first half of August. Within days of his arrival, Wiley Hale wrote to his mother describing the rough environment, thorny plants, and dangerous creatures. "Innumerable insects and reptiles of every hue, size and appearance infest our camp. Rattlesnakes are more abundant here," he thought, "than in any other place upon the globe." A tarantula bit Jackson native Thomas Spurrier, whose critical condition eventually caused him to be sent home. As for their health in general, members of the Second Tennessee seemed to fare pretty well initially. The first companies to arrive were those that had been raised in the western counties closest to steamboat transportation on the Mississippi, and after several weeks in Mexico, their sick lists remained relatively short. However, when the East Tennessee companies arrived, having come from the more rural mountainous region of the state, disease spread rapidly. The decimation of some of its companies contributed to the later decision to leave the Second Tennessee at Camargo when Taylor advanced on Monterrey.[24]

Gideon Pillow arrived at Lomita on August 9. By that time, Taylor had already occupied Camargo with part of the army and had set up his headquarters there. The rest of the army, mostly volunteers, were preparing to follow when Pillow arrived. The boys of the First Tennessee got their first glimpse of Pillow at Lomita. The new volunteer general was gracious to his men; he was articulate and captivating in conversation, and members of his new command were impressed with his bearing. They also appreciated the care that he took for the sick and his regular visits with the infirm of his command. He also did away with the drudgery of day-guard duty, a decision that, while militarily unwise, was well-received by the men. Pillow's deficient military knowledge and his enormous ego became obvious only later.[25] For the time being, all seemed well between Pillow and his men as the First and part of the Second Tennessee continued their journey to Carmargo in mid-August.

"The Rio Grande is certainly the crookedest River in the world," thought Pillow.[26] And worse, the steamers kept running aground along the shallow bank, making it a frustrating trip. Not until the twenty-fifth of August did all of the First Tennessee arrive at Camargo. The army stayed there only three weeks, but long enough for attitudes to change about General Pillow. When he proposed that two companies from the First Tennessee be detached from that regiment and reassigned to the Second Tennessee, giving each regiment an equal number of companies (ten), his field officers protested. Eleven angry captains sent a "Remonstrance" to Pillow, arguing their case against the reorganization. Soon after his arrival in Camargo, Taylor invited Pillow to dine with him at Taylor's headquarters. Pillow's desire to reassign two companies was likely a topic of conversation for afterward "Pillow cooled down very much and said it was not his wish to interfere" with the organization of his regiments.[27]

This interference is likely what Colonel Campbell was referring to in an August 28 letter when he complained that Pillow "seems not to know what to do & is often directing & interfering in matters which he properly has nothing to do with." Campbell had been around Pillow for less than a month but had already developed a negative opinion of him. Perhaps influenced by his Virginia relative's characterization of Pillow as an unprincipled demagogue, Campbell quickly surmised that Pillow was "one of the smallest caliber that has ever been elevated to so high a command." Pillow and Taylor's first meeting caused the commanding general also to come away with an unfavorable opinion of the Tennessean. Two days later in a letter, Taylor asserted that Pillow had "much to learn as regards his new profession."[28]

The last half of August was a waiting game at Camargo, with occasional drill but mostly boredom. The hot sun made unnecessary activity rare, but the travelers did take the opportunity to explore the town of three thousand and its environs. John Robertson from Nashville expressed surprise over two discoveries. When he visited the local cathedral, he had expected to find elaborate gold images which he understood to be common in Mexico. He was disappointed to find none. The other surprise that Robertson recorded in his *Reminiscences* was not couched in terms of disappointment. He and his comrades quickly discovered that the female residents of Camargo went to the river daily and bathed in the nude. They did not appear to be the least embarrassed as they laughed, sang, and shouted during their bathing ritual. Their unabashed behavior shocked the young American soldiers, who had very different beliefs regarding modesty and propriety. "A merrier set of nymphs it would be hard to find," Robertson concluded. In addition to this novelty, there were the usual mainstays of army life, with its abundant camp followers providing whiskey, gambling, prostitutes, and the like.[29]

In late August, the number in Taylor's army was approaching fifteen thousand, as remnant units continued to be shuttled up the Rio Grande into Camargo, while the general struggled to rectify his shortage of land transportation, medicine, and other supplies. When the Georgia volunteers were loading onto a steamer, a fight broke out among the various companies, and the Indiana Regiment was called in to restore order. The fight resulted in at least eight deaths and several other injuries, including the commander of the Indiana volunteers who was shot in the neck. Several Tennesseans became casualties from a boiler explosion on board the *Enterprise* prior to its arrival at Camargo. Enoch Tucker and Alexander Boswell, both of Lawrence County, were killed and several others were severely scalded. When the men determined that the cause of the accident was solely the fault of a drunken engineer, they administered justice via the "Lynch code," one Tennessean remembered.[30]

While the troops waited for marching orders, the sick list grew. The drinking water at Camargo was putrid, and within two weeks after their arrival dysentery and typhoid were wreaking havoc in the camp. Measles persisted and became even more wide spread, and the debilitating effects of diarrhea had become a chronic malady for many of the men. An army doctor aptly described disease as "our invincible enemy."[31] All of this misery was made worse by deplorable conditions: inadequate housing, scarce hospital stores, lack of basic camp sanitation, and a daily fight against snakes, scorpions, centipedes, tarantulas, frogs, and insects. The regular army had less sickness than the volunteers, but even General Taylor had been ill in mid-August, along with other regulars like Lieutenant Ulysses S. Grant. Inadequate accommodations, an insufficient number of doctors, and a multitude of raw recruits proved to be a deadly combination among the volunteers. They had no training and little knowledge of how to care for themselves. In Camargo, practically every volunteer unit had a sick roll that included at least 30 percent. Colonel Campbell reported in late August that among the First Tennessee there had been thirty-two deaths with dozens more "discharged from disease and broken down constitutions from disease." He lamented that his regiment was "fast wasting away in this tropical climate." There were dozens of First Tennesseans (according to Adolphus Heiman, seventy-five) buried at Lomita and Camargo. Having arrived on the Rio Grande two months earlier with over a thousand men, the First Tennessee now had barely five hundred fit for duty.[32]

Captain Frank Cheatham from Nashville wrote to his brother that he had been sick for four days and that he had just discharged twenty-one men from his company for illness. Among them was Lieutenant George Maney, about whom Cheatham wrote of his fear that "poor Geo . . . will not recover he has been suffering for 2 weeks with a severe attack of inflamed bowels which is the most dangerous diseas that a man can have in the country." Maney did not want to go home, but friends convinced him that he must. "A more noble highminded generous hearted boy never lived," wrote Cheatham, half expecting that Maney would not live to see home again. But he did live, and a decade-and-a-half later, he again served as a subordinate to Cheatham in the Confederate Army of Tennessee. Maney was twenty years old when he volunteered to fight in Mexico. He was a native of Franklin, Tennessee and a graduate of the University of Nashville. After returning home and recuperating, he received a commission as a lieutenant in the Third Dragoons in March 1847 and returned to Mexico in June 1847 in time to participate in the closing battles of the war. When Cheatham wrote this letter at the beginning of September, he reported that Tennesseans were now dying at a rate of four or five a day.[33]

Sickness in the First Tennessee also affected the Wynne brothers from Castalian Springs. Bolivar, the one who had fathered a child out of wedlock before the war, received a surgeon's certificate and was sent home from Camargo on September 9. Also, the younger brother, Bruce, somehow ended up in New Orleans in the same month, and remained there for several weeks before appearing back in Mexico in early November. How he got there is unclear. One source said his enlistment expired, and he went to New Orleans to visit family on his way home only to reenlist during his stop there and return to the army. That is unlikely because the May and June enlistments had all been for a year. It is plausible that Bruce received a leave of absence to escort his sick brother as far back as New Orleans before sending him on his way to Middle Tennessee. During his month-long visit in the Creole City, Bruce did indeed spend time in the home of an aunt and uncle, Mr. and Mrs. James W. Breedlove. While there, he also courted a young lady named Susan Carlin, and in keeping with his brother's example, Susan became pregnant and bore Bruce's child during the summer of 1847. However, when the war ended, he returned to New Orleans to marry Susan and care for his child, and later moved the family to Tennessee.[34] Because of his brother's illness and his own extended leave from the army, both boys missed the one major battle in which the First Tennessee participated.

At the beginning of September, Taylor realized that he could no longer remain along the bank of the Rio Grande. With over fourteen thousand men in the area of Camargo and Cerralvo, he had to begin his push to Monterrey—public opinion back home demanded it, and so did the president. Not sure that the enemy would even fight for Monterrey, he identified the units that he wanted to take south. They were mostly regulars but with a sizeable number of volunteer regiments. The First Tennessee would accompany Taylor as would Colonel Jefferson Davis's Mississippi Rifles as well as volunteer regiments from Kentucky, Ohio, and Texas. Six thousand in all comprised the army that Taylor marched to Monterrey, and they struck out in the first week of September. But thousands were left behind—both able-bodied and sick—mostly volunteers from Alabama, Georgia, and elsewhere. Among the regiments ordered to remain at Camargo was the Second Tennessee and the lawyer-turned-general, Gideon Pillow. Taylor named Pillow military governor of Camargo perhaps to placate him, but he was not happy and neither were the Tennesseans. They had stood on the bank of the Mississippi River in Memphis and watched their compatriots in the First Tennessee sail by, and now they watched again as the other Tennesseans left them behind. Members of the Second Tennessee would have to wait until later for their opportunity to achieve glory.[35]

Taylor had begun his two-step move toward Monterrey in late August when he set up a forward base at Cerralvo, some sixty-five miles southwest of Camargo and about halfway to his objective. After pushing forward 160,000 rations to Cerralvo, he began to move his army there one division at a time beginning with General William J. Worth's regulars. In the first two weeks of September, the rest of the army made the arduous march to Cerralvo: General David E. Twiggs's division of regulars, General William O. Butler's volunteer division, and General James P. Henderson's Texas division, altogether about six thousand five hundred men. Butler's division was comprised of two all-volunteer brigades: Brigadier General Thomas L. Hamer's, which was made up of the First Kentucky and First Ohio Regiments, and Brigadier General John A. Quitman's brigade, consisting of the First Tennessee and First Mississippi Regiments.[36] Butler, Hamer, and Quitman from Kentucky, Ohio, and Mississippi, respectively, were all civilian Democrats who received their appointments from the president.

The march to Cerralvo proved torturous for the volunteers. A baking sun and thick dust kicked up by thousands of pounding feet made the daily trek oppressive. They covered fifteen to twenty miles a day, but water was scarce and thirst was relentless. Along the way, the undisciplined volunteers wiped away the yellow-green scum floating on any pool of water that they happened upon and drank liberally. Not surprisingly, they continued to send back to Camargo daily those overcome by illness. They also had to contend with prickly cacti and sharp, pointed grass, and one Nashvillian remembered that even the frogs had horns. When given a few minutes to halt and rest, the men could not even sit in the grass without being stabbed. "D——n such a country" a soldier was heard to shout after being thus goaded. The Tennesseans arrived in Cerralvo to find fresh spring water and tall trees, two things they had not seen in quite a while. They rested in the town for a couple of days, but while there, several of the men suffered scorpion stings, four of them became too incapacitated by illness to continue, and one man died twelve hours after being bit in the face by a tarantula.[37]

As they departed Cerralvo, the Sierra Madres, which had appeared as a faint, hazy outline several days earlier, now loomed tall and ominous in their front. The remaining sixty miles took them through the town of Marin, which was the last population center before reaching their destination. The Tennesseans had been saying since leaving Camargo that they were headed for a great fandango in Monterrey and, as they got closer, the prospects of a battle rejuvenated their excitement. Lieutenant Patrick Duffy from Sumner County had bought a mustang in Camargo so the march was not as onerous for him, but soon he would find that his fine horse was of little use to an infantryman in combat. Taylor's army began arriving in force a few miles north of Monterrey on September 19. The distant thunder of cannon indicated to the Tennesseans—who were miles back in the column—that the army's advance units had arrived within range of Mexican guns. An anonymous Marshall County volunteer wrote in his diary, "our ears were saluted for the first time by the firing of [the] enemy's cannon."[38]

*Chapter Four*

# FANDANGO IN MONTERREY

Monterrey sat in a picturesque valley surrounded on three sides by looming volcanic mountains. The approach from the north was open and relatively flat, except for a gentle descent toward the city. And from this northern approach, the American troops could see the city from several miles away. Sitting on what was essentially a vast plain, Monterrey dominated the scenery, and the fertile soil surrounding the city was heavily cultivated. Taylor's army stretched for eight miles, and he was near the front of the column when it began to arrive at the open end of the valley. From a few miles away, he surveyed the city and its surroundings, but he could see little from that distance. Not sure if the Mexicans would defend Monterrey, he took his staff officers and mounted guard and rode forward to get a closer look, and as he ventured within cannon range several booming rounds from a fortified position gave him his answer. These were the shots heard by the Tennesseans who were still a few miles back in the column.[1]

As the rest of his army continued to arrive, Taylor sent out his engineers to the east and west to reconnoiter the city's defenses. Meanwhile, Texas Mounted Volunteers brought in Mexican prisoners lurking in the area who were suspected of being spies, because they had been captured and released previously while the army was at Camargo. They had obviously been trailing the army for weeks. The Texans shot one of them who tried to escape, and the papers they found on him detailing the size of Taylor's army confirmed their suspicions. They extracted information from another captive by tightening a noose around his neck and threatening to hang him if he remained silent. From reconnaissance and "interrogation," Taylor's scouts gathered the necessary information.[2]

The Mexican army had prepared an impressive array of defenses. They had fortified several peaks and ridges west of the city, through which ran the road to Saltillo; most notably Independence Hill and Federation Hill. On the south side and stretching the entire one-mile length of the city ran the Santa Catarina River, a natural defensive barrier. The eastern approach was partially obstructed by a northward bend of the river, which wrapped around part of Monterrey's flank, and added to that were two forts that defended the city's northern and eastern approaches called Fort Tenería and Fort Diablo. La Tenería was a three-sided earthen fort that stood near a tannery, which was built of stone and gave the earthwork its name. It contained two hundred defenders and mounted three guns, which had a clear field of fire on the open plain north of Monterrey. Its sister fort, El Diablo (devil's corner), which stood on a hill three hundred yards to the southwest, was smaller but its elevated position gave it a commanding presence. El Diablo contained about 150 to two hundred defenders and a pair of guns. Just behind Fort Tenería stood the stone tannery that had been fortified and protected an open sally port on the back side of Tenería. Its sandbagged windows and rooftop made it a strong position. A tributary of the Santa Catarina River ran through the northern part of the city and between these forts before emptying into the river near Tenería. To the west of El Diablo was the Purísima Bridge, which led to the heart of the city and the main plaza. Therefore, Mexican engineers heavily fortified the northern end of the bridge. But the most formidable fortification stood a thousand yards due north of Monterrey and adjacent to the main road that entered the city from Marin. It was a partially completed cathedral, now in ruins, which is labeled on most maps as the Citadel, but Americans called it the Black Fort. It was manned by four hundred soldiers with at least eight cannon, and dominated every possible approach from the north. In all, General Pedro de Ampudia commanded a Mexican force of 7,300 with which to defend the city and its ten thousand inhabitants. A week later, after the Americans had occupied the city, George Nixon from Lawrence County wrote to his wife that Monterrey was "the best fortified place

I expect to ever see." Nixon and other Tennesseans referred to the city as a Gilbraltar.[3]

The Tennesseans arrived in the vicinity excited about the prospects of a battle. While the engineers scouted and mapped the area on Saturday the nineteenth, the army set up camp four miles north of Monterrey in a grove of oak and pecan trees. The hospitable area, known as Walnut Springs, had clear, bubbling springs of fresh water, and the residents of the city often used the grove as a picnic destination. The cool, fresh water, the abundant shade and the generally pleasant surroundings made Walnut Springs seem like anything but a combat area, and the volunteers spent two nights comfortably bivouacked there.[4] As the Tennesseans and the rest of the army settled into their new campsite, General Taylor formulated his attack plans.

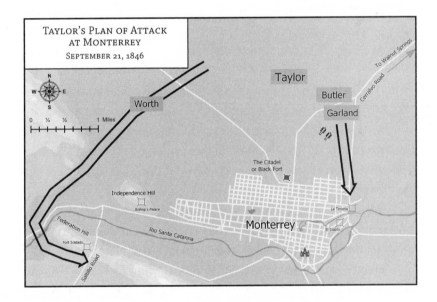

Saturday evening, Taylor gathered a council of his generals, where he decided on his battle plans for the following day. He ordered General William Worth to lead two thousand men in a westward march in order to flank Independence Hill and seize the Saltillo Road. Rather than "ordered," it may be more accurate to say that Taylor agreed to a flanking move by Worth since some believe the movement was someone else's idea. Worth was to move his men to the west of the city on Sunday in preparation for an all-out assault on Monday. The remainder of the army, General Twiggs's division of mostly regulars and General Butler's division of volunteers, would remain north of Monterrey at Walnut Springs and await orders. Worth's flank attack seemed the most likely to dislodge the enemy, given the opinion of one of Taylor's topographical engineers, Lieutenant George G. Meade, who argued that the east side was more heavily defended and thus more dangerous to attack.[5]

In the early afternoon on Sunday the twentieth, Worth began his flank march led by Colonel Jack Hays and his mounted Texas volunteers. Hays made his name as a Texas Ranger, but his roots were in Tennessee. Born in Wilson County in 1817, Hays's father, Harmon, had fought with Andrew Jackson in 1814, serving in a dragoon unit under one of Jackson's most trusted lieutenants, John Coffee. In fact, Harmon named his son John Coffee Hays, but a relative gave him the nickname Jack. At fifteen, Jack lost both of his parents, and four years later (1836), he ended up in the newly established Republic of Texas. On this day in 1846, it was Hays's Texans who were among the first engaged when Mexican troops, having spotted Worth's column, came out of the city and attacked. In was a minor skirmish in late afternoon, and it did not alter Worth's plan. That evening, however, he did send word back to Taylor asking for a strong demonstration on the northeast side of the city the next morning.[6]

That night, as Worth's men camped west of town, the Tennesseans sat around campfires with foreboding thoughts. They knew that next morning they would advance on the north face of the city as part of the diversionary assault that Worth had requested. They had made litters to carry the wounded off the field—a foreboding chore that had sobering implications. That evening was filled with anxious anticipation, and a Nashvillian remembered that "the camp presented a scene of universal solemnity." Here, one soldier pulled another aside to "unburden to him his irrepressible thoughts"; there another gave to a comrade a message to be passed on to loved ones if he did not survive; still others kept to themselves and wrote what they thought might be their last letter to family. Only those who were apathetic or oblivious to what the morrow might hold could sleep soundly on the eve of the battle.[7]

At dawn, as the eastern sky gradually turned from gray to blue, a haze floated at the base of the mountains and over Monterrey. But low-lying fog did not obscure the sublime sight that Nashvillian Adolphus Heiman described as "a beautiful morning, the sun had risen in all its splendour, throwing the Sierra Madre with its lofty peaks in bold relief against the clear blue sky." Already Worth's men were beginning their assault on the west side of town. Closer to the American camp—and 1,400 yards north of the Citadel—three pieces of light artillery (a ten-inch mortar and two twenty-four-pound howitzers) began to lob shots toward the Mexican fortification, with little effect. Taylor had ordered the placement of the cannon the previous day, but he had no heavy siege guns that could do damage to the enemy fort. When the long roll sounded, soldiers emerged from Walnut Springs, formed into ranks, and began marching forward. This secondary assault would consist of regulars from Twiggs's division and volunteers from Butler's division. As they began to move forward, 350 men of the First Tennessee unfurled the blue eagle pendant, which fluttered in the breeze, reminding them of the celebratory send-off they had experienced three-and-a-half months earlier in Nashville. But the pageantry and speeches were over. Dreams of glory and talk of exploits were over, too. This was the real thing, and the gravity of the moment hushed all chatter. Now it was bravery and patriotism, along with the fear of letting down comrades, that forced one foot in front of the other as forward they marched, closer to the city in preparation for the attack. Several years later, Heiman remembered that it was just such a day that they had all anticipated and now that the moment had arrived, it caused their "ambitious hearts to seek on that day, their reputation at the cannons mouth."[8]

In the early morning, Taylor ordered Twiggs's division, temporarily commanded by Lieutenant Colonel John Garland, to attack with his First and Third Infantry Regiments along with a battalion of Maryland volunteers. Taylor's parting instructions to Garland were: "if you think (or if you find) you can take any of them little forts down there with the ba'net you better do it." Taylor, of course, was referring to La Tenería and El Diablo, along with several other well-fortified buildings in the area. With eight hundred men, Garland headed toward the northeast face of the city. Initially, their advance was covered by cornfields, but as they emerged into the open, enemy guns from all across the front of the city opened fire. They veered right and soon found themselves in a deadly crossfire from Fort Tenería to their front-left and the Citadel to their right. They made a dash for the city streets to seek shelter among the houses. It was a mistake, for Mexican soldiers lined the rooftops and windows, firing at the trapped Americans. Officers valiantly tried to keep their units organized to advance on hot spots of enemy resistance, but with Mexican soldiers firing from every window and rooftop, it was a deadly undertaking. Americans were pinned down throughout the northeastern portion of Monterrey, with some trying to press deeper into the city while others fell back. Major Electus Backus had the greatest success among Garland's struggling troops, as he and two companies fought their way through the streets east toward Fort Tenería's west flank.[9]

Most of Garland's men were pinned down in the city's outskirts. Outside the city streets and in the open field to the north, Dr. N. S. Jarvis, surgeon for the Third Infantry, found a "quarry pit" that was deep enough to shield him from fire, and he directed that the wounded be brought to him there. When the Mexicans discovered that the wounded were being congregated there, they opened an intense fire on the pit, forcing Jarvis to move his aid station to the rear. The situation quickly became desperate, so General Taylor ordered Captain Braxton Bragg's four-gun battery into the city to provide support. Bragg quickly learned that he could not maneuver and fire his guns with affect in an urban setting. After Taylor rode closer to the city to see for himself what was happening, he ordered the Fourth Infantry and the First Ohio Volunteers into the fray. Lieutenant Ulysses S. Grant, regimental quartermaster of the Fourth, had been ordered to stay back in camp to guard the regiment's equipment, but when the shooting started that morning, he had ventured forward to get a glimpse of the action. He was present when his regiment was ordered to attack, and as he later wrote, "lacking the moral courage to return to camp," he went in with his unit. What was supposed to be a strong demonstration had turned into an all-out assault, probably because of Garland's interpretation of the commanding general's instructions.[10]

While Garland's men fought in the suburbs, the Tennesseans, Mississippians, and Kentuckians had been ensconced behind the three-gun battery and in an indentation of the ground, hidden from the enemy and relatively safe. They were introduced to combat incrementally. First, although they could not see anything from their position, they could hear the fighting, especially the occasional menacing whizz of cannon balls flying overhead. Then stretcher bearers made their way through the huddled Tennesseans headed for the rear with an artilleryman whose leg had been taken off by a solid shot. The reality of their situation was beginning to sink in when the order came for the Tennesseans and Mississippians to go forward and reinforce Garland's outgunned men. They were at the fandango, and it was time to dance.[11]

Apparently, none wavered. Immediately, the order to load was shouted up and down the line and instantly the rattle of ramrods and the click of hundreds of locks briefly rang out over the distant sound of battle. "Left face, double quick time," came the order, and the Tennesseans filed past the Mississippians. When the order "forward march!" rang out, the First Tennessee gave a "huzzah!" and quickly lurched forward with Jefferson Davis's Mississippians right on their heels. "[O]ur Regiment was in front," one soldier wrote to his mother after the battle.[12] Twenty-three-year-old James Burkitt from Lawrence County looked over at his eighteen-year-old brother, Joseph, and later recalled that his young "face [was] all lighted up with the joy of battle." They ran forward in column formation, one company then the next and the next, and so on, and after two hundred yards they emerged from the sunken topography that had provided shelter. They were now on the open plain and the entire panorama of battle appeared before them. Two thousand yards in front of them lay the city, and their course was aimed at the northeast corner near where Garland's men had gone in. To their right at a forty-five-degree angle stood the Black Fort "shrouded in smoke" and "blazing like a volcano," as one soldier put it.[13]

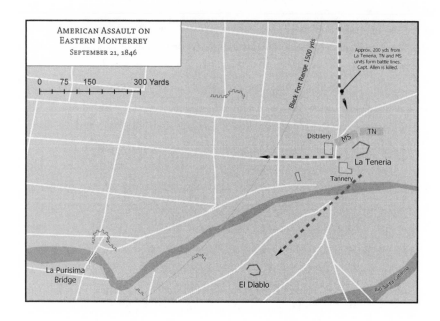

Several members of the First Tennessee reported being in a crossfire from the Citadel and Tenería during the charge, but that depiction calls for an analysis of the three principle forts, along with their armaments. The largest cannon mounted in Tenería and Diablo were nine pounders, and their effective range was seven hundred to nine hundred yards. The Citadel (Black Fort) mounted twelve pounders with a range of 1,500 to 1,600 yards. As the Tennesseans advanced, they came within artillery range nine hundred yards north of Tenería, and pressing forward another three hundred yards, they fell within the range of the guns from Diablo, which was located behind Tenería. As they advanced, they could see the Black Fort on their right, but their course appears to have taken them no closer than perhaps 1,600 yards from that fort, placing them barely at the extreme range, or perhaps just beyond range of its guns. However, seeing both fort's guns belching fire resulted in the obvious conclusion that they were in a crossfire. In addition, bouncing solid shots were lethal, and even from that range, the Black Fort's guns could do considerable damage. Recreating the regiment's path and using satellite imagery georeferenced with an 1846 map indicates that when the regiment reached a point approximately six hundred yards north of

Tenería, it may actually have been—if only briefly—in a position to be hit from all three Mexican forts.[14]

Crossing the deadly ground, about a mile in distance from the depression in the terrain to the outskirts of the city, took perhaps twenty minutes. For the First Tennessee, it was the bloodiest twenty minutes of the entire war. Their pace quickened as they ran across the open plain, and each step they took placed them closer to the deadly guns of Tenería and Diablo, along with the menacing Black Fort always on their right. Although the latter was nearly out of range, soldiers' accounts indicate that they were close enough to see and feel the effects of its fire. The converging fire created "a perfect hurricane of balls," remembered John Robertson. George Nixon later recounted to his wife that "cannon balls passed in every direction several passed within less than one foot of me." When over halfway to their objective a solid shot passed through the front of the column killing four and wounding three from Lawrence County's Company M. Because a column formation is narrow and deep, the shot likely came from the front. The entire column had to pass over the ground where these seven dead and wounded lay, but "they passed on rapidly without much disorder," reported Colonel Campbell. This stalwart resolve was particularly noteworthy for James Burkitt, who pressed on with his comrades even though one of the seven was his brother Joseph. A Mississippian, following on the heals of the Tennesseans, passed by this grisly scene and remembered "how it made the soul shrink in, to see the broken limbs, the blood, to hear the groan." Most horrifying was his memory of one of the seven "sitting on a rock, holding in his bowels, and singing a psalm!"[15]

When they reached 150 to two hundred yards from Tenería on the edge of town, Campbell halted the column and attempted to deploy the companies into linear formation. However, they were now within range of small arms, and a sheet of musketry tore into the ranks of the Tennesseans, causing them to waver. The young volunteers, whose four months in the army had afforded them little training and no experience, responded instinctively in the face of withering fire. According to Campbell's battle report, the fire "was so galling and destructive at this time, that it caused my whole line to recoil and fall back 15 or 20 paces." But instinct also told them to shoot back. So, for several bloody minutes they remained stationary without cover while they loaded and fired as quickly as they could amid growing confusion and mounting casualties. According to Captain Frank Cheatham, "we found ourselves under a deadly cross fire of cannon Balls, shells, grape and musketry, from three different forts," and another soldier concluded, "God only knows how I escaped."[16]

Captain William B. Allen's company of Lawrence County boys had been so positioned as it ran the mile to the city that it had been "cut to pieces" even before the deadly stall. Here, at this spot, Allen was killed. When he left home, Allen's father gave him the sword that he had carried as a soldier in the War of 1812. Now standing on the Monterrey plain with that sword in hand, trying to get his men aligned and moving forward, Allen was shot in the breast. He died instantly, still clutching his father's sword. An 1844 graduate of the University of Nashville, Allen was intellectually and oratorically gifted. Immediately upon his graduation at age twenty, he had been elected to a seat in the state legislature. Because of Allen's ability and reputation, the Lawrence County boys had chosen him as their company commander, and his death was devastating. The unintended pause lasted only a few minutes, but that period of time meant "death to a great many," remembered one soldier.[17]

Nearby, Dr. William Dorris helped the wounded. His grandfather, Joseph Dorris, had been a well-known Baptist preacher who had served as a chaplain in Andrew Jackson's army in the previous war. Grandson William was a religious man but found his calling in trying to heal the body rather than the soul. He was a native of Middle Tennessee and a graduate of Transylvania University in Kentucky. Dorris did not hesitate to put himself in harm's way on the Monterrey battlefield. At one point, while he knelt over a wounded soldier who lay on the bloody ground, his probe was shot out of his hand, so he cut a stick to the size he needed and used it to continue probing the man's wound. He extricated the musket ball, and the man survived.[18]

During the halt, Colonel Campbell and Lieutenant Colonel Samuel Anderson remained busy trying to get the companies reorganized and moving forward in line of attack. Still on horseback, and thus conspicuous targets, they rode through the ranks shouting directions at their men and imploring company commanders to get their units deployed. Anderson later reported that a musket ball passed through his cap, one passed through his coat and another one went through his horse's mouth. Thirty-seven-year-old adjutant Adolphus Heiman also performed heroically in moving up and down the line trying to keep the regiment organized and moving. Writing about the battle a dozen years later, Heiman said that the events of that day were "as vivid in my mind as if it was done yesterday." Unfortunately, all of the shouting and cajoling by the officers did little good because the noise of battle coupled with the fervor with which the Tennesseans were loading and firing, prevented them from hearing the commands.[19]

Finally, after several bloody minutes, a lull in the thunder of battle allowed the officers to regain a semblance of control. The same instinct that caused them to reel in the face of withering fire now told them that to stay where they were would be disastrous. Anderson knew that their only two choices were to "storm the fort or retreat in disgrace," and later he proudly wrote, "You may very well know which course we took." Cheatham, too, surmised that he and his men were "without any chance of extricating ourselves except by charging at the mouth of the cannon, the forts in our front."[20] Campbell also understood that with his men falling all around, it was more expedient to rush the fort than to get the companies properly aligned, so he ordered an immediate charge. Company commanders quickly obeyed, including Cheatham, who bellowed, "Come on men! Follow me!" and just as he would do a decade-and-a-half later at places like Shiloh and Stones River, he led his men straight into enemy fire.[21]

Jefferson Davis's First Mississippi had come up and formed to the right of the First Tennessee, and now both regiments made the last 150-yard dash simultaneously. Relentless Mexican fire continued to wreak havoc. According to Lieutenant Patrick Duffy, "it seemed like a sheet of fire from east to west all along the north side of town." Describing the attack to his wife the following month, Lieutenant George Nixon wrote, "I pressed forward to the *charge* and as to the muskett balles that passed . . . if you had had a hand full of pees and threw them at me at ten pases, they couldent be any thicker." As Cheatham charged forward, sword in hand, he saw a cannon ball hit the ground in front of him. (The low muzzle velocity of nineteenth-century artillery often made cannon balls visible to soldiers.) He recounted how his fast reflexes saved him: "as quick as lightning I dropped to my knees to let it pass over me. I had scarcely touched the ground, when a musket ball wized across my back, just breaking the skin, but it burnt me at the time as if a coal of fire had have been dropped upon my back." He knew how lucky he was, for had he not ducked "I should have been shot through." Cheatham survived while three men near were shot during the day, and he later wondered how he made it through the battle alive.[22]

When they were within thirty yards of Fort Tenería, the Mexicans discharged their cannon one last time before abandoning the guns. Within seconds, the Americans were swarming over the walls and into the fort as the defenders ran "pell mell in every direction." The Tennesseans took a few prisoners but fired on those trying to escape, many of them fleeing to the nearby stone tannery behind the fort. When Nixon scaled the top of the rampart, he encountered a Mexican trying frantically to load a cannon for one last shot. Nixon fired his pistol and "he instantly fell. . . . I sent him to another wourld." Minutes after Tenería fell, the First Tennessee's blue eagle banner was flying over the ramparts—the first regimental flag to do so.[23]

Although the fort's defenders were fleeing, the Americans contin-ued to be subjected to deadly fire from Mexican soldiers, who lined the rooftop of the fortified tannery just beyond. So, some of the attackers, instead of entering Tenería, swung around it and surged on to the source of the musketry. Many of these were apparently from the Mississippi Regiment, and Colonel Jefferson Davis followed the Mexicans so closely on their heels that he burst through the door of the building right behind the last enemy soldier, and there received the surrender of all those inside. Mississippians, along with a few intermingled Tennesseans, attempted to press on toward Fort El Diablo but soon were ordered back. It was late morning, and Taylor's army now held a strong lodgment in the northeast corner of Monterrey. Of the soldiers who had launched the initial attack that morning (First, Third and Fourth Infantry along with Maryland and Ohio volunteers), some had retreated when they encountered the withering fire, but others had remained in the suburbs of the city, fighting to hold on to the streets they occupied. In fact, members of the First Infantry had worked their way over to a nearby building flanking the tannery, seized it, and had been firing at the fort's defenders as the Tennesseans and Mississippians charged.[24]

The danger remained but not with the same level of intensity as their bloody dash across the plain. With Tenería in American hands, the Tennesseans remained under fire, but now they at least had the benefit of cover inside the fort. They had just run a mile under heavy fire, and the shelter offered an opportunity to catch their breath and perhaps reflect on what they had just accomplished. In the days that followed, the question would arise, who was first to go over the rampart of the fort? Patrick Duffy claimed with pride to be the first American in Fort Tenería—"I believe I was the first man on the fort." But Lieutenant George Nixon from Lawrence County also claimed the recognition in a letter to his wife Sarah, asserting that he "had the honor of waving the first sword" over the fort, and another member of the regiment remembered Nixon being the first. A month later, in another letter to Sarah, he restated his claim: "I was the first man on the rampart of Monterey." Another source asserts that Frank Cheatham was the "first captain" in the fort, a claim that does not necessarily contradict Duffy's or Nixon's.[25] Clearly, for a man to be able to declare that he was the first was to allow him to lay claim to a higher magnitude of honor and glory. But the real debate over who was first was not among the Tennesseans; it was between the Tennesseans and Mississippians, and that dispute became fully engaged soon after the smoke had settle over Monterrey.

After taking Tenería, James Burkitt was not concerned about who had been first. His thoughts were of his brother, Joseph, who had been struck by a solid shot during the charge. James returned to the spot where his brother had gone down and accompanied litter bearers who carried him back to camp. Joseph was conscious but badly injured, and back at camp he survived only a short time, all the while being cradled in James's arms. In his final minutes the eighteen year old expressed to James pride in the way his life was ending. "I am dying satisfied, for I fell at my post. Tell mother how I died, and not to grieve after me." After pausing and struggling for breath, he instructed James to "Get the money due me and give it to mother." Then as he looked into his older brother's eyes, he crossed his arms over his chest and died.[26]

Back in Monterrey, the Americans had gained a toehold on the eastern side of the city. It was early afternoon when General Taylor, hoping to press his advantage, gave orders to push deeper into the city. In response, the Ohio volunteers, whose earlier attack route had taken them into the suburbs farther west or to the right of the Tennesseans and Mississippians, began to work their way southeast in an effort to flank Fort El Diablo. Colonel Garland rounded up some regulars to assist in the effort as General Butler took personal command of this urban flank attack. But the going was slow. As they fought their way from block to block, they encountered dead and wounded Americans from that morning's desperate street fighting. The Mexicans had blockaded the streets and turned every house into a sandbagged fortification. America's introduction to urban warfare was a bloody experience.[27]

As the soldiers made their way toward El Diablo, they "met a nasty surprise," as Colonel Garland put it. A hundred yards to the south, two cannon from the fortified Purisima Bridge unleashed a deadly fire on them. Garland shifted his attention to the bridge and moved his men in that direction in an effort to knock out the enemy guns, but the task was difficult and the toll on his men was heavy. Then orders arrived at Fort Tenería for Tennessee troops to support Captain Randolph Ridgely's battery in an attempt to knock out the troubling Mexican guns at the bridge. To do so, Ridgely needed to position his battery directly north of the bridge, which meant the Tennesseans had to work their way from the fort in a westward direction six hundred yards to support the artillerists. Captain William Blackmore did not hesitate as he led about fifty of his Sumner County company into the dangerous streets of eastern Monterrey.[28]

From this mission comes one of the most poignant examples of loyal comradeship during the entire war. When they had gone about two-thirds of the way to their objective, Corporal Julius Elliott fell wounded in the street. Two comrades, Nimrod Smith and Hynds Martin, picked him up and carried him into a nearby house for protection before the company continued up the street. When they reached their designated place, they quickly learned that Ridgely's guns could not maneuver through the streets without great difficulty and that their numbers were not sufficient to turn the lopsided battle at the bridge in their favor. So, the Tennesseans began to retrace their steps back to Fort Tenería. They stopped to check on Elliott, but because they had nothing with which to carry him, Captain Blackmore decided to leave a few men with him, return to the fort with the bulk of his company, and send back a stretcher. Accordingly, Smith, Martin, and Private James Cartwright stayed behind with Elliott. Because there were still U.S. soldiers up the street, the men felt safe being left there in the house. Soon, however, a strong contingent of Mexican cavalry (lancers) began to push their way down the streets, sweeping all Americans back as they advanced. As U.S. troops retreated past the house that sheltered the Tennesseans, Smith and Cartwright chose to fall back with them, but Martin declined to leave. Elliott insisted that Martin retreat with the rest and leave him there since there was nothing that Martin could do for him. But Martin, determined to accept whatever fate befell Elliott, would not go. With that, Smith and Cartwright left their friends. When the lancers reached their location, they entered the house and killed both men. Martin's loyalty, explained Blackmore in a letter to the Martin family, "turned into a personal sacrifice. . . . His bravery was an honor to the family name."[29]

The actions of the lancers enraged the American soldiers. As they advanced up the narrow cobblestone streets, they killed every wounded American they encountered, usually by cutting their throats. Sometimes they mutilated their bodies but always they robbed them of their valuables. All the while they shouted: *"Es esta el fandango de Monterey, eh? Esta una fandango mucho!"*[30] When the Sumner County boys got back to the house where they had left Elliott, they found that enemy soldiers had "cut him almost to pieces and then striped him of every thing." After retrieving the bodies, the Tennesseans buried them beside each other.[31]

Later in the afternoon, the Ohio and Kentucky volunteers relieved the First Tennessee, which was ordered back to camp at Walnut Springs. On their way back across the plain, they saw the carnage created a few hours earlier during their attack. The dead and wounded lay all around. "Oh! How can I ever forget the heart piercing cries of the poor fellows, who were suffering from their wounds." They saw, too, that wagons had come forward, and attendants were loading as many of the wounded as possible to take to the rear. While the grisly task was underway, Mexican gunners from the Black Fort continued to lob shots across the plain trying to pick off medical wagons, and at least one ball found its target, smashing into a wagon and killing the wounded inside. As the rest of the regiment moved to the rear, Captain Frank Cheatham volunteered to stay behind on the plain to make sure all the Tennesseans were gathered and loaded.[32]

There had been hard-won success on both sides of Monterrey on the twenty-first. West of town, General Worth's flanking column had seized the road to Saltillo, crossed the Santa Catarina River and successfully captured Mexican fortifications atop Federation Hill. Jack Hays's Texans, fighting dismounted, led the attack that morning. Worth's men assaulted and captured two enemy forts on Federation Hill and turned the captured guns on other Mexican fortifications on Independence Hill. Their elevated location made the forts difficult to attack, but Worth's accomplishments had come with less than twenty casualties. Balie Peyton had been with Worth on his western approach, having offered his services as a voluntary aide since the disbandment of his Louisiana unit. Early in the engagement, Worth had sent Peyton to deliver a message to Taylor, a task that Peyton undertook while under fire. Being on a swift thoroughbred, the accomplished horseman from Tennessee lit out on a "dead run" and succeeded in his mission.[33]

As the sun faded that evening, the weary boys from Tennessee settled back into their camp at Walnut Springs. Just twelve hours earlier, with a spring in their step, they had courageously marched forward to see the elephant. Those who had escaped uninjured returned drained and exhausted—and different. They had experienced combat, seen friends die, perhaps killed other men, gone through the fire that tested their courage and, in so doing, had lost their innocence. They had done their duty with honor, and they would never be the same. A cold rain fell that night and that, coupled with the steady cries and moans of the wounded punctuated by the sporadic boom of artillery, made sleep difficult. Adolphus Heiman remembered that "The night . . . was gloomy in every respect, . . . it was dark and rainy, and the sufferings of the severely and mortally wounded were painful to behold."[34]

Throughout the night, surgeons worked to repair the damage done on the battlefield. Doctor Edmund Kirby Chamberlain described that night: "I was, therefore, ordered into camp, and performed eight amputations, as fast as I could get along. . . . My work of extracting, and excising balls, securing blood-vessels, and dressing contused wounds, continued during the livelong night." Chamberlain was with the First Ohio volunteers, but his duties were not confined to Ohio's wounded. "I have amputated for the Tennessee, the Mississippi, and my own regiment, and three regulars,—besides, there are a number of limbs, that, in all probability, must yet come off. It seems all blood,—blood,—blood!—and I am heartily sick of it."[35]

Next day, the Tennesseans were ordered back to Fort Tenería. On their way, they ran across Colonel George Croghan, whose bold defense of a fort on the Sandusky River in 1813 had brought him fame along with the sobriquet "hero of Sandusky." Heiman recognized him and half-jokingly commented that another day like yesterday and there would not be enough men left to bury the dead. To which Croghan responded, "Oh! . . . your Regiment might get into forty Battles, but you will not suffer so again." Back at Tenería for the day, they enjoyed the relative safety of the fort's walls. Enemy guns from El Diablo lobbed an occasional shot in their direction but with little effect. They did not venture into the city nor did Mexican troops try to retake the fort, but across town American forces continued to press their advantage by capturing fortified positions on Independence Hill. Lieutenants James Longstreet, George G. Meade, John Pemberton, Daniel Harvey Hill, and other men of future Civil War prominence participated in the attacks on the western heights. With all of the enemy strongholds west of Monterrey under Worth's control by the afternoon of the twenty-second, and the investment of the city complete, the captured Mexican guns were turned on the city.[36]

During the night of the twenty-second and in the predawn hours of Wednesday the twenty-third, the Mexican commander, General Pedro de Ampudia, ordered his troops to fall back from their positions around Monterrey's extremities and constrict their lines to form a tighter, more concentrated defense in the heart of the city. Consequently, on Wednesday morning, the Americans on the east side were surprised to find El Diablo and other fortified positions abandoned. Taylor viewed this as an invitation to push deeper into Monterrey, so at his instruction, Quitman ordered two companies of the First Mississippi and two companies of the First Tennessee to begin working their way west toward the main plaza. From block to block they began pushing the defenders back.[37]

It was a grisly day of urban combat. Patrick Duffy from Sumner County described his company's actions: "into the street we went and commenced our day's work, shooting and slaying, and driving them before us out of the streets and yards and house tops." He described the fighting as "hot" and went on to explain how they fought "the enemy in their own houses and killing and driving them from their own firesides, cutting down their doors and running them from their wives and children. . . . The havoc made . . . was terrible." The fighting was desperate, and at times the Tennesseans used axes and bayonets to dig through the adobe walls from house to house so as to avoid exposing themselves to deadly fire in the streets. After a while, Taylor ordered a unit of Texans to reinforce the volunteers. The Texans came in like an "avalanche," Duffy explained. "They hate the Mexicans so bitterly that they seem to think it no crime to shoot or kill them. These men fought with the fury of fiends from wall to wall, from house top to house top, killing every man they found." General Taylor was on the east side of the city, and he gave the following rather bland summary of the events he observed: "Our troops advanced from house to house, and from square to square, until they reached a street but one square in the rear of the principal Plaza, in and near which the enemy's force was mainly concentrated."[38]

Meanwhile, General Worth's men were doing the same thing from the west. On both fronts Taylor's army pressed together toward the center of Monterrey like a deadly pincer. In the evening, Taylor ordered a halt so that he could consult with Worth about a concerted attack on the morrow. The Mexican army had pulled back so that it occupied only the area around the main plaza, and with all hope of defending the city lost, General Ampudia knew that surrender was his only option. At 3:00 a.m. Thursday, Taylor received Ampudia's request for surrender terms, and in the afternoon Taylor sent three commissioners, General William Worth, Colonel Jefferson Davis, and former Texas governor and commander of the Texas Division General J. Pinckney Henderson, to treat with their Mexican counterparts. Ampudia's army began to evacuate the city two days later, and under the generous (and controversial) terms of the capitulation, they carried their muskets with them and one six-gun battery. They agreed to retreat forty miles below the city, and Taylor settled that he would not advance for eight weeks.[39]

Burial details went out on the battlefield on Friday the twenty-fifth to collect and bury the dead. The rocky ground made digging difficult, so the dead usually ended up in shallow graves, and they were buried, remembered one Tennessean, "upon the spot where each had fallen, without even the ordinary ceremonies that attend a soldier's burial."[40] It was a sobering and sad task, but it had to be done, and many times over. Captain Robert Bennett from Sumner County reflected that "many a brave Tennessean, . . . now sleeps near the enemies batteries." Colonel Campbell reported twenty-seven killed in his regiment, but within a few days two of the wounded had died bringing the number of Tennesseans killed at Monterrey to twenty-nine with another seventy-six wounded. The regiment's casualties were 22 percent of the army's total losses (488). A Lawrence County soldier lamented the loss of his messmates who shed their blood "for their country's glory." Glory was on Captain Bennett's mind, too, as he assuaged his melancholy mood by remembering that his fellow Tennesseans "won a glorious grave, and died a glorious death while charging upon the enemies of their country."[41]

Several of the wounded would die in the days ahead, and those who suffered with their wounds likely did not consider it glorious. Private William Young from Smith County was fatally wounded during the charge on the twenty-first. He was shot in the groin, and his injury was described by the Third Infantry surgeon, Dr. Jarvis. After the ball entered the lower abdomen, it "ranged diagonally across the pelvis, inclining downwards, wounding both the bladder and rectum, and passing out . . . just above the os coccygis; urine and fæces passed from both orifices of the wound." Attendants inserted a catheter and dressed the wounds. "In this condition he lingered *twenty-three* days, when he expired, worn out . . . by long-continued suffering."[42]

It took Richard Gifford, another Smith Countian, two years to die from his Monterrey wound, and his story is tragic. When he volunteered in 1846, he and wife Mary had been married for twenty-eight years and had four children, ages seven to twenty-one. Gifford was seriously wounded during the charge on the fort—shot in the "thick part of his thigh" near the hip joint, reported company commander William McMurray, and the ball could not be extracted. He remained in a makeshift hospital for two weeks, and while there, he became "badly deranged," threatening others with a knife, musket, or whatever weapon he could get his hands on. A guard had to be assigned to watch him at all times lest he hurt someone. On November 10, he was discharged and sent home. Over the months, Gifford's irrational behavior worsened, and controlling him became an increasingly challenging task for Mary and the children. Sometimes their only resort was to tie him down. As Mary later stated, Richard eventually "became a raving maniac" and the only recourse was to lock him up in the Carthage jail, where he died on December 5, 1848, twenty-five months after returning home. A physician's statement gave the cause of death as "derangement." Mary died three years later.[43]

In the days following the battle, some of the Tennesseans wrote home, telling family about the riveting and bloody experience; their letters were filled with reflection and pride. Frank Cheatham told his Nashville family, "The Mexicans say that we are the first people, that they ever saw, run up into the canons mouth, they wanted to know where we came from, and what kind of people we were." Patrick Duffy was particularly effusive in a letter to his brother Francis. Capturing the fort "was a glorious moment for Tennessee . . . [whose] military fame was already high." Foremost on his mind was the regiment's obligation to uphold the state's honor and prove itself worthy of the home folks' pride. "[W]e knew that the eyes of all our noble state was turned towards us and watching eagerly every movement with breathles anxiety and expecting much at our hands." Everyone knew, he continued, that given the opportunity the First Tennessee "would give a good account of its self." In capturing Fort Tenería at the point of the bayonet, they proved that their generation was capable of maintaining the volunteer state's legacy. This was "the proudest moment of my life," Duffy wrote.[44] The state's honor had been upheld.

Duffy's letter not only expressed pride in his regiment, but also informed his family of the safety and conduct of his nephew, Tom. Duffy's greatest fear during the battle had been the fact that Tom was by his side throughout. He worried for his kinsman's safety and stated that he "hoped never to have to go into battle agan with a relation." The parting warning Tom's family had given him before he left home was to not get shot in the back. Now Patrick wrote to assure them that Tom had "acted nobly showing himself to be a Duffy and worthy of the name." Family honor also had been upheld.[45]

Hometown newspapers confirmed that the state's honor had been preserved. The Lebanon *Banner* spoke of "unfading laurels," and went on to assert that the Tennesseans "have indeed proved themselves the sons of those brave sires who triumphed at the horseshoe and at New Orleans. While our state is doomed to mourn, she may be allowed to indulge an honest pride." General Quitman used similar terminology in describing the Tennesseans who attacked with "characteristic valor," proving they were sons of the men who fought under Andrew Jackson and were "worthy of their sires." Some of the volunteers were so anxious that the folks back home know what they had done at Monterrey that they wrote directly to newspapers, which then spread the story. On November 17, Lieutenant Colonel Samuel Anderson wrote a letter to the Gallatin *Union*, which was later reprinted in the *National Union*, wherein he informed the mid-state readers that the Sumner County boys "bore a noble part in this desperate contest, and were amongst the very first on the fort." A newspaper account the following spring alluded to "the glory resulting to our country" as a result of the battle and the "individual heroism" of the boys from Tennessee.[46]

The fandango at Monterrey had won the regiment the moniker "The Bloody First," a label it would carry with pride for the remainder of its service and back home afterward. However, as word spread of their gallant storming of Fort Tenería, not everyone agreed with the Tennesseans' version of the battle. Jeff Davis and his Mississippians were confident that theirs had been the first regiment to reach the fort, and that their Lieutenant Colonel Alexander McClung was the first man on the ramparts. They took exception to the claim made by the Tennesseans. They were also offended that the Tennesseans had lifted their regimental banner over the fort as it fell, an honor, they contended, that should have gone to the actual first regiment to enter the fort.

The controversy began when Colonel Campbell clearly laid claim to the honor on behalf of his regiment in his battle report and in a letter to his Virginia relative. To David Campbell, he described the capture of the fort thus: the Mississippi regiment "rushed forward with my men, but my Regt. being more directly in front of the fort and nearer to it than the Miss. Regt. reached it sooner and were the command that stormed the fort." In his report to General Quitman, Campbell wrote; "From the position I occupied (for I was on horseback) I could see that my regiment were the first to enter the fort as a body of troops, although individuals of another regiment may have entered with the first of my regiment." This statement provides latitude for interpretation and leaves open the possibility that a few Mississippians may have entered the fort simultaneously with his men (maybe even just ahead of them), but that the majority of the early arrivers were Tennesseans. In letters home, however, he clearly asserted that his regiment was the first in the fort and the Mississippians played a supporting role.[47]

While there is no definitive evidence one way or the other, in fact, most sources tend to favor the Mississippians' account placing their regiment and McClung as winners of the race to the fort. Because the First Mississippi was to the right of the First Tennessee during the charge, their position put them more directly in front of the west side of the fort and thus closer to the open embrasure, perhaps giving them quicker and easier access to the fort's walls and interior.[48]

Campbell wrote his report and letters with the best recollection he had of a chaotic battlefield, and although he did not intend for his correspondence to be published, one of his letters appeared in newspapers. Campbell had written honestly and with no ill intent, but Colonel Davis turned the disagreement into a vitriolic crusade. Davis was angry, and he wrote letters to the press back home denouncing Campbell's claim and asserting that Campbell's version was "improbable, unjust, and injurious to us." The brigade commander, General John Quitman from Mississippi, tried to remain neutral in the debate, but at length he succumbed to pressure from fellow Mississippians and sided with their position.[49]

When Tennesseans learned that the Mississippians were trying to "steal" their glory, the debate was fully engaged. Captain Cheatham vented in a letter to family: "It is the most rascally, ungentlemanly, and unsoldier like piece of conduct that was ever heard of to undertake to rob us of the honor and glory that we had won at the cost of so many of Tennessees noble sons." He went on to write that everyone in the army knows that "we have the *honour* of having been first in the fort, after one of the most desperate charges ever heard of." They are trying "to appropriate to themselves the '*first* honor' in the capture of the fort," wrote Sergeant James McDaniel from Nashville, who asserted complete confidence in the "facts." John Robertson believed that Davis's claim was a "glaring injustice" to Tennessee.[50] Balie Peyton, who had deep Tennessee roots and sympathies, had been with Worth's division throughout the battle and thus was not an eyewitness to the Tenería charge. Nevertheless, he sided with his native state in a letter praising the Tennesseans as "the first regiment which stormed the fort." When the letter was published in newspapers, Davis demanded that Peyton correct his false statements. Lieutenant George Meade, also with Worth's division and not an eyewitness, had no such native sympathies, and he too sided with the Tennesseans. In a letter to his wife, he proclaimed Campbell's men to be "the first to enter."[51]

While Campbell had given the Mississippians a share of the credit in his telling of the attack, Davis hardly mention the Tennesseans in his version except to say that they were engaged in a maneuver and not within his sight during the final charge. When someone asked Davis why his regiment had only seven killed while the First Tennessee suffered four times more deaths, he supposedly responded that when the Mexicans fired at the oncoming Americans, the Mississippians were so far ahead of everyone else that the shots went over their heads.[52] It was an extended debate. Five months after the battle, Campbell promised to correct "the claim which Col. Davis has set up for the First Mississippi in taking the fort No. 1 at the battle of Monterey. It is most presumptuous, and as soon as I have time to devote to the subject, I will expose his false statements." But the dispute was never adequately settled. That Davis was an ardent Democrat and Campbell a prominent Whig only exacerbated the issue. According to a Mississippi Whig, Davis's motive in this imbroglio was "to make a little Locofoco capital at home for Mississippi consumption." One of Davis's biographers, William Cooper, accurately identified the twin motives behind the dispute as pride and politics.[53]

Both regiments had performed admirably in their first test of combat and both deserved credit and praise. A Texan accurately asserted that both regiments had "distinguished themselves" and that their attack on the fort was among the most "noble charges ever know[n] in the histories of Battles."[54] John Robertson decided not to be so partisan about it because, he contended, praising Mississippi was like paying an indirect compliment to Tennessee. "To detract from . . . Mississippi would be to detract from Tennessee, for more than one-third of Davis' rifle regiment were from Tennessee." Among them was Major Alexander B. Bradford, a native of Madison County, who "does not pretend to claim the honor" of beating the Tennesseans into the fort.[55] Together, Tennessee and Mississippi, along with the support of regular troops, had contributed significantly to the outcome of the battle and in so doing had demonstrated that there was ample glory for all involved.

*Chapter Five*

# CAUGHT IN THE IDLENESS OF WAR

The controversy over who got there first did not trouble members of the Second Tennessee back in Camargo. Rather, their concern was with who got there at all. On September 27, a report of the battle arrived, detailing the heavy involvement and losses of the First Tennessee. The news of the decisive role played by volunteers from Tennessee and Mississippi, as well as the involvement of Ohio and Kentucky troops, was a source of pride for the volunteers in Camargo, but it was also a crushing blow to their ambitions. Learning that the army had won a major battle, and with the help of volunteers, meant that those left behind a few weeks earlier had missed a grand opportunity. An Alabamian expressed what could have been written by scores of Tennesseans when he penned in his journal that his comrades "are mortified at not being at the battle. They say that they have been cheated out of their just rights." Tennesseans, indeed, expressed similar sentiments. In a letter from Camargo, John McClanahan from Jackson, Tennessee, shared the frustration that he and his companions felt. "I am sure he [General Taylor] will never receive the forgiveness of the Second [Tennessee] Regiment for not moving them on and giving them an opportunity to share in the danger and participate in the glory of their friends and brothers of the First."[1]

Some of the Tennessee officers were also unhappy about being left behind. Two weeks prior to Taylor's march from Camargo to Monterrey,

General Gideon Pillow wrote his wife expressing how much he missed her and the children. "Duty to my country calls me here," he wrote, "and that duty must be met and will require . . . great Privation." When he learned that he must remain at Camargo as the army moved forward, Pillow could add disappointment and frustration to his list of privations. He was "greatly dissatisfied" with Taylor's decision to leave him there. Pillow's friend and aide-de-camp, Captain William Caswell from Knox County, felt cheated also. In a letter to his family, Caswell wrote explaining that he had been "compelled to remain here . . . under what I consider a very unjust decision of Genl. Taylor." Consequently, he could only "curse my luck & sweat here under the burning sun of Carmargo."[2]

Wiley Hale's letters to his mother indicate that he had several things on his mind. He was quick to inform her that "our boys are very bitter against Genl. Taylor for not ordering us up to Monterey before the battle." But he also relayed to her other news from the Second Tennessee's Avengers at Camargo. William Goodrich, Benjamin James, and O. W. Stillwell had died of disease, but overall the company enjoyed improving health. Regarding his friend and mentor, William Haskell, Hale instructed his mother to "tell Mrs. Haskell that the Colonel enjoys excellent health" and that he is "a most excellent officer." Clearly, Hale was thinking about his return home and likely about Caroline Haskell, who was waiting for him. "All my hopes are now centered in Jackson for the present." In one of his letters, he enclosed some wild flowers that he had picked along the bank of the Rio Grande with instructions for his mother to give them to Caroline. In an October 3 letter, he opined about what he might do for a living when he returned, and he expressed his desire that the family "keep my horse fat. I want to keep him." The young officer obviously was thinking about his future, but he had one objective to fulfill before leaving Mexico, which he shared with his mother at the conclusion of that October 3 missive: "All that I care for here is that we may get into one hard battle before we return. . . . If we *do* I shall do something to be mentioned for in dispatches or die."[3] Unfortunately for Wiley Hale, it would be the latter, for he was destined to return home in a coffin.

Rampant disease persisted at Camargo, adding to the depression of the healthy who were left behind. Taylor had failed to provide hospitals for the sick who were packed by the half dozen into hot tents. In addition to measles and dysentery, which dominated early sick reports, now yellow fever ravaged the ranks. The Second Tennessee, already decimated by illness when it arrived at Camargo, added between twenty-five and thirty to its sick rolls every week after its arrival. By September, only 317 in the regiment were fit for duty. Among the Georgia volunteers only 370 out of 795 were fit for duty, and 324 out of 754 in the Alabama regiment. Sensitive to the comfort of the men, Pillow seized several large houses in the town and moved the sick Tennesseans in, promising to pay the homeowners out of his own pocket if the U.S. government did not reimburse them. He visited the sick regularly, and some of the Tennesseans credited his care with saving lives.[4] Nonetheless, the Tennesseans died at an alarming rate, and so many were sick that Pillow had to requisition men from the Alabama regiment to bury Tennessee's dead. Altogether approximately 1,500 Americans died at Camargo.[5]

Even without the problem of disease, Camargo remained a dangerous place. Mexican guerrillas kept an eye on all the roads in the vicinity and were a constant threat to troops and supplies traveling between Camargo and Monterrey. It was not uncommon for American soldiers who fell behind on a march or wandered away from the safety of the army to fall prey to bandits and guerrillas. On September 29, two days after news of the battle arrived, the bodies of two Tennesseans from Memphis were found. They had gone hunting—a common activity for soldiers trying to supplement their meager rations—and, when found, they had multiple stab wounds in the chest, slit throats, and gunshot wounds. The manner of their death was "shocking." A host of volunteers vowed revenge, and the next day Colonel Haskell, accompanied by his adjutant, Captain Hale, and sixty other mounted troops, rode out in a vain search for the guilty Mexicans. A few weeks later, a Mexican civilian was indiscriminately murdered near the Tennessee and Alabama camps and not long afterward two more Mexicans were found dead. Most people assumed that it was in retaliation for the two dead Tennesseans. Pillow and other officers condemned the vigilante killings and promised to hang the perpetrators, but the offending persons were never identified.[6]

With sickness all around and the generally deplorable conditions in Camargo, depression was common place. Caswell worried endlessly about the prevalence of disease and about missing his chance for combat, and if that was not enough to affect his performance as a staff officer, he borrowed money from Pillow habitually, referring to his superior as "a good financier." That problem, coupled with his despondency, caused Pillow to replace him as aide-de-camp. Pillow's servant Alfred was also affected. To try to buoy his mental state, Pillow offered him his freedom if he wanted to remain in Mexico, but Alfred declined, saying that he would rather go home.[7]

Demoralization over the missed opportunity for battle also contributed to a breakdown in discipline among the volunteers. The relationship between Pillow and the Alabama regiment became particularly strained, stemming from the fact that Pillow blamed the Alabamians for the wanton murder of the Mexican civilians mentioned previously. On one occasion when Pillow and General Robert Patterson ordered the Tennesseans and Alabamians into formation, the Alabamians reportedly "howled and brayed like jackasses" in a blatant show of disrespect. The following day, Pillow addressed the regiment concerning its undisciplined conduct, but there is no indication whether his appeal helped. They were volunteers who lacked the training and discipline of regular soldiers, they were hundreds of miles from home, and they had just been deprived of an opportunity to fight, which was their reason for being there. Furthermore, they were stuck in a miserable place with little to occupy their time. It was, as one writer put it, a case of volunteers being "caught in the idleness of war."[8]

With hostile guerrillas roaming the countryside and reports that the surrounding farmers had joined partisan bands, alarms occasionally interrupted Camargo's daily boredom. To guard against possible attacks, officers ordered streets barricaded and defensive positions constructed. Other precautions were taken to keep the men alert, and Pillow established a regular system of drill and instruction for the volunteers as further training in the art of soldiering. It was in this atmosphere that Pillow made an amateurish blunder that would taint him during the remainder of his Mexico service and dog him for the rest of his life.

During the construction of a breastwork, he ordered the men to dig the ditch on the inside of the wall rather than the proper location on the outer face where it would impede an attacking force. The regulars in Camargo had a great time making fun of the volunteer general. To the regulars and especially the West Point trained officers, Pillow was the epitome of the political appointee, a friend of the president, who lacked the rudimentary knowledge of how to lead troops. The story of Pillow's ditch was retold many times in the fall of 1846 until the Tennessean was a laughing stock, and years later, memory of the story persisted.[9]

The Pillow case was but a single example of the general friction that existed between volunteers and regulars that reared its head during the idleness that followed the Battle of Monterrey. Volunteers were notoriously undisciplined in every aspect of military life—from camp sanitation, which contributed to their lengthy sick rolls, to disrespect for the lives of Mexican civilians, which led to assaults, rapes, and murders. They were the ones who, more so than regulars, sought out fandangos and saloons in search of personal entertainment, and because their drunkenness and rowdiness were renowned, officers routinely stationed military guards at such locations to keep the troops in line.[10]

The idleness that permeated Taylor's occupation of Monterrey also took its toll on army discipline there. Regular officers were quick to point out the deficiencies of the volunteers. Daniel Harvey Hill, an 1842 West Point graduate, wrote extensively in his diary about his disdain for volunteers. "Volunteers had committed outrages of every kind," he wrote. They are most often the perpetrators of rapes and robberies, Hill asserted, and they commit their crimes "in the broad light of day." Several weeks after the battle, he wrote that "the excesses of the Volunteers in Monterey" are "frightful." When Hill and others mentioned specific volunteer units in connection with such depredations, they rarely—if ever—mentioned Tennesseans as participants in such acts. The most common accusations seem to have been leveled against Kentucky, Arkansas, and Texas volunteers. Their actions were so bad that a Mexican priest referred to them as "*vomit from Hell.*"[11]

Maltreatment of the civilian population often resulted in retaliation and, as mentioned previously, exacting such revenge often happened when soldiers were lured away from the main body of troops. When a Kentucky and Indiana volunteer ventured too far from camp, they were attacked, and their bodies were found later in a gully with their "skulls . . . beaten in." Such actions, thought Hill, were the "consequence of the atrocities of the Volunteers."[12] One Tennessean, who obviously had some kind of run-in with a resident of Monterrey and lost his life for it, was William Forrest of Nashville. He apparently had a disagreement with a Mr. Armstrong who owned a tavern and boarding house in the city. The origins of the encounter are unknown and the local man's name does not indicate Mexican nationality. All that is recorded is that Armstrong killed Forrest.[13]

Although it did not have rampant disease to deal with like the Second Tennessee, the First Tennessee nevertheless dealt with its own hardships. In addition to sickness, several of the wounded died in the weeks following the battle. The Tennesseans knew that their regiment had taken the lion's share of the army's casualties, a fact that produced both pride and remorse. Sickness and casualties combined caused Frank Cheatham, in an October 16 letter, to characterize the Bloody First as "the unlucky Regiment of the army." Robert Green from Nashville had been wounded in the knee and had since died. Cheatham wrote his family about the death, calling Green "a brave and gallant young man," and asserting that "his death has cast a gloom throughout the Regiment."[14]

In addition, some of the Tennesseans struggled financially. Those who did not have the resources of a prosperous family from which to draw found it difficult to get by on a private's pay of seven dollars a month. Some of the men owed so much to sutlers that when the paymaster came around with their pay, they used it all to retire their debts. Cheatham did not have that problem, but he sympathized with those who did. In a letter to his aunt, he explained the situation and concluded, "that is a sight hard upon a poor Soldier a thousand miles from home." Cheatham was also concerned about "a beautiful pair of Silk Mexican bridle ranes" that he purchased for his father and that somehow got sent to Hartsville instead of Nashville. And one more thing troubled him—the infrequency with which his family wrote to him. In December, Cheatham had just received his first letter in eight weeks, and in his rejoinder, he complained: "I do think it is the strangest thing imaginable that I cannot get letters occasionally from a house that contains a dozen or more writers." After scolding his family, Cheatham resolved not to write again.[15]

Although the volunteers liked General Taylor, in the weeks following the battle some offered a critique of his generalship. Patrick Duffy believed that Monterrey "would have been one of the greatest victories won in modern warfare had it not been for Taylors armistice." Allowing the enemy army to retreat unmolested was a mistake that he characterized as "the cow kicking over the pail of milk." Especially puzzling was his decision to advance on Monterrey without heavy siege guns. Cheatham was not alone among the Tennesseans in the opinion that "Old Taylor committed one of the greatest blunders that ever a General was guilty of in coming here to attack one of the strongest fortified towns in Mexico, with nothing in the world but small artillery for open field fighting." A surgeon in the regular army described Taylor as "the poorest Genl. in all christendom." Colonel Campbell had never been impressed with Taylor's ability, but he did note with interest the nature of the post-battle criticism leveled at the commanding general. Many of the officers, he wrote, are "here on a political tour to gain reputation" for their return home. In addition to being "jealous of each other . . . these Democratic Gen's, and Col's, and Major's . . . are striking at Genl. Taylor whom they fear may be taken up for the Presidency and whose fame they are now jealous of."[16]

In their free time, the men sometimes ventured into Monterrey to explore, and that provided a diversion from camp drudgery. Within days after the city's capture, Mexicans came out in large numbers to sell to the Americans in open-air markets. One Tennessean noted the "rare harvest" from which the men had to choose: goat milk, exotic fruit, and the like. The residents even came out of the city and brought oranges and other items to sell in the American camps, and by selling at exorbitant prices they made quite a profit. The young ladies of Monterrey were a fascination with their "dark lustrous" eyes and "long raven hair," which complimented their low-cut white tops and short dresses that revealed well-shaped ankles. Most fascinating of all was that these beauties often walked around smoking a "cigaritto."[17]

The Tennesseans also took note of other aspects of the city. Local men seemed to take great pride in their mounts, or, to be more precise, the saddles on their mounts. Many of them were elaborate and ornate, and oddly enough, those who rode donkeys often sat behind the saddle instead of on it, which provided a full view. The architecture was also a curiosity and, according to John Robertson, it provided cultural insight. The flat-roofed houses looked unfinished, and the white stucco walls always formed right angles at the corners and when rising up from the ground. The houses had no chimneys nor did windows have glass or shutters but grates instead. The high exterior walls and grated windows, thought Robertson, served as "forceful commentaries upon the jealousies and faithlessness of this mixed nation." In general, he described the architecture as "half Moorish, half Mexican."[18]

As October passed into November, the Tennesseans were thinking increasingly about home and about the fact that their twelve-month commitment was almost half over. "The remainder of our time," wrote George Nixon to his wife, Sarah, "I hope will not seem half as long as the first six months." When he returned home to Lawrenceburg, he assured her, he would find fulfillment in "enjoying your sweet company for the remander of my days." But while away from her, a month seems like five, and "time cant fly too swiftly for me when I am from you and the children." In a November 8 letter, he obviously pined for his children, and he expressed to Sarah his desire to "bring them up in the way of christianity . . . and I hope by the assitance of the supreme being we will be enabled to raise them in the way of honesty & prudence." Tell the children, he concluded, that "pa will be to see them before very long."[19]

Back home, family and friends celebrated the news of the victory at Monterrey and the exploits of Tennessee's brave sons. On October 28, citizens gathered at the courthouse in Nashville to honor the volunteers. Whig congressman Edwin H. Ewing presided, and another Whig, who the following year would be elected to Ewing's seat in the House, George Washington Barrow, gave a speech. Ewing introduced and the group endorsed several resolutions commemorating the courageous deeds of their native sons, and one commended the Tennesseans who "covered themselves with glory" during the charge at Monterrey. The group also supported the idea of erecting a monument in honor of the Tennesseans killed in the battle, and Ewing oversaw the appointment of a committee of twenty-five prominent citizens to explore the possibility. Barrow was on the committee as were Alfred O. P. Nicholson and Thomas Claiborne Sr. Ironically, the party that most opposed the war (Whig) took a prominent role in the victory celebration, and as for Nicholson, he was leader of the anti-Polk wing of the Democratic Party in Tennessee. Claiborne, however, was a loyal Democrat, a veteran of Jackson's army, and the father of Thomas Claiborne Jr., who had received his commission as a second lieutenant in the regular army directly from his friend President Polk. The residents of Nashville and Davidson County never followed through on the monument, but if they had, one of the fallen who would have been honored on the edifice was Private James Hart Allison, son of Nashville mayor Alexander Allison. The family had James's body brought home, where it was buried in the Nashville City Cemetery in January 1847.[20]

It was not just Nashvillians. Patriotic citizens met all across the state and passed resolutions commending the gallant Tennesseans at Monterrey and praising their exceptional conduct in battle. At one event, a speaker went so far as to assert that the Tennesseans' accomplishment at Monterrey surpassed that of Bunker Hill. At a gathering in Lawrenceburg, resolutions specifically noted the bravery of William B. Allen, captain of the Lawrence County company, who was killed in the attack, and George H. Nixon, who survived the battle and became the company commander.[21]

Sumner County residents came together in Gallatin on November 21, the two-month anniversary of the storming of El Tenería. The courthouse was packed as Balie Peyton, who had been a volunteer aid in Taylor's army at Monterrey and was back in town for a visit, gave a speech about the battle that lasted an hour. In keeping with what other groups were doing, they passed resolutions of pride and honor. Then they expressed support for the Davidson County proposal to build a monument, and they likewise committed to erecting their own monument in honor of Sumner County's Monterrey dead. County residents committed a considerable sum of money for the enterprise. Among them was

Mary Elliott whose son Julius had been the one wounded in the street on the afternoon of September 21 after the fort had been captured and then had been taken into a house for cover only to be killed by Mexican lancers, along with Peter Hynds Martin. There is no indication of how much Mrs. Elliott donated, but she specifically wanted to memorialize her son as well as Martin, who remained by his side even unto death.[22]

Both the Elliott and Martin families had the comfort of the return of Julius's and Peter's bodies a few months later for interment in the Gallatin Cemetery. They were appropriately buried beside each other. Their story became renowned in Sumner County because of the unselfish display of sacrifice and heroism. The *National Union*, after recounting their death, concluded: "They were associates in life, they were associates in death, they will this day occupy the same honored grave; I hope and pray to God that they are now associates in heaven."[23]

State-wide adulation caused some people to begin to think about politics. Wesley Nixon, George Nixon's cousin, apparently became quite excited about the prospects of his hero relative running for office. "You have won for yourself imperishable glory & renown," Wesley wrote to George. After assuring his cousin that he held "a deep intrest for you," he admonished George to "preserve that good name" and stick to his democratic principles and do not make enemies. His status now would allow him to seek any office he chose, and the Democratic Party had a decided interest in him running for the legislature. From Mexico, George responded with gratitude for "the good feelings that I see manifested toward me in Tennessee," but "when I return home I expect to pursue a domestic life and not medle in politics." His primary motive, George wrote, was "to serve my country in the best way that I know how."[24]

The Tennessean who lived at 1600 Pennsylvania Avenue was also thinking about politics. A war that was not universally popular to begin with was now six months old, and despite American victories at Palo Alto, Resaca de la Palma (in May before volunteers arrived) and Monterrey, the Mexican government showed no signs of capitulation. President Polk knew that the war's expense, both money and lives, was taking a political toll on the Democrats. By the fall of 1846, it was becoming apparent that the war was raising up a military hero with the potential to be a presidential contender in 1848. Zachary Taylor's army had dominated the news since spring, making the general familiar to every household in America. Companies had named apparel after him, saloons had named drinks after him, poems and songs had been written for him, and most astonishing of all, two biographies of Taylor had come off the press even before the Battle of Monterrey. All of his life, Zachary Taylor had been apolitical, never having even voted in an election, but now the rumblings of presidential politics became connected with Taylor's name. That the hero-general identified as a Whig was a troubling development for Polk and the Democrats.[25]

Polk already held a low opinion of Taylor before the Monterrey victory. Several times in the fall, the president discussed with the cabinet his lack of confidence in Old Rough and Ready, and he followed up those discussions by recording his opinions in his diary. "General Taylor, I fear, is not the man for the command of the army," wrote Polk on September 5, because he lacks "grasp of mind enough." A week before the battle, the president recorded, "He does not seem to possess the resources and grasp of mind suited to the responsibilities of his position." Then the news arrived of the battle, but accompanying it was the dampening acknowledgment of Taylor's armistice with the enemy army, allowing them to retreat from Monterrey unmolested, an arrangement that Polk believed prolonged the war. The president's opinion of his general plummeted. Taylor had committed a "great error," and the cabinet agreed with Polk that the armistice had to be terminated immediately. Now the president believed that Taylor was "unfit for command." Polk's sagging opinion, coupled with Taylor's surging political popularity, served to accelerate discussions within the administration about a change in military strategy that would effectively remove Taylor from the limelight.[26]

Needing the war to end as quickly as possible, the administration began to discuss an invasion of Mexico at Veracruz on the east coast and six hundred miles below Monterrey, followed by a march inland to capture Mexico City. Taylor was quickly dismissed as the potential commander of the invasion force, and after considering other possibilities, Polk settled on Winfield Scott, the commanding general of the army and War of 1812 hero. Scott was itching to go to Mexico, and as a more sophisticated professional, he shared the president's low opinion of Taylor. He believed, indeed, had shared with a friend three months earlier, that Taylor's "intellect . . . is limited." Given that Scott wanted field command and was knowledgeable and competent, the choice made sense, but Polk and Scott had clashed earlier in the year and the commanding general had been in Polk's doghouse since May. In addition, two commonly known facts about Scott made the choice risky for the president and his party: Scott was an ardent Whig and a zealous presidential aspirant. A third fact about the general should probably be added: his pomposity and arrogance made him difficult to work with. These were issues that Polk would have to deal with later, but for the time being, Scott appeared to be the lesser of two Whig threats.[27]

The Mexico City Campaign, as it would be called, did not begin until the following spring. Plans needed to be made, and more importantly new troops needed to be raised for such an expansion of the war effort, and that would take time. Meanwhile, Scott would accumulate what troops he could from available units and more importantly from the transfer of about half of Taylor's existing army, which forced Taylor to assume a defensive posture in northern Mexico. In the closing days of December, Scott was en route to Mexico and ordered Taylor to transfer to him 4,500 regulars along with several volunteer regiments including the First and Second Tennessee. Scott designated the coastal town of Tampico as the rendezvous point for the concentration of his troops.[28]

Earlier that same month, Taylor had put in motion a major southern advance to Victoria 250 miles below Monterrey. Then Taylor learned of the new strategy and command changes that would necessitate sending his troops 150 miles beyond Victoria to Tampico, where they would fall under Scott's command. Taylor was furious over the reallocation of troops, and he was convinced that the motivations behind it were politics and jealousy. When the Tennesseans received their marching orders in mid-December, they did not know their ultimate objective, but they were happy to be on the move after weeks of idleness. Learning that Victoria was their destination and that General José Urrea commanded Mexicans troops there heightened the sense of excitement for some of the Tennesseans, because it was Urrea who had captured the Texas soldiers at Goliad in 1836. It was actually Santa Anna who had ordered the execution of the prisoners (including William Haskell's brother Charles), which became known as the Goliad massacre, but many of the Tennesseans believed that Urrea was the guilty party. Wiley Hale from Jackson reported during the march to Victoria, "We are anxious to meet with the gentleman [Urrea]. . . . If we find him at Victoria we will pay him up for old scores."[29]

It was in Victoria that the three Tennessee regiments came together under the same command for the first time, for this is the point at which Tennessee's mounted volunteers reentered the story. The Mounted Regiment had undertaken quite an arduous trek since leaving Tennessee in late July. They crossed the Mississippi River and galloped into Arkansas over nine hundred strong with a wagon train in tow. Half of the companies were armed with flintlock rifles and the other half with percussion carbines (probably 1833 model smoothbores) and pistols. Their journey took them through Little Rock then south through Shreveport, Louisiana, before crossing into Texas in the first week of September, and it took another month to reach Port Lavaca south of Houston. Soon after reaching the Lone Star state, a massive two-day storm engulfed them, scattering the companies as well as supply wagons for miles. Some of their cargo was lost in the relentless winds— when it finally subsided, a general state of chaos and exhaustion prevailed. While their fellow Tennesseans were fighting the Battle of Monterrey, they were at Port Lavaca, three hundred miles north of the Rio Grande.[30]

Day after day, the Tennessee horsemen trudged through south Texas dodging Comanches, rattlesnakes, and wolves. Wild game was abundant for hunting but drinkable water was often in short supply. By the end of October, the column had made its way through Corpus Cristi and beyond when, one day, a rider came galloping toward them warning of a host of mounted enemy soldiers ahead. They halted the wagon train and moved it to safety while the Tennesseans formed for battle. It was their first real threat and, in their haste to prepare for a possible attack, some of the men suddenly realized that shooting at deer and geese had exhausted their implements of war. Some were out of cartridges, others found that they had no percussion caps, and others needed flints.

Quickly the men borrowed and traded with comrades for what they needed. During the commotion, one DeKalb County boy in Company I, called "Preacher Smith" by the others, accidentally discharged his musket. Within minutes, a cloud of dust arose in the distance indicating the enemy's approach, and the men braced themselves for their first combat experience. However, as the horde approached closer, they saw that the attackers were merely a herd of wild horses.[31]

Finally, on November 9, almost ten weeks after leaving Memphis, the Mounted Regiment of Tennessee volunteers crossed the Rio Grande. They joined the U.S. encampment outside Matamoros called Camp Ringgold after Major Samuel Ringgold, the first American officer killed in the war. Their stay at Matamoros lasted six weeks, and without ever having seen an enemy soldier some were deciding that they had been through enough. Disease had become an issue before they reached the border. Some grew ill enough to be sent home and others, having lost their excitement for war, tried to appear sick. As for Captain Joseph S. Lenow, commander of Company A from Fayette County, he went on leave, returned home and sent in his resignation. There were probably others who would have done the same thing except for honor and a sense of duty.[32]

They rode out of Matamoros on December 21 and began a two-week march to Victoria, which was uneventful except that, halfway there, one of the companies was sent back to Matamoros to serve as escort for a supply train of sixty wagons. It was the Marshall County boys of Company E that went back, and they finally reached Victoria ten days after the rest of the regiment. Along the way, they experienced a conflict in the town of Santander with several dozen Mexican males who were caught trying to steal rifles, swords, and other equipment. Some of the missing weapons were returned but not all, so the Americans bound the men and began to march them off to Victoria with them until their wives and daughters and other town people caught up with the column and begged for their release. When the town alcalde arrived and promised to pay for the missing items, the Mexicans were untied and allowed to return home.[33]

By early January 1847, all three Tennessee regiments had reached Victoria along with several others. Box-shaped adobe houses with flat roofs filled the town, giving it a neat, orderly appearance from afar. However, closer inspection in the streets and around the houses revealed "various kinds of rubbish" and generally dirty conditions. The appearance of Victoria did not matter to the Tennesseans, who were finally all together for the first time and with their new designation, the Tennessee Brigade. Brigadier General Gideon Pillow, who recently had been sick in Camargo, was there also, and he assumed command of the Tennessee Brigade, which made up part of General Robert Patterson's volunteer division. The new organization gave the Tennesseans a sense of pride and unity, and their buoyed spirits were reinforced by rampant rumors that they were to be part of a new army under Scott destined for new military objectives to the south. They were confident that more battles lay ahead.[34]

While the prospects of more adventure excited the men, transferring from Taylor's to Scott's command received mixed reviews. Notwithstanding some of the criticisms leveled at the general after Monterrey, Taylor remained a favorite among the men and his sobriquet "Old Rough and Ready" was representative of his personality as a "down to earth" hard fighter. But Scott was "Old Fuss and Feathers," a famous but pompous general known to be a stickler for discipline. While Scott "always wore all the uniform prescribed or allowed by law," wrote Lieutenant Ulysses S. Grant years later, "General Taylor never wore uniform, but dressed himself entirely for comfort."[35]

The result of Taylor's attire was that sometimes his men did not recognize him as the army commander, as illustrated by this story that took place while at Victoria. Taylor had accompanied the troops there, having received orders to transfer part of his army to Scott, and did not return north until his departing units continued their march south to Tampico. One day, Taylor was riding through the Tennessee camp in his nondescript attire and a member of the Mounted Regiment, admiring his mount called to him, "Hallo, stranger, how will you swap that pony for this horse[?]" Taylor politely told him that he did not want to swap, and at about that time a staff officer rode up revealing the identity of the commanding general. The embarrassed Tennessean apologized, but Taylor brushed it off with a smile then engaged the young man in conversation, complimenting the trooper on the bravery and martial spirit of his home state. The incident bought Taylor a measure of good will with the men especially after their haughty division commander had another member of the Mounted Regiment arrested for a similar inquiry.[36]

The Tennessee Brigade was buzzing with activity on the evening of January 14. Orders had arrived instructing them to prepare to march to Tampico the next morning. Letters from home had also arrived that day, two hundred of them, and the men who were not packing camp supplies sat around sharing information about family and friends. Those who received letters were overjoyed, but those who had not were disappointed and angry and some swore that they would not write to their families again. Others took the opportunity before starting the march to write a letter home since they did not know when the next opportunity would arise. "I hope the time will not be long when I can have the pleasure of your sweet company," George Nixon wrote to his wife in Lawrenceburg.[37]

Next morning, the Tennesseans and the rest of Patterson's division started early. Staggered over three days, more that 4,700 troops marched out of Victoria and headed for Tampico. In addition to Patterson's division was David E. Twiggs division and John A. Quitman's brigade (William Worth's division would join Scott's army later). Soon after they left Victoria the road began to ascend the spur of a mountain. After a while, the Tennesseans could look back from whence they had come and see the town far off and below them in the distance along with the tiny white tents of the troops left behind clustered on its outskirts. Stretching back across the plain was the long line of soldiers trudging through the cloud of dust kicked up from the dirt road. The view behind them provided a beautiful scene that "attracted universal attention." On the second morning of the march, General Patterson stepped into a hole and twisted his ankle. Seeking relief, he sent an aide to fetch his bottle of brandy only to discover that it had gone missing. Sources do not reveal the identity of the culprit, but it is assumed that some Tennesseans enjoyed a "fine merriment" as a result of the heist.[38]

Much of the twelve-day march was uneventful except for occasional discipline problems that arose. A member of the First Tennessee in Captain Robert Foster's company slipped away from the column one day to hunt game, but when he fired his weapon, the ball struck near a group of officers. General Pillow had the man tied to a wagon wheel as discipline, but Foster came along later and released him, which resulted in Pillow ordering Foster's arrest. Most of the soldiers thought that Foster had done the right thing, and a fellow soldier later wrote to Foster's mother explaining what had happened and confirming the rightness of her son's action. However, Foster was not court-martialed and the matter was allowed to die, presumably because his father was prominent Whig politician Ephriam H. Foster. Eighteen-year-old John V. Wright of the Mounted Regiment also got into trouble, but he too was let off without harsh punishment because of the general's "high regard for Wright's father." Other young soldiers felt the sting of Pillow's punishment during the march as the sentiment in the Tennessee Brigade, once largely favorable, began to change. The men began to see their general as selfish, stubborn, and unpopular.[39]

Tampico was a beautiful tropical town of 15,000 inhabitants located seven miles from the coast and on the bank of the Panuco River. Rich soil, tall timber, beautiful flowers, and lush vegetation abounded, all accented by parrots, mackaws, and other species of exotic wild life. It was a paradise for the weary troops. In addition to its beauty, Tampico was a prosperous town. Numerous Americans and other foreigners lived there, and they appeared to conduct the majority of the local business, giving the town something of a commercial air. The lively atmosphere reminded some of the soldiers of Yankee enterprise, and one Nashvillian described it as "the most American town to be seen in Mexico." The town had become quite "Americanized" thought a West Tennessean who assured his sister that he had enjoyed "some luscious dinners" in Tampico.[40]

Campbell's First Tennessee, Haskell's Second Tennessee, and Thomas's Mounted Regiment set up camp outside of the city on a picturesque plain along the river, but the men wasted no time in exploring the lovely town. They also wasted no time in finding ample supplies of liquor. A variety of establishments with names like *La Luna* (The Moon) and *El Caballo Blanco* (The White Horse) became favorite haunts for the volunteers. Ranking officers tried to get ahead of potential problems by ordering the saloons to sell nothing stronger than wine to American soldiers, so upon ordering a drink of hard liquor, the proprietor usually responded that he had no brandy. However, the determined Tennesseans learned that if one asked for "strong wine" the owner would then pour them a glass of brandy.[41]

Such idleness was not all that occupied the troops' time while waiting for General Scott and the rest of the army to arrive. A deserter from Dekalb County warrants mention. Calvin W. Hill volunteered in the Mounted Regiment and had been with the unit on the long, overland trek, but never befriended any of his comrades. Some thought he had behaved suspiciously all along, and on one occasion he, perhaps unintentionally, mentioned that he had lived with a wealthy Mexican family in Puebla and Mexico City a few years earlier. He spoke Spanish fluently, and in each Mexican town they entered he was quick to locate the alcalde and strike up a friendship. After they arrived in Tampico, Private Hill slipped away and took an officer's coat with him. The whole army knew that the Mexican government had offered lucrative inducements of land and money to any American who would desert and fight for Mexico. And in some instances, worthy deserters who joined the Mexican army could receive an officer's commission, which probably explains why Hill took an officer's coat. The Tennesseans later heard that he indeed had been commissioned a captain in the enemy army, but such rumors were never proven. From that point forward, "scamp" was the word used in reference to Hill.[42]

Their month-long stay in Tampico ended in the waning days of February, when the Tennesseans drew twenty-five days' rations and began loading on steamers that would take them south. Six thousand troops congregated in Tampico and others were already at anchorage near Veracruz waiting for the assemblage of the army to be completed. It took several days for the Tampico contingent to embark, and because of the lack of transport, the Mounted Regiment had to leave their horses behind for the time being. Excitement surrounded the beginning of this new military campaign, but Tennesseans offered varied predictions about what lay ahead. Some thought the war was nearly over, with little fighting left, while others likened Veracruz and its defenses to a Gibraltar that would require heavy fighting to capture. "We will have a bloody time of it," thought Captain William B. Walton of the First Tennessee.[43] No matter—all were determined to go and write the next chapter in Tennessee's martial history.

*James K. Polk portrait by George Healy. Courtesy of Tennessee State Museum—Tennessee Historical Collection.*

*Vines Lucas "Luke" Collier Jr. (1822–1900) from Sumner County was an officer in the Tennessee militia when he volunteered for service in Mexico. He was a devout Methodist and father of ten children. Courtesy of Nathan Knight.*

*Thomas W. Collier (1823–1873) was the youngest of the Collier brothers who were both members of the First Tennessee Volunteer Regiment. He was one of the many Americans incapacitated by disease at Camargo and was discharged with a surgeon's certificate. He later served in the Confederate army. Courtesy of Nathan Knight.*

*John Whitfield (1818–1879) was born in Franklin, Tennessee, and served as a captain in the First Tennessee Volunteers. In the 1850s, he lived in Missouri and Kansas and ended up in Texas, where he joined Confederate forces as an officer in a Texas cavalry regiment. Courtesy of the Tennessee Historical Society Collection.*

*Balie Peyton (1803–1878)*
*was an early member of the*
*Whig Party in Tennessee.*
*He was a volunteer aide*
*in Zachary Taylor's army*
*at Monterrey. Courtesy of*
*Tennessee State Museum—*
*Tennessee Historical*
*Society Collection.*

*William B. Campbell*
*(1807–1867) served*
*admirably as the colonel*
*commanding the First*
*Tennessee Volunteers. He*
*was elected governor in*
*1851 with the campaign*
*slogan, "Boys, follow*
*me!" which was intended*
*to remind voters of*
*the charge he led at*
*Monterrey. Courtesy*
*of United States Army*
*Don F. Pratt Memorial*
*Museum, Fort Campbell.*

Samuel R. Anderson (1804–1883) was lieutenant colonel of the First Tennessee and later a general in the Confederate army. Courtesy of Tennessee State Museum—Tennessee Historical Society Collection.

Adolphus Heiman (1809–1862) was the Prussian-born adjutant of the First Tennessee who had lived in Nashville since 1837. He became a noted architect after the Mexican War. Courtesy of the Tennessee Historical Society.

*Benjamin F. Cheatham
(1820–1886) from
Nashville was captain
in the First Tennessee
and later colonel of the
Third Tennessee. He
fought with distinction
in the Civil War as
a division and corps
commander. Courtesy
of the Tennessee
Historical Society.*

*William B. Allen
(1824–1846) from
Lawrenceburg,
Tennessee, was
killed in the charge
at Monterrey while
leading his company.
This 1853 sketch is in
the public domain.*

*William T. Haskell (1818–1859) from Jackson, Tennessee, was a lawyer, poet, and Whig politician with great promise prior to serving as the colonel of the Second Tennessee Volunteer Regiment. Courtesy of the Tennessee Historical Society.*

*Gideon J. Pillow (1806–1878) was an ambitious lawyer, planter, and close friend of James K. Polk. His political appointment as brigadier general in 1846 received wide-spread criticism. He was brave and twice wounded in Mexico, but he proved in both the Mexican War and Civil War that he lacked the qualities necessary for effective military leadership. Courtesy of the Tennessee Historical Society.*

William B. Walton (1824–1908) was the grandson of the founder of Carthage, Tennessee. He served in the First Tennessee and returned home with a souvenir piece of coral from San Juan de Ulua. In the late nineteenth century, he remained active in the Tennessee Mexican War Veterans Association. Graphite sketch by Jennifer Pepper, 2017.

*Ticket to the 1882 veterans reunion. Courtesy of The Tennessee Historical Society.*

*Veterans of the Third Tennessee Volunteer Regiment taken at the home of James Guthrie in Gallatin, Tennessee. In this 1902 photograph, their ages ranged from seventy-five to eighty-one, and they would all be dead within six years. Seated from left: Jacob H. Wise, Littleberry Moncrief, James Guthrie. Standing: Daniel Calgy and William M. Stewart. Courtesy of the Tennessee Historical Society.*

*Moscow Carter (1825–1913) from Franklin, Tennessee, was a member of the First Tennessee. This image of young Carter is believed to have been made in about 1850. Courtesy of the Battle of Franklin Trust.*

*Moscow Carter served briefly in the Confederate army before being captured then paroled in 1862. He returned home and became a farmer. This photograph was made in about 1890. Courtesy of the Battle of Franklin Trust.*

*Sarah and James Polk at the end of his presidency looking forward to retirement in Nashville. Courtesy of James K. Polk Memorial Association, Columbia, Tennessee.*

*Polk Place located on Vine Street (today it is 7th Avenue N.). Before its destruction at the turn of the twentieth century. Sarah still lived there when this picture was made in the 1880s and James's grave is visible on the right. Courtesy of James K. Polk Memorial Association, Columbia, Tennessee.*

*Chapter Six*

# MEXICO'S GIBRALTAR

Veracruz was an important and busy port city on Mexico's east coast, 260 miles from Mexico City. In 1847, it had a population of about fifteen thousand, and its strong defenses made it a formidable objective. A fifteen-foot high brick, coral, and granite wall surrounded the city with artillery bastions built into its fortifications. The most impressive part of Veracruz's defenses was the San Juan de Ulúa castle perched on a coral reef a thousand yards offshore and dominating the approach to the city. The castle walls stood sixty feet high, and the impressive structure housed 150 cannon of various sizes along with over a thousand defenders. The city itself held another 1,400 Mexican soldiers. Capturing the city would provide a supply base for Scott's army as he marched inland to capture Mexico City—but everyone knew that Veracruz was a powerful and potentially bloody obstacle.[1]

Captain William Walton was from Carthage, Tennessee, a town on the Cumberland River that was founded by his grandfather and namesake who was a Revolutionary War veteran. A letter that Walton wrote to his father makes clear that he was worried about what lay ahead. "If they dispute our landing with anything like equal numbers there is no other alternative but for us to Suffer Severely." As a member of the Bloody First, he already had seen the elephant, so his expectations were more realistic than idealistic. Perhaps he thought of his grandfather or of the prominent place that his family name held in the community. If he did, he knew that regardless of what lay ahead, he had to push on. Nimrod Smith from Sumner County also thought that difficult fighting lay ahead.

He believed that the Veracruz garrison would "defend it to the last," but he expressed stern resolve when he concluded that "the last will come."[2]

Dozens of naval vessels and transport steamers cluttered the horizon on March 9. It was eighty-five degrees that day and the waters were calm—ideal conditions for an amphibious beach landing. Looking far beyond Veracruz, a hundred miles inland, Mount Orizaba rose up from the horizon. Early that afternoon, the armada anchored near Sacrificios Island, a thousand yards from Collado Beach, which lay two miles south of the city. At about 5:00 p.m., a signal gun fired and sixty-seven landing craft carrying just over 2,500 men started for shore in an awesome display of coordination. Scott's old friend William Worth won the honor of having his division go ashore first. The Tennesseans, along with the rest of the army, packed the decks of the transports, watching with suspense as the boats plied their way to the shoreline, expecting at any moment to receive fire from the sand dunes that lined the beach. "Surely a more magnificent sight could not be imagined," remembered John Robertson. The anxiety and anticipation of the climactic event "lent to the scene a glorious grandeur." Worth's men jumped out of their surfboats and waded unopposed onto Collado Beach. "The landing . . . was a most magnificent scene. We received no opposition," was Lieutenant Colonel Samuel Anderson's laconic report.[3]

The boats rowed back to the transports, and the Tennesseans climbed over the side of their steamers and descended into the surfboats. By the time all of the volunteer division had relocated into the landing craft and headed for shore, the "sun had already sunk behind the grand and lofty snow capped Orizaba . . . [but] the luster of his brilliant golden rays . . . [added an] additional beauty to the magnificent scene." Darkness was quickly approaching when the volunteers jumped into waist-deep water and waded ashore. The boats shuttled back and forth late into the night until nine thousand men had made it to land without incident. Gideon Pillow's Brigade was no longer the Tennessee Brigade, for it now included the First and Second Pennsylvania Volunteer Regiments, and was part of Robert Patterson's volunteer division. The regiments spread out along the beach and wet men tried to sleep in shifts that night. The combat-experienced First Tennessee received orders to move down the beach to guard against a night attack on the army's extreme left. It was an uneasy night with frequent alarms and infrequent sleep, but no attack came.[4]

Next morning, when the army formed on the beach to receive orders, some of the First Tennessee felt a bit out of place. The regiment looked haggard in their well-worn and tattered uniforms and standing next to other units whose appearance was neat and clean was embarrassing for some of the men. However, they felt their pride return when an unknown soldier came along and said, "Ah! That's the 1st Tennessee! They've seen hard times. They are the Monterey boys, and they do look like they'd fight."[5] The Monterrey boys stood a little taller.

That morning, Scott issued orders not to attack the city but to encircle it. First, Worth's division of regulars would move forward and take a position along the sand dunes south of Veracruz. Next, Patterson's volunteers would dig in along a siege line west of the city, with the Tennesseans resting at the end of Worth's line and with the Pennsylvanians on the other side. And beyond them, General David E. Twiggs's men would stretch the line north until it reached the coast again, bringing the siege line to a length of six miles. Due to the difficulty in negotiating the sandy slopes and to the weather, which did not always cooperate, it took several days for the Americans to complete the encirclement of the city on the land side.

As the Tennesseans were pushing on beyond Worth's men, the undulating ground dipped down into a ravine where stood the ruins of an old hacienda called Malibran. Upon the Tennesseans' approach, Mexicans opened fire from the main house and out-buildings, as well as from nearby hills. Pillow ordered the First Tennessee to push forward and capture the buildings, and then he ordered the Second Tennessee to drive the enemy off of the hills. The Tennesseans accomplished both objectives with only light skirmishing and no casualties, but members of the Second were particularly jubilant to have their first opportunity to exchange shots with the enemy regardless of the severity of the test. With "one continual shout of defiance," they rushed up the heights negotiating the tangled chaparral as best they could by pulling themselves up the steep grade with bushes. The Mexicans retreated as they

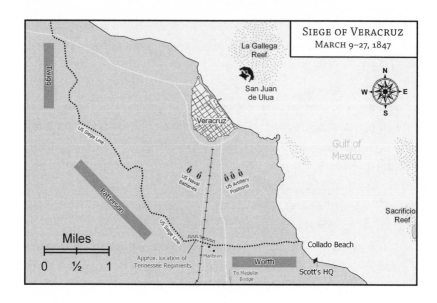

reached the top, and the first man to the summit, Lieutenant Frederick
Nelson of the Memphis Rifles, planted his company's flag, as the proud
soldiers shouted "*three cheers for Tennessee and Col. Haskell!*" The following day, as regulars from Twiggs' division filed past headed north, the
cocky volunteers boasted about their Malibran skirmish the day before,
to which a member of the Fourth Artillery, Lieutenant Daniel Harvey
Hill, sarcastically noted that they failed to injure a single enemy soldier.[6]

Two days after landing on the beach, Patterson's division was in
position in the center of the line facing the city. As they began to dig
in along the sand dunes a mile-and-a-half west of Veracruz, they could
clearly see lush green suburban groves surrounding the city, and jutting
up from the maze of buildings were steeples and domes. Spanish and
Moorish architectural features were evident. The Alvarado Road exited
the city and ran through the Tennesseans' portion of the siege line; to
block its access to the city, Pillow ordered that a strong barricade be
erected. Then he positioned some of the Pennsylvania men to guard a
railroad track, and his alignment of troops revealed once again the general's lack of experience. He posted his men in lines on both sides of the
track about twenty yards apart, which would have compelled them to fire
in each other's direction at point blank range had a skirmish erupted.

General Patterson quickly averted a potential disaster by repositioning all the soldiers on the same side of the road.[7]

As American troops solidified the investment line, several army engineers, including Captain Robert E. Lee, began to prepare the placement of heavy siege guns to bombard the city. The Mexican response to all of this activity outside the city walls was to occasionally lob artillery fire toward the besiegers. Most of the shots were ineffectual but some found their mark. Several soldiers who ventured up on a hill to get a better look at the city were killed by a shell, and the Second Tennessee's Adjutant, Wiley Hale, was ten feet away from a drummer boy who had his arm taken off by a solid shot. The Tennessee campsite was surrounded by hills and sand dunes that offered protection from enemy fire, and their "excessive hard duty," as one soldier put it, strengthened their trench works daily. But hygiene and camp comfort were not among the daily routines. One Tennessean went nine days after the landing without taking off his clothes and eight days without sleeping in a tent.[8]

With three batteries made up of twenty guns preparing to open fire on Veracruz on March 22 and two more batteries scheduled for completion soon after, General Scott worried that he had insufficient firepower to force the city's timely surrender. So, on the twenty-first, he met with the navy commanders and secured their agreement to loan the army six of their heavy guns, which would have to be hoisted off of their ships and pulled with drag lines across sand, mounted on large wooden wheels, and pulled over dunes for more than two miles. These guns, three sixty-eight-pound shell guns and three thirty-two-pound solid shot, would comprise what came to be known as the Naval Battery, and its location was in front of the volunteer division seven hundred yards from the city. Immediately, the Tennesseans and Pennsylvanians were sent to work under the supervision of army engineers to construct the embrasures for the new battery. At night, under the cover of darkness, hundreds of Tennesseans participated in work parties to pull the three-ton guns to their destination, an enterprise that ultimately required 1,500 men.[9]

Pillow had been under Scott's command for less than a month, but already he felt the boldness that his friendship with the president afforded him. Despite Scott's orders to move the big guns only at night,

Pillow, in order to hasten the last gun to its location, ordered that it be done in daylight. This was open insubordination to the commanding general but it was not the first instance. When the Tampico troops were preparing to load on ships for their voyage to Veracruz, Scott ordered that officers leave their mounts behind for the time being because of the army's limited transport space. Pillow, however, took his horse anyway, using a recent illness and his inability to get around on foot as an excuse.[10] Pillow may have been an amateur soldier but he was no amateur politician, and he knew that his friendship with Polk gave him enough clout to protect him from repercussions, or perhaps more accurately, to make repercussions non-existent.

The initial landing on the beach had been a week-and-a-half earlier, and as the Tennesseans worked on the batteries, their unlucky sister unit, the Mounted Regiment, was only just arriving. It had left Tampico a few days after the infantry regiments and without their horses, which were to follow in a week or two. Otherwise, all seemed well. On the way, one of the men stood on the deck of the ship and gave a long and loud speech to the others standing around about Texas and the causes of the war and about why he had volunteered. His primary reason for leaving home to go to Mexico was to make a name for himself. He intended to trade a year of his life, and even the chance of losing it, for a large enough portion of recognition and glory to enter politics. This unnamed soldier intended to return home and parlay his veteran status into a seat in the state legislature and after that, hopefully, Congress.

But the man would have to wait a few more days to get his chance at glory because on March 12, prior to the regiment's arrival at their landing point, things took a turn for the worse when a storm hit and blew their ships off course by over twenty miles. The ships struggled in strong winds and rough water for days, and many of the men became frightened and ill. The Churchwell brothers, Daniel and Ephraim from Columbia, worried that the ship they were on, the *Virginia*, would not stay afloat, and worse than that they were hopelessly seasick. They both wished that they were back home. The regiment did not get to Veracruz until March 20, and it was two days after that before the Mounted Regiment off-loaded to dry land.[11]

Tennessee's mounted volunteers reached land in time to witness the brilliant display of sight and sound as the bombardment began. As soon as the U.S. batteries commenced, Mexican guns in the city and in the harbor castle responded, and as night fell the scene became even more spectacular. When the opening salvos signaled the beginning of the bombardment, the Tennesseans cheered with approval and amazement. "It is really a pretty sight to see the bomb shells winding their deadly way through the air upon their message of destruction!" wrote Wiley Hale to his mother. John Robertson provided a more vivid description in his *Reminiscences*: "During the whole night the mortars on both sides were in constant activity. The contest now presented a splendid spectacle of grand and awful sublimity." Among the limited arsenal of guns available for the bombardment were ten ten-inch mortars; short, fat, muzzle-loading guns designed to lob exploding shells at low velocity. Their projectiles have a high trajectory and they can be loaded and fired relatively quickly, making them ideal for siege warfare. Robertson went on to describe the arching path of a mortar shell: "There was the red flash as the belching flame shot upwards from the mortar's mouth;" he wrote, "then the dull, heavy boom broke on the ear, and the bomb with its flaming fuse rose high in the air, rapidly at first, then slower and more slow till reaching its greatest height it bends and moves down, like a shooting meteor, until hid within the city walls, when up bursts the fitful, lurid glare."[12]

Near the end of the siege of Veracruz, Tennesseans had an encounter with Mexican troops that was more than incidental. It was common for groups of men to leave their camp areas a go hunting for food. Sometimes these were official expeditions done under the auspices of contractors who were constantly scouring the countryside looking to buy animals for army consumption. At other times, these "beef parties" consisted of hungry soldiers who, absent authorization, went out looking for cows, pigs, chickens, or anything else that would satisfy necessity. Just as "beef parties" were common, so too were rumors that enemy forces were gathering behind American lines intent on breaking the siege.

On the afternoon of March 25, members of the First Tennessee were out "beaving" when they stumbled into two dozen Mexican lancers. They were able to get word of the encounter back to camp, and General Scott immediately dispatched a hundred dragoons under Colonel William S. Harney to ascertain if the sighting indicated the presence of a larger body of enemy troops. Harney was the commander of the Second Dragoons, and he also had Tennessee roots, having been born just outside of Nashville. In case infantry was needed, several companies from the First and Second Tennessee along with one company from Tennessee's Mounted Regiment accompanied the horsemen. After going about three miles, they discovered a strong contingent of Mexican troops, at least 150, barricaded on a stone bridge, Puente de Moreno, or as some sources refer to it, the Medellín Bridge. Because of the enemy's strong position, Captain Frank Cheatham suggested the need for artillery, so Harney sent orders back to camp requesting a battery. When it arrived, the Americans deployed for battle.[13]

Cheatham and Colonel Haskell moved their Tennesseans off the road and into the brush and chaparral to the right and began to advance, using the vegetation as cover. When they were within musket range, they opened fire, and the Mexicans responded in kind, severing branches overhead without inflicting casualties. After the artillery unlimbered in the middle of the road and fired several rounds of grape shot, the Tennesseans, led by Cheatham, rushed forward—"our boys raised the Tennessee yell and charged the bridge," remembered one. The dragoons soon followed, but the footmen, having started the attack from closer proximity, reached the bridge first and began simultaneously tearing down the blockade and firing at the retreating enemy troops. When the bridge was cleared, the dragoons took up the chase and killed several dozen enemy during a four-mile pursuit.[14]

The Tennesseans had once again proven their metal under fire. After the engagement, the typically reserved General Patterson, their division commander and ranking officer on the scene, rode past the boys from the volunteer state, stood up in his stirrups and tipping his hat exclaimed, *"Hurrah for Tennessee!"*[15] The action at the Medellín Bridge might have been an opportunity for the Second Tennessee to win much-desired laurels, but it turned into another shining moment for the Bloody First, especially Frank Cheatham, who was at the forefront of the attack. Cheatham's boldness in counseling his superiors against an attack on the bridge without supporting artillery was prudent and timely advice, which did not go unheeded. A fellow Tennessean from the Mounted Regiment wrote a letter to Cheatham's brother John, in which he concluded that Frank was "always in the hotest and thickest of the danger."[16] It appears that Cheatham was already laying the foundation for his Civil War reputation as a hard-fighting division commander. As for Haskell and members of the Second Tennessee who were present, they too acted bravely but their actions were overshadowed or blended into other units so that they were unable to distinguish themselves as a regiment. They would have to wait for their opportunity.

Apparently, success and celebration was becoming a weakness for some of the Tennessee boys, because on their way back to the siege line they engaged in unwarranted destruction. Passing some rancheros, they assumed that because the houses were deserted, they must belong to hostile locals, so they took what they wanted and burned the dwellings to the ground. Next day, the city garrison signaled its desire to surrender, and negotiators from both armies were designated to discuss terms. After hearing of the capitulation, the Tennesseans once again set a bad example as celebration turned into ugly exuberance. Two Tennesseans, the source did not identify persons or even which regiment they were from, got into a fight, which ended with one of them seriously wounded in the back with a pistol shot.[17]

When the bombardment ceased on March 26, the American guns had fired 6,700 rounds of solid shot and exploding shells in six days. Scott appointed Pillow, along with Worth and two other officers, to serve as peace commissioners to negotiate the city's surrender. Under the terms agreed upon, the garrison of the Castle of San Juan de Ulúa filed out of their bastion on the same day as the troops defending the city, and all Mexican soldiers were given their parole, meaning they pledged to go home and not fight anymore. The negotiators also agreed upon the twenty-ninth as the day that Mexican forces would evacuate and turn the city over to the Americans.[18]

The siege of Veracruz was a brilliant success made all the more impressive by the fact that so few U.S. soldiers were lost; thirteen killed and just over fifty wounded. After the surrender, Colonel Campbell wrote in a letter that this "affair has been a brilliant one and eminently successful." One of Campbell's men, Private Samuel Lauderdale, asserted to his brother that "a more splendid nor bloodless victory ever adorned the historic page." An artillery officer in the regular army named Thomas J. Jackson was impressed with the outcome, and he wrote that the capture of Veracruz and the army's performance "excell any military operations known in the history of our country." The young Virginian, who a decade-and-a-half later would earn the nickname "Stonewall," concluded that Scott was "the most talented and scientific" general in the army.[19]

Pillow was beginning to feel his self-importance, and he contemplated his future and possible promotion in the army. As a mere brigade commander, his assignment to the peace commission seemed to position him within the commanding general's inner circle. Indeed, Campbell thought that Scott, Worth, and Pillow were seen together so often that they had become "a sort of triumvirate." Pillow knew that the administration was pushing a bill through Congress calling for the organization of ten new regiments—it was commonly called the Ten Regiment Bill—and that new generals would be appointed. Because Democrats wanted a major general "to counter-act that . . . which is exclusively whig," he believed that he was the best candidate for the elevated rank, and he anticipated his promotion. He also knew that he had a powerful ally in Polk, which gave him considerable confidence. And it did not hurt that Pillow was an adept self-publicist. He made sure to funnel information back home for publication in Tennessee newspapers. Less than a month after the fall of Veracruz, the *Nashville Daily Union* ran a story about the American victory, and in it described Pillow as one of "the most conspicuous officers of the army in the recent bombardment and siege of the city of Vera Cruz."[20]

Campbell did not share his brigade commander's high opinion of himself, and in fact had already formulated his own assessment of all three in the triumvirate. That Scott acted favorably toward Pillow was simply an effort on the commanding general's part to show deference to Polk's friend, thought Campbell. It was no secret that Pillow was the president's eyes and ears in Mexico and that he was communicating directly with Polk without regard to the chain of command. Given Scott's rocky relationship with the administration, and Polk's initial decision to keep Scott in Washington, the general appeared to be trying to better his own standing by showing a preference to Pillow. In "putting forward Pillow on all occasions," Campbell believed that "Scott [was] . . . paying Polk for letting him come here." The whole affair affected Campbell's opinion of both Scott and Pillow. "I like Genl. Scott very well, but he is a very vain, and light man, but of great acquirements and genius," wrote Campbell on March 28, and on the same topic the next day he penned that Scott can "be reached by flattery." About Pillow, Campbell simply wrote that he was particularly unsuited for the military. As for the third member of the triumvirate, Campbell wrote, "Worth has gained great eclat for his conduct in this whole affair." "Éclat" is a French term that can mean "brilliance" or "conspicuous success," but it also carries the meaning of "a showy display" or "publicity seeker." It is left to the reader to decide Campbell's true meaning. Campbell was resigned to endure the remaining two months of his service commitment, but "to be under Scott and Pillow longer," he asserted, and "I would be forced to resign. But I will hang on and do my duty."[21]

By previous arrangement, the Mexican army's evacuation of the city occurred on March 29. Two parallel lines of U.S. troops stretched for a mile on both sides of the Alvarado Road: Worth's men on one side and Patterson's on the other. When a cannon fired signaling the beginning of the procession, the city gates opened and out poured thousands of soldiers, local militia and civilians; military wives, residents, and the like. The appearance of their vanquished foe filled William Caswell with pity for "the poor, abject, poltroons, & slaves which constitute the rank and file" of the Mexican army. As the last of the Mexican soldiers exited the city and the harbor castle, the American flag went up as guns fired a salute. Soon after that, some of the Tennesseans went inside the city walls to explore. Evidence of the devastation caused by the bombardment was everywhere. Debris filled the streets and sandbags had been used to shore up damaged sections of the city wall. Equally obvious, upon close inspection, was the formidable defenses that the Mexicans had prepared to beat back an assault. Barricades, ditches, walled forts, and cannon made Caswell thankful that the city fell without need of an attack.[22]

Sergeant Henry W. Hart and Lieutenant William B. Walton, both from the First Tennessee, were on a special mission after Veracruz changed hands. They approached Colonel Campbell and asked for permission to go out to the San Juan de Ulúa castle to look around—a primary purpose of their mission was also to search for relics to take home. Campbell granted their request, so they found a rowboat and rowed themselves out into the harbor and tied off next to the castle fortification. The sixty-feet-high walls of the quadrangle San Juan de Ulúa castle sits on a coral reef, which serves as its foundation. Upon reaching their destination, they noticed pieces of coral lying around, which they assumed had been broken away during the bombardment. Hart and Walton both found as large a chunk as they could comfortably handle and carried them back to camp and ultimately back home. In March 1888, a newspaper reporter in Nashville was interviewing Hart for an article commemorating the forty-first anniversary of the surrender of Veracruz, and the old veteran intimated that both he and Walton still had their pieces of coral.[23]

A week after the surrender, Scott issued orders for his troops to prepare to march to Jalapa, sixty miles inland. Getting the army moving as quickly as possible was imperative because of the imminent arrival of yellow fever season, which was particularly ravenous in the coastal regions. General David Twiggs's division of regulars left Veracruz on April 8 as the lead element of Scott's army of invasion. The next day, Patterson's volunteers, including the two Tennessee infantry regiments, were trudging through deep sand as they marched away from Veracruz in oppressive heat. Left behind was the hapless and horseless Mounted Regiment along with several sick. Within a few days, William Caswell's company of Knox County cavalry—who were fortunate enough to have horses—were allowed to follow the army inland, however, most of the regiment would never get horses. As the army pushed inland, Caswell's troopers guarded wagon trains, escorted officers, and relayed orders to disperse elements of the army. Soon the volunteers reached the National

Road and within a couple of days they were marching up into higher elevations and through more picturesque scenery. On the third night, they camped at National Bridge, which crossed the Antigue River halfway to Jalapa. It was, and remains today, an impressive stone structure fifty feet wide and several hundred yards long with five arches supporting its massive weight. Here the terrain was uneven but the surrounding landscape was green with vegetation.[24]

On the next day, April 12, the Tennesseans started early and covered sixteen miles, arriving at a small village called Plan del Rio in the evening where they set up camp. Five miles farther was the village of Cerro Gordo, but between the Tennessee volunteers and the Cerro Gordo hamlet were hills and ridges and ravines where, within a few days, one of the great battles of the war would be fought. Earlier on the twelfth, before the Tennesseans reached their camp sight, Twiggs's vanguard had run into a strong Mexican position just ahead and, after an initial skirmish, Twiggs pulled back to consider his options. His first instinct was to attack with the troops on hand, but wiser council prevailed, and he opted to await the arrival of Scott and the rest of the army. In the days that followed, Captain Robert E. Lee, Lieutenant George McClellan, Lieutenant P. G. T. Beauregard, and other army engineers conducted extensive reconnaissance to ascertain the enemy's positions and strength. Meanwhile, Scott rushed to the scene and the bulk of the army was in the vicinity by the sixteenth. With scarcely six weeks left on their one-year term of service, the Second Tennessee Volunteer Regiment was finally on the eve of its opportunity for glory.

*Chapter Seven*

# AN HONORABLE
# MARTYRDOM: CERRO GORDO

Antonio López de Santa Anna had recently returned from his Cuban exile thanks to an interesting "under the table" negotiation worked out with the Polk administration. The president had facilitated Santa Anna's return to Mexico, and in return the *generalissimo* had agreed to a generous peace settlement. However, rather than bring about a speedy end of the war, Polk unwittingly prolonged the conflict, for when Santa Anna returned to Mexico City, he orchestrated a *coup* that put himself back in power, then he organized renewed military efforts against the North American invaders. Personally commanding the Mexican army, Santa Anna set a trap for Scott's army using the best resource available— geography. The National Road ran in a northerly direction at Plan del Rio where it crossed a swift stream called Rio del Plan. Continuing on beyond the village, the road wound back and forth through hilly terrain for about two miles before turning west and passing through a three-mile-long gorge with steep walls more commonly known as the Cerro Gordo Pass. Upon exiting the gorge and continuing westward, the road soon came to another village called Cerro Gordo. Hills and ridges dominated the countryside on both sides of the road, and the thick vegetation made off-road travel virtually impossible, or so Santa Anna thought.

So, he laid his plans. At the western mouth of the pass and just north of the road was a prominent hill called El Telégrafo, which offered a commanding view of a long stretch of the road, and upon which Santa Anna placed four guns and a handful of soldiers. He also blocked the road below with more cannon (six) and infantry (1,400). Adjacent to El Telégrafo was La Atalaya, another hill of roughly equal height, which Santa Anna left undefended because he believed it was inaccessible through the rugged countryside. To the south, three ridges ran roughly parallel to the road like three fingers pointing east. Santa Anna had fortified each of the fingertips with a combined strength of nineteen guns and two thousand men. Here the Mexicans had felled trees and thorny underbrush to provide a clear field of fire to the east and upon the road to the north. Santa Anna's formidable position would be difficult to assail. An American advance up the road might prove suicidal and an assault on the ridges to the south would certainly be a bloody undertaking. Furthermore, Santa Anna's flanks appeared secure with the river through a deep gorge south of the ridges protecting his right and the rugged terrain to the north protecting his left. Scott's army had few viable options, so from April 13 to 16, his engineers extensively and carefully scouted all of these enemy positions in search of weaknesses.[1]

While the engineers reconnoitered the area for military purposes, the volunteers had time to reconnoiter the area for leisure and dietary purposes. They found orange, peach, and lime trees and took advantage of the Río del Plan and other clear streams to bathe. In addition to plucking an occasional piece of fruit, the Tennesseans participated in beef parties; both official and unofficial. On April 16, a Pennsylvania volunteer recorded in his journal that one of the Tennesseans was brought into camp with seven gunshot wounds. A group of friends had gone out of camp looking for cattle when two of them became separated from the rest. They were attacked by lancers, and one of them was killed while the other was shot multiple times. This was the poor fellow carried back to camp by his comrades. He died soon after his arrival. In a separate incident on the same day, John Roberson was killed while serving as a member of an official escort for army contractors in search of beef. John and his brother, Rufus, were from Knoxville and were members of the Mounted Regiment—Company K, the Knoxville Dragoons—and they were together when John was shot in the thigh by a lone Mexican soldier hidden in the brush alongside the road. Rufus shot the Mexican as he ran away, and the Tennesseans carried John back to camp in a wagon. He had been hit high on the thigh and the musket ball had shattered the bone. John survived for two pain-filled days.[2]

By the sixteenth, the engineers had provided Scott with the information necessary for him to determine his next move. Captain Robert E. Lee and Lieutenant P. G. T. Beauregard had located a goat trail north of the road that, if cleared and widened for troops and cannon, could be used to march by stealth through the hills, ridges, and vegetation around the Mexican army and into its left flank and rear. Using skill and sweat, the Americans did, in fact, turn this narrow trail into a path sufficiently wide, thus defying Santa Anna's conclusion that a rabbit could not pass through that terrain. So, five thousand infantrymen led by General Twiggs began an arching flank march on April 17 in preparation for an attack on the Mexican left the following morning. Nashvillian Thomas Claiborne, a lieutenant in the Mounted Rifles, saw Lee for the first time in his life on the morning of the seventeenth and was struck by his bearing. Claiborne's unit was with the flanking column, and he came across Lee and Scott sitting on their steeds where the National Road started into the gorge. They were there showing the troops that this was the point at which they were to exit the road and follow the path that had been cut through the brush. Years later, Claiborne remembered that Lee "looked in the fullest vigor of manhood a most striking figure" who sat upon his horse "with superb grace." Claiborne concluded that Lee made an impression on him that morning that "I could not forget."[3] Mexican troops spotted the flanking force and quickly positioned troops atop La Atalaya, the hill just north of and adjacent to El Telégrafo. In the afternoon, American troops captured La Atalaya after a sharp skirmish that resulted in several dozen U.S. casualties. This premature engagement spoiled the surprise intended for the next morning but not the ultimate outcome.

While these events unfolded north of the road, Gideon Pillow prepared to lead the First and Second Tennessee and the First and Second Pennsylvania regiments in an attack on the three fortified ridges south of the road. This assault, to be executed simultaneously with the flank attack

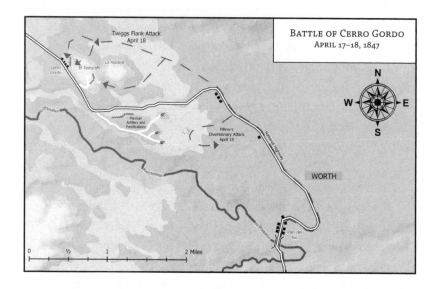

the next morning, was actually intended as a diversion. Lieutenants Zealous B. Tower and George McClellan, both engineers, had conducted extensive reconnaissance in this region over the previous days, and at least part of the time they had been accompanied by Pillow and other volunteer officers as they charted the path that the volunteers would take to get into position for the attack. That evening, as Twiggs's men hunkered down around La Atalaya just north of El Telégrafo, Pillow called his four regimental commanders, Campbell, Haskell, Francis M. Wynkoop, and William B. Roberts, to his headquarters to apprise them of the plans and the role that each regiment would play. They would leave camp early in the morning, march up the road to a designated point where they would file off to the left (south), and follow a path to a point facing the fortified ends of the three parallel ridges. At 8:00 a.m., the Second Tennessee and First Pennsylvania would lead the assault supported by the First Tennessee and Second Pennsylvania.[4]

As they settled down on the night of the seventeenth, the volunteers of the Second Tennessee knew that their opportunity had come. Finally, they would get their chance to fight their way onto an equal par with their First Tennessee brethren. Monterrey had been a source of pride for Davidson, Lawrence, Sumner, and other Middle Tennessee counties. If all went well in the morning, Cerro Gordo, as the battle would come to be known, would provide a similar opportunity for the boys of Carroll, Madison, Shelby, and other counties outside the mid-state to bring glory home to their communities. Although Colonel Campbell's regiment would play a supporting role the next day, he believed that hard fighting lay ahead. That night, he wrote to his wife that "tomorrow will settle the affair between Genl. Scott & Genl. Santa Anna." Ivory Kent was thinking more about past transgressions than about a chance at heroism. Kent was the Carroll County volunteer who had gotten uncontrollably drunk on the march to Memphis the previous summer and had pulled a knife on his superior, Lieutenant Isaac Hawkins. In a somber frame of mind, Kent found Hawkins by a campfire that evening and, pulling him aside, told him that considering the uncertainty that lay ahead, he wanted Hawkins to know that he harbored no ill will toward him. Hawkins reached out his hand and the two men shook then parted without another word. Kent was mortally wounded the next morning.[5]

Pillow's men were up and moving at 6:00 a.m. the next morning with Wyncoop's First Pennsylvania in the lead followed by Haskell's Second Tennessee. Campbell's "Bloody First" took up the line of march next, and Roberts's Second Pennsylvania brought up the rear. After a couple of miles, they reached the spot where they were to leave the road and follow a predetermined path for the last mile; there they found Tower, McClellan, and a cohort of a dozen men waiting. The engineers knew the path and they, along with their men had been designated to lead the volunteers through the rough terrain, clearing rocks, branches, and other debris along the way. But there were actually two paths leading away from the road—one veered left and the other right. The path to the left had been chosen after extensive reconnaissance as the best route to get Pillow's men, under cover, to the spot where they were to launch their attack, but when Pillow arrived he indicated that he wanted to take the path to the right. Although it was somewhat shorter, Tower protested because Pillow's preference would take the volunteers along a route that would be more easily detected by the enemy. An exchange of disagreements went back and forth between Tower and Pillow for several minutes. While the troops waited on the road, General Patterson rode by, giving each regiment words of encouragement, but he apparently did not intervene in the argument. Tower eventually acquiesced to Pillow's order and the men took the path that inclined to the right.[6]

Pillow's last-minute decision to take an alternate route was a critical mistake. Although shorter, it was so narrow that his two thousand men had to walk in single file, which significantly hampered their progress. At 8:30 a.m. they were still trying to reach their designated starting position. As the engineers worked feverishly to cut through the dense chaparral and thorny brush with billhook machetes, they heard the distant sound of cannon and musketry indicating that the flank attack was underway. This added a sense of urgency as their tardiness now threatened to turn their diversionary assault into an afterthought. It was about 9:00 when the volunteers finally began to arrive at their appointed location three hundred yards from the enemy's position.[7]

The Tennesseans and Pennsylvanians were now close enough to hear the faint shouts of Mexican officers as they barked orders to their men. They remained mostly concealed in the underbrush, but in places where one could see through the vegetation, the sight was foreboding. The volunteers were directly opposite the tip of the three fortified ridges where the Mexicans had a combined strength of nineteen guns and two thousand men, and they could see that the Mexicans had cut down the brush across a two hundred-yard front to give themselves a clear field of fire. And the stacked vegetation, consisting largely of thorny bushes and cacti, formed a crude abatis to further imped the attackers. Scott had ordered Pillow to attack the ridge on the far left, which, with the Rio del Plan running through a deep canyon at the base of its steep wall, provided a secure right flank for the Mexicans. Attacking the end of the enemy line offered the Americans the advantage of limiting the directions from which they would face enemy fire—meaning that when the Tennesseans and Pennsylvanians advanced, they would receive fire from the far left ridge directly in their front and perhaps from the middle ridge to their right, but their own left flank would be safe because of the river gorge. At this time Pillow made his second bad decision of the morning. Because the path he insisted on taking brought his men into position a little further to the right, he decided to deploy in a manner so as to attack both the middle and the left ridges simultaneously. That decision would be costly for it gave enemy gunners on all three ridges a line of fire on the advancing Americans.[8]

The events of the next half hour were perhaps the most confusing of the war for any of Tennessee's participants, and making sense of the conflicting accounts is difficult at best. Given the rocky, uneven terrain, the thick underbrush and an obstructing ravine, deploying for the attack was fraught with confusion. In trying to form its assault lines, the Second Tennessee's flank somehow lost proper alignment, and Haskell had to turn his men and straighten up the mess. Meanwhile, stragglers arriving and joining their units late had to be "literally shoved into their places one by one."[9] It was noisy and confusing and quite remarkable that they had not yet been detected. While Haskell was struggling to get the Second Tennessee up and in line, Pillow sent orders to Wynkoop in an effort to get the First Pennsylvania properly positioned alongside the Second Tennessee, but negotiating the terrain made it difficult to properly orient the companies. The confusing situation prompted one officer to note derisively that Pillow was trying to get his men aligned in a "novel order." Haskell had formed less than half of his regiment when a frustrated Pillow shouted, "Why the Hell don't Colonel Wynkoop file to the right?" Pillow's shout may or may not have been what alerted the defenders to American troops in their front, but within seconds a Mexican bugle sounded, and moments later the guns on the ridges opened fire.[10]

The deafening thunder of cannon added an additional layer of confusion to the situation. Ready or not, their part of the battle was now underway so Pillow ordered Haskell to charge the enemy works. But Haskell's entire regiment was not yet deployed and remained scattered in the chaparral. One Tennessean, William Lacy of Fayette County, later stated that not a single man of the Second Tennessee was out of place when the attack started, but this assertion was certainly untrue. George McClellan recorded in his diary that "Haskell's Regiment became at once 'confusion worse confounded,'" a description that was exaggerated at the other end of the spectrum but not entirely inaccurate. Despite the disorganized state of his command, Haskell ordered the attack, and

Tennesseans—at least those who had not taken cover—rushed forward through the brush and up a steady incline until they emerged out of their concealment and into open sight. Their location placed them right in front of the middle ridge with its nine guns, making it the most stoutly defended, and what was worse, they were in sight and range of the guns on the other two ridges. As soon as they came out into the open field of fire, the Mexicans opened with musketry also, and the converging fire resulted in "devastating showers of balls" that decimated the Tennesseans.[11]

When Haskell's men went forward, Wyncoop's Pennsylvanians were supposed to advance on their left, but they were nowhere in sight. They were still disorganized, and Wyncoop apparently did not receive the order to attack. So, with both of their flanks exposed and the other supporting regiments still too far in the rear to assist, the Second Tennessee was all alone and the recipient of concentrated enemy fire. In less than five minutes, the regiment suffered dozens of casualties including all of its field officers except for Haskell. Although he had not been hit, Haskell's hat had been shot from his head, releasing his long, flowing hair. Enemy fire was every bit as intense, perhaps more so, as that received by the First Tennessee at Monterrey seven months earlier. Determined to reach the enemy works, the Tennesseans "went on bravely," as a Pennsylvanian put it, "till they came within 50 yards of the works, when they began to falter."[12] Private Austin McAdoo of Carroll County's Company B, remembered that about 350 members of the regiment went forward and those not yet killed or wounded got to within sixty yards of the enemy while "all the time exposed to cross fires of grape and canister from about 20 pieces of artillery, and to the incessant fire of some thousands of muskets." The situation was becoming desperate for the twenty-eight-year-old Haskell. He had come to Mexico in part to avenge the murder of his brother, but this was not the kind of revenge he had anticipated.[13]

Meanwhile, Pillow was back at the staging area trying to salvage some degree of order out of the chaos. The rear was a dangerous place with various types of projectiles whizzing through the brush. Even the First Pennsylvania, which never joined the attack, sustained casualties, including the death of a donkey that carried medical supplies for the regimental surgeon. It was only minutes into the battle and things were going badly when Lieutenant McClellan sought out General Pillow to get orders. He found the general squatting behind a bush with his back to the battlefield. While conversing there, a canister ball struck Pillow's right arm above the elbow, breaking the bone and tearing muscle. The general and an aide immediately moved farther back to the rear, and along the way he ran into Colonel Campbell, who was pushing to get his regiment up to the front to support the attack. Pillow ordered Campbell to assume command of the entire brigade and try to press the attack forward.[14]

Campbell "was in a most furious humor" over the way the battle had commenced before he had been able to get the First Tennessee close enough to support. Now he tried to hurry his men up to the sound of the fighting, and he went on ahead of them to take command of troops at the front. However, Campbell's efforts to get the First Pennsylvania moving fell on deaf ears, because Wyncoop refused to recognize Campbell's right to give him orders. While the First Tennessee worked its way through the brush to get to its designated location, Samuel Lauderdale stopped to wipe the sweat from his face when a canister shot struck him in the forehead. He survived two hours in a comatose state but never spoke a word. (It was Samuel's father William who, as an army major during the Seminole War, built a fort on the coast of Florida around which grew the town of Ft. Lauderdale.) Meanwhile, Pillow decided he was well enough to continue in command (or maybe he realized what an early and ill-advised departure from the field would do to his reputation) so he returned just in time to face an angry William Haskell.[15]

Having gotten close to the enemy's line, the depleted number of attackers, thinned by relentless fire, caused the Second Tennessee to lose momentum. Haskell realized the precarious nature of the affair and ordered a retreat. This was an order his men were happy to obey, and some of them rushed to the rear so fast that they blew through the lines of the Pennsylvanians, creating more confusion in the process. Before the attack, the Tennesseans had been ordered not to fire until they reached the enemy works, but they never reached the works before being thrown back. Ironically, most of the men never fired a shot. As his regiment scattered to the rear, an angry Haskell, his hair waving "wildly in the wind," found Pillow and the two men had a heated exchange. Pillow was agitated and in pain (and probably shifting into face-saving mode). He accused Haskell of neglecting his duty by leaving his regiment and ordered him to return to his men and reorganize them for another attack. Haskell fired back that his regiment had been badly mauled, because it had gone into battle alone and without the promised support. After witnessing the verbal salvos of their exchange, Lieutenant McClellan took it upon himself to "beat the bushes" in search of Haskell's men and begin the effort to reorganize the regiment. After locking horns with Haskell, Pillow turned his wrath on the Pennsylvanians, blaming them for hanging back and not doing their duty, and he ordered them too to prepare for another attack. Campbell also pointed an accusing finger. He thought the actions of Wyncoop's regiment were reprehensible and he "damned the Pennsylvanians for a set of cowards."[16]

Toward the rear, men of the mounted Knoxville company, which Pillow had brought as additional reinforcements, were close enough to the action to ascertain what was happening. One member of the unit kept a diary, and while it has survived, the name of the diarist has not. In writing about the battle, he wrote that Haskell's charge was one of "gallantry" and "desparation." However, moments after the repulse, "Men all bloody from the wounds received came staggering along the path supported by their comrades." Others were being carried back to the surgeon's station. Also, the anonymous writer expressed "shame to say some cowards came running in great havic," but he was quick to point out that only a few were Tennesseans. One of the injured stumbled toward the rear holding his wounded buttocks and exclaiming "Oh! I am killed. . . . I believe I shall die." When he reached the medical staff, the doctor assured him that he would only experience pain when he sat down and that it would go away in a few days.[17]

Next Pillow dispatched McClellan to the other side of the battlefield with a request that General Scott send regulars to assist with a second attack on the ridges. When McClellan found the commanding general and apprised him of the situation on the Mexican right, he was "not much surprised and not much 'put out' that Pillow was thrashed," according to McClellan. Furthermore, Scott seemingly "attached no importance to

[Pillow's] future movements," because Twiggs's flank attack had over-run El Telégrafo and the entire Mexican left had crumbled. Scott knew that the Mexican position on the ridges was now untenable and that they would be forced to surrender or retreat. Scott simply instructed McClellan to tell Pillow to attack or not attack—whichever he wished. Indeed, at about the time McClellan returned to Pillow's sector, Mexican troops atop the ridges, aware that the rest of their army was in full flight, raised a white flag. The battle was over, but Wyncoop seemed not to know the meaning of a white flag, and when told that it meant the Mexicans had surrendered, he vowed that he was going to attack anyway—with or without orders. It was, of course, too late for Wyncoop and his men to participate in the battle.[18]

During Pillow's brief time in the army, he already had cemented a reputation that he would never be able to shake. Cerro Gordo was his first major test under fire, and he failed. He tried to act independently by changing the assigned route and the point of attack, and in both cases his judgment was flawed. Haskell and the Second Tennessee men blamed him for the failure and their anger persisted for a long time. Patrick Duffy, a member of the First Tennessee thought that "the attack [by] . . . Pillows Brigade was badly planned. . . . There is great responsibility rest-ing on someone in regard to this matter." That evening after the battle, Campbell described his superior officer in a letter to his uncle, writing that Pillow "is no Genl. and on the field of action, has no decision or judgt." McClellan considered it a "misfortune" that he had been assigned to the Tennessean during the battle, and he referred to Pillow's volun-teers as the "whipped community." Furthermore, McClellan believed that the failure on the American left was entirely due to Pillow's "puerile imbecility." Another West Point–trained officer, Daniel Harvey Hill, wrote a diary entry that referred to "that fool Genl. Pillow."[19]

Pillow's men paid the price for his mistakes. The Second Tennessee suffered sixteen killed and forty-five wounded, and the First Tennessee, having been briefly in the line of fire as it made its way to the front, had one killed and eight wounded. Approximately 8,500 American sol-diers were engaged at Cerro Gordo, and sixty-three were killed in the battle while 368 were wounded.[20] Sixteen percent of all U.S. casualties were Tennesseans, but even more worthy of note was that Tennesseans made up 27 percent of the deaths. Haskell's regiment had suffered fewer deaths at Cerro Gordo than had Campbell's regiment at Monterrey, but that was because the Second Tennessee had been exposed to enemy fire for only a few minutes as it charged across two hundred yards of open terrain. The Bloody First had been exposed for about twenty minutes as it traversed a mile-long open plain and was within range of artillery for 1,500 yards. The engagements were not dissimilar in intensity, the only major difference being the duration of time under fire.

But Pillow did not receive universal condemnation. Nashvillian John Robertson, an admittedly sympathetic Tennessee volunteer, asserted that "to no one can blame be attached for the failure." The fault lay in the fact that Mexican strength on the three ridges had been badly underestimated, wrote Robertson, a misfortune that resulted in Pillow attacking the strongest portion of the enemy line with the weakest contingent of American troops. He concluded that since Pillow's attack began simultaneously with the flank attack at the other end of the battlefield, it had served its intended purpose as a diversion. Objectivity requires that some credence be given to Robertson's argument, at least until his last point about the timely start of Pillow's attack, which was patently false. In Nathaniel Hughes and Roy Stonesifer's even-handed biography of the general, the authors try to give Pillow the benefit of the doubt by praising his willingness to be aggressive on the battlefield, but ultimately it was his "amateurish command decisions" that led to the failure of his command at Cerro Gordo. Furthermore, the authors contend, if Mexican strength had been underestimated prior to the attack, it was Pillow himself who had done it.[21]

Pillow's debacle became merely a footnote to the Battle of Cerro Gordo and was not enough to stain the significance of the outcome. It was a lopsided victory with over three thousand Mexicans captured, including five generals and two hundred other officers. The flank attack on the left end of the enemy line had been spectacular, causing those who were not captured to scatter in every direction, including Santa Anna who fled the battlefield in such haste that he left behind a carriage containing one of his prosthetic legs. General Scott commented to

McClellan that Twiggs's attack was "the most beautiful sight that he had ever witnessed"—a statement that is reminiscent of one made by Lee at Fredericksburg in 1862, when he said, "It is well that war is so terrible, or we should grow too fond of it."[22] Mounted troops pursued what was left of the retreating Mexican army, killing many more along the road before halting fifteen miles away at Jalapa.

Another Tennessee casualty, this one from the ranks of the regular army, justifies brief treatment. Tom Ewell was from Jackson, Tennessee, and he had set up a recruiting office in his hometown the previous year. Then, just as Thomas Claiborne had done, he secured a lieutenant's commission in the Mounted Rifles, a new regiment being organized in the regular army. Ewell and Claiborne had taken part in the attack on El Telégrafo that morning, and by some accounts Ewell was the first to reach the Mexican works at the summit. After killing two enemy soldiers in hand-to-hand combat, he received a gunshot wound in the abdomen. When the hilltop had been cleared of retreating Mexican soldiers, Claiborne found Ewell nearby on his hands and knees in agonizing pain and did what he could to make him comfortable. His deportment impressed Claiborne who related the story to family back home: "He behaved with the greatest courage, and when suffering the greatest agony, would only press firmly his lips together and close his eyes. . . . He disdained to groan, and refused to mention his misfortune." Ewell told Claiborne that he knew he was going to die, and he asked for opium to ease his pain. Soon Ewell's brother, future Confederate general Richard (Dick) Ewell, who was a lieutenant in the dragoons, joined the group of comrades who had gathered around Tom. The brothers exchanged words, and Tom repeated to Dick that he was dying and asked him to write a letter to their mother. Dick gave what assurances he could then rejoined his unit in pursuit of the Mexican army. At some point, General Scott happened upon the huddle of men around Ewell and stopped to offer an encouraging word. Knelling by Ewell's side and taking his hand, Scott said, "Mr. Ewell you are an honor to your name, an honor to the service to which you belong." After proclaiming the Tennessean a hero, Scott concluded, "you must not die." That evening Dick returned from Jalapa and reunited with Tom on the battlefield, remaining beside him until he died soon after midnight. Friends buried him in a "rough coffin" on the side of El Telégrafo.[23]

In an honor-driven society, one's bearing under trying circumstances reveals insight into their character. Even in death, it was important to be remembered for bravery. During their conversation on El Telégrafo, Claiborne gave assurances that he would let others know of Ewell's courage: "[I]f I live I will let your friends in Tennessee know of your gallantry." Ewell thanked him. And Claiborne kept his promise by writing an account of Ewell's final hours that was published in newspapers back home. In it, he not only spoke of Ewell's bravery but he implored folks back home not to leave his body in a foreign land. "Will not Tennessee claim his remains? He fought for her honor." "He gave his life to the glory of his country," eulogized a Memphis paper. Indeed, Ewell's remains were repatriated back to Tennessee and reburied in the Riverside Cemetery in Jackson.[24]

Unfortunately, it was only in death that members of the Second Tennessee found honor. Those who survived faced disappointment, and disappointment turned to bitterness by the thoughts that their part in the battle had been mismanaged by their commanders. Theirs was the only part of the battle wherein one could find second guessing and thoughts of "what if." The blood that the regiment shed had been in a failed effort, and because of that failure they had missed their opportunity for glory. As one account asserted, "Haskell's 2d Tennessee had been humiliated" at Cerro Gordo.[25] Gideon Pillow would get another chance to redeem himself, but William Haskell and the Second Tennessee would not. Members of the regiment had expected to return home filled with pride at their accomplishments, but the only glory was for those who died a glorious death in a "forlorn hope."

Two months later, after folks back home had heard the story of the Second Tennessee's misfortune, newspaper accounts put the best spin possible on the situation but often with a sympathetic tone. The *Republican Banner* asserted, "These brave men were prepared to sacrifice themselves for the honor of their State and the glory of the United States, and they will not be the less cherished by their fellow-citizens for that, the most devoted chivalry, when misdirected, would only achieve an honorable martyrdom." The *Knoxville Tribune* likewise tried to make the botched attack seem more palatable by asserting that the Mexican surrender had "deprived the Tennesseans of the opportunity of avenging their loss."[26] When they returned home a month after the battle, they would be honored by their fellow Tennesseans, but they would never possess the glory they had sought.

The results of the battle hit William Haskell particularly hard. He was devastated to hear of Thomas Ewell's death. Although fighting in different units and at opposite ends of the battlefield, Haskell and Ewell had grown up together in Jackson. After returning home, Haskell wrote the following about Ewell in the Memphis *Daily Eagle*: "He was my intimate, personal friend, and school boy companion. Will not Tennessee erect a mausoleum to his memory and consecrate him to immortal glory?" Haskell finished his memorial with the following lines: "Sweet sleep the dead, who sink to rest; By all their country's wishes blest!"[27] Haskell would be disappointed to visit the Riverside Cemetery today and discover that Ewell's gravesite is nondescript and its location difficult to find.

Equally devastating was the death of his good friend and adjutant, Wiley Hale, who had been by his side since the formation of the regiment and who likely intended to marry Haskell's sister, Caroline. Haskell had kept Hale close as a way of insuring the latter's safety so that he could return home to Caroline. Hale was wounded in the battle, but initially the injury did not seem serious, and for several days the young adjutant had been walking about camp, visiting the injured, and apparently not experiencing pain. However, on Saturday the twenty-fourth of April, he suddenly became incapacitated and died two days later, likely from tetanus. Hale's death was yet another symbol of Haskell's failure in Mexico, but he was not the only one who suffered from the loss. All of the Jackson boys, indeed the entire regiment, was "deeply shrouded in gloom" over Hale's death.[28] A total of seven Madison County comrades serving in the Second Tennessee died at Cerro Gordo. These losses coupled with the other casualties in his regiment were sufficient to debilitate Haskell's spirit, but add to that the death of his wife's brother, William Porter, who had volunteered for the Mounted Regiment, endured the long trek to Mexico by land, and at Matamoros, after suffering an extended illness, resigned his captaincy only to die in New Orleans on his way home.[29]

The army quickly resumed its inland push toward Mexico City, and on April 20 Pillow's volunteer brigade left Plan del Rio to join the march. They marched through the Cerro Gordo gorge and passed by El Telégrafo, which was "dotted with the blackened and bloody corpses of three hundred dead." Already the stench of decaying flesh hung over the battlefield. The road leading out of Cerro Gordo was strewn for miles with debris, Mexican corpses and animal carcasses. The Second Tennessee did not leave with its sister units, but rather it stayed behind to care for its wounded, bury the dead, and see to the destruction of captured weapons (the Americans had captured four thousand muskets and forty cannon). In other words, the regiment was given the menial task of cleaning up the battlefield. First Camargo and now Cerro Gordo; members of the Second Tennessee were growing accustomed to being left behind. After the army's departure, one more misfortune befell Colonel Haskell. When attempting to burn a pile of muskets, he accidently touched off a powder magazine and the resulting explosion burned him severely.[30]

The first leg of the army's march was just fifteen miles to Jalapa. Between Cerro Gordo and Jalapa was one of Santa Anna's grand estates called El Encero, which several Tennesseans stopped to explore. As they marched into Jalapa, it seemed that eyes were gazing at them from every window. Some of the eyes appeared angry, some presented only a blank stare, and others appeared to be snickering at the "ragamuffin and tatterdemalion appearance" of the Tennesseans. They marched through the town to their designated campsite just beyond, and along the way, many of the Tennessee boys took note a one particular young lady who sat in a chair and watched them pass. John Robertson thought she deserved special mention, and he offered this vivid description in his *Reminiscences*. "She was a perfect picture of beauty. There she sat, neatly and richly clad, with her light and gracile form bending in the symmetrical curves of graceful beauty; her dark, luxuriant hair passing along her forehead and falling in a shower of raven tresses upon her neck." She held a book in her lap and pretended to read it, but Robertson thought that she was obviously more interested in the passing Americans. He concluded a lengthy description with; "suffice it to say that the bright beauty of that black eyed brunette made the eye of every beholder glow with admiration."[31]

Jalapa was a delightful, picturesque town. When Pillow's men arrived, much of the army was already there, and the Second Tennessee would arrive within days. The town had an elevation of four thousand feet, and its pleasant climate was a striking contrast to the *tierra caliente* of the coastal lowlands. The rich soil of the region produced lush vegetation and all manner of exotic fruits. After exploring the town, one Tennessean concluded that Jalapa was "one of the finest places we had seen in Mexico." Colonel Campbell thought that Jalapa was "one of the cleanest places I ever saw." He also concluded that the town's "population is more of the European than in any town I have seen."[32]

Over four decades later, Nashvillian Thomas Claiborne of the regular army wrote about a Jalapan family that opened up to him and his comrades. They lived in a house within sight of Claiborne's quarters where he and his friends sat every day. When the Americans first arrived, the house appeared deserted with its doors and windows shut, but after a few days children ventured out and the inhabitants opened the front door and shutters. In time, the children warmed up to the strangers, and one day a servant brought a tray of fruit out of the house and took it to the Americans. Soon the soldiers became regular guests in the home where a daughter played the harp and sang for them and where they discovered a grown son who had learned English as a student at Columbia College in New York. As it turned out, this aristocratic family actually lived in Veracruz but owned and lived in the Jalapa house during the yellow fever season.[33]

When the Second Tennessee arrived, the month of April was quickly passing by and the end of their twelve-month commitment was rapidly approaching for all three of Tennessee's volunteer regiments. On May 6, General Scott sent the Tennesseans home, along with volunteers from three other states. With scarcely a month left of their enlistments, the timing was such that the soldiers would remain under army command— that is to say, under military discipline during their return trip. Having seen the elephant, along with the blood and suffering that accompanied it, there was little protest when they received orders to march back to Veracruz and load on transports. The members of the Mounted Regiment who had finally gotten mounts and had joined the army late, covered the sixty-three miles back to Veracruz in two days. Once there, they sold their horses to the quartermaster department before boarding the waiting steamers. It took the foot soldiers four days to retrace their steps to the coast, and along the way they passed back through the Cerro Gordo battlefield where vultures were plentiful and the hills and ravines were replete with howling coyotes and wolves that had been feasting on the decaying flesh.[34]

The question many soldiers were asking after Cerro Gordo was how much longer the war would last. Many thought the end was near. General Scott even wrote to Taylor after Cerro Gordo that "Mexico has no longer an army." However, some of the Tennesseans were not so sure. John Robertson was disappointed that he would not make it to the Halls of the Montezumas, but more importantly he believed it was a "shortsighted" mistake to send the volunteers home. Lieutenant William Lacy from Fayette County headed home with the conviction that the war would continue for quite some time. Because Scott's pacification policy forbade pillage and plunder and required payment for all goods taken from civilians, he believed that the army was too lax and generous, and as a consequence had failed to induce the Mexican government to sue for peace. Mexicans must feel the sting of war, thought Lacy, and the war would continue until they saw the U.S. forces as "an army [come] *to conquer* and *to punish*." He continued in a letter that was published in a Memphis newspaper: "The Mexican people do not *feel* our power, we are all the time preaching up that we are friends, giving them every protection, and [paying] the most exorbitant prices for every article we got of them." In short, thought Lacy, Mexicans must approach us "begging for peace."[35]

Although pleased to be heading home, both Tennessee regimental commanders were unhappy with their military experience. Campbell vowed never to serve in a volunteer unit again, because volunteers never get the credit they are due and regulars always receive better supplies and comforts. He resolved that if he ever entered the army again it would only be with a commission as a regular officer. Haskell was devastated over his personal losses at Cerro Gordo and was seething over the leadership fiasco that handicapped his regiment. As soon as he arrived in New Orleans on May 19, Haskell and his officers aired their grievances publicly by publishing in the *Picayune* a diatribe against Pillow, whom they blamed for the botched attack. They charged that Pillow was unfamiliar with the terrain and with the enemy position that was attacked, and furthermore that Pillow bungled the march that morning and was at fault for the chaos that accompanied their attempt to deploy for battle. They also wanted to correct an assumption among the general public that Pillow had led the attack at Cerro Gordo and had received his wound at the head of his command. Haskell and his comrades clarified by noting that Pillow "neither led nor followed in the assault," and never got closer to the enemy line than the beginning point of the attack. Four regimental officers from Memphis joined Haskell in signing the statement before its publication, and they went so far as to demand Pillow's court martial.[36]

Haskell's publication was not the end but rather the beginning of an acrimonious exchange that, while starting in the New Orleans press, was picked up and reprinted in Tennessee newspapers. When Pillow saw Haskell's account of the battle in the *Picayune*, he immediately wrote a rejoinder. In his initial report immediately following the battle, Pillow had written that Haskell's men were met with "the terrible fire of the enemy" but that they nevertheless "sustained the shock—both officers and men—with firmness and constancy worthy of high commendation." Now his tone changed. In his lengthy newspaper essay, Pillow countered each of Haskell's charges: the order of march, the alignment of regiments, the number and location of enemy batteries, and other particulars. Pillow took special care to explain and justify the point of attack on the morning of April 18. The assault, he wrote, had been aimed at an angle between two of the enemy batteries, believed to be the weakest point of the Mexican defenses, which was a determination based on reconnaissance done with the engineers and, as Pillow pointed out, in the presence of Haskell, who had joined the reconnoitering party. In his account of the affair, Pillow referred to Haskell's "inexplicable confusion of mind," and at one point wrote this stinging rebuke: "To suppose him so ignorant of the principles of military science, would show him utterly unfit for the command of a regiment."[37]

Also, Pillow's associates solicited through newspapers other accounts from people who had witnessed Haskell's behavior during the battle, and members of the First Tennessee responded with damning critiques. They said that Haskell appeared "very much confused" and "greatly excited" when his regiment was repulsed, and for some reason they felt compelled to mention Haskell's loss of his hat during his regiment's retreat and how he occasionally ran his hand through his hair during his animated exchange with Pillow.[38] The personal aspersions and caricatures would have taken a toll on anyone no matter how resilient his psyche.

Questioning Haskell's state of mind and competency was an insulting condemnation. Within days, he responded to Pillow's "provoking language," claiming to be mystified by Pillow's reconstruction of events, especially his description of the enemy works and the number of batteries. As to Pillow's assertion that he ordered an attack on a weak angle in the Mexican line, Haskell responded, "the truth is, there were no such angles as he describes there." Furthermore, rather than being the weakest portion of the enemy works, Pillow actually ordered an attack on the strongest part. Like an attorney, Haskell pointed out contradictory statements in Pillow's version. Moreover, he condemned his superior's failure to solicit battle reports from the regimental commanders, which was "contrary to all courtesy and military etiquette." The reason for this was clear to Haskell, because such "reports would have elicited the truth" about what happened at Cerro Gordo. Haskell concluded his rejoinder by stating, "I have contended, and still contend, that Gen. Pillow exhibited a total want of ability to command."[39]

The Memphis press also took on a more belligerent tone as the Pillow/Haskell feud heated up in mid-summer. The *Daily Enquirer* joined the anti-Pillow chorus with an article titled "Our Volunteers and their General," in which it recounted how Pillow's "military capacity is impeached by the regiment." It characterized the Cerro Gordo attack as a "fearful and needless slaughter," and asserted that the general "neither led nor followed in . . . that assault." Instead, he "hastened from the battle field and received the firstlings of the public gratitude for the glories of Cerro Gordo." Further implying that Pillow had received undeserved credit and honor, the article speculated that his arm wound had garnered him sympathy. The newspaper continued its invective the following day by claiming that Pillow had deceived General Scott regarding his pre-battle reconnaissance, had attacked in the wrong place, and in sum was a failed commander.[40]

Polk straightaway heard that Haskell had launched stern criticisms at Pillow, so Pillow felt the need to write to the president in his own defense. Haskell's attack was unprovoked, wrote Pillow, but "I have so completely turned the tables upon him as to have floored him." Pillow was confident that he had destroyed Haskell's "military reputation, if any he had."[41] It is interesting (or perhaps a better word is revealing) that when Pillow clashed with someone, he not only tried to set the record straight, but also sought to ruin the reputation of his antagonist. The episode with Haskell was just a foretaste of what Pillow was capable of when he set out to damage someone who crossed him. Indeed, Pillow would demonstrate by the end of the war a penchant for feuding with fellow officers in the aftermath of major battles—always to accomplish the goal of securing his personal legacy.

Pillow won the short-term argument but the long-term verdict of history would go against him. Haskell's opinion that Pillow lacked the ability to command was an assessment that remains intact a century-and-a-half later, as evidenced by the following twenty-first century assertion: "It was at Cerro Gordo that Pillow first showed a propensity to get rattled on the moment of action."[42] Returning members of the Second Tennessee shared Haskell's sentiments. They were disappointed and angry about the Cerro Gordo failure, and as far as they were concerned, the blame for their missed opportunity rested with a fellow Tennessean, the president's friend.

*Chapter Eight*

# OPPOSITION IN
# THE VOLUNTEER STATE

The Tennesseans arrived back home in early June and were treated to banquets, barbecues, and parades. City officials in Nashville organized a major reception and parade to honor the heroes of the Bloody First. Members of the regiment returned the Blue Eagle flag to the Nashville Female Academy in a ceremony that included patriotic speeches. The motto affixed to the bottom of the flag had admonished the men to "strike for their country" in order to avoid the stigma of timidity, and they had not disappointed their family or community. The flag was returned "*unsullied* & *consecrated* by the blood of some of the noblest sons of Tennessee," said Campbell in a speech that emphasized the regiment's keen desire "to preserve its [the flag's] honor untarnished." The colonel went on to talk about the pride that his men felt for their flag and the sensation it produced through the ranks whenever it was unfurled. In praising the ladies of the academy for honoring the regiment with the flag, he assured them that they were not forgotten each time the unit went into battle. "[S]o vividly," Campbell proclaimed, "we could almost fancy, that, like guardian angels, they were hovering over their favorite regiment."[1] Following the flag ceremony the companies disbanded, and the men returned to their respective homes, forever changed and in many people's eyes, forever heroes.

One part of Campbell's speech at the Female Academy warrants discussion for the political tinge it contained. He began his address with words that reflected his own doubt about the war's true origins. Tennessee's brave sons volunteered out of patriotism, "no matter by what means the conflict between the two nations had been caused—whether by the reckless & grasping spirit of the one, or by the sullen & obstinate refusal of justice from the other." Clearly "reckless & grasping" was meant to represent Polk's actions. Campbell continued: "No matter which was the aggressor in the beginning of the contest, it was sufficient that we knew our country to be at war . . . [and] that the blood of our fellow citizens had been shed. We cheerfully offered our services, for right or wrong we will stand by our country in all its emergencies."[2] Campbell obviously remained unconvinced that Polk's actions in taking the nation to war had been blameless, however, he was firmly convinced of the duty that honor required.

The Second Tennessee returned to similar fanfare but their home-coming was tainted by the Cerro Gordo repulse. Within a week of their return, a Memphis newspaper printed this reminder: "For the first time, we believe, in the military history of our country, a regiment of TENNESSEE VOLUNTEERS was repulsed in battle." The article was not intended to cast aspersions on the Second Tennessee, but rather to show sympathy to Haskell and his men who were, at that moment, engaged in a war of words with Pillow. They deserved an opportunity to explain what happened to a curious public, the article continued, because of the "renown of the gallant State whose honor was in their keeping" on the battlefields of Mexico.[3]

Despite the simmering Pillow/Haskell feud, the returning volunteers were treated to lively galas. Memphis officials invited the officers of the regiment to an elegant dinner at Gayoso House. At the event, Colonel Haskell spoke to the gathering, where he expressed appreciation to the Memphians for the joyous reception, and showed off trophies of war like a brass six-pounder captured at Cerro Gordo. But his speech was not entirely a recitation of the regiments martial exploits. He turned somber and reflected on comrades who did not return, offering such a touching eulogy that spectators cried. Haskell seemed consumed by thoughts of the loved ones he had lost. In stark contrast, Campbell's homecoming speech contained references to "victory" and "noble hearts" and a flag that was "never . . . forced to retire before an enemy." Sadly, Haskell could not use such words with West Tennessee crowds.

On June 15, the city held a large celebration at Court Square to honor all of the city's returned veterans. There were speakers, bonfires, and a barbecue dinner, and after sundown, all the houses in Memphis were illuminated for the occasion. Scattered rain showers during the day dampened some of the festivities, which for the Second Tennessee was symbolically appropriate. However, that was not the worst thing that happened during the celebration. At some point, Nathan Ursery, who had served in Shelby County's Company E, used vulgar language in the presence of a lady. A prominent resident of the city, Joseph Aiken, chastised Ursery for his foul mouth, and in the fight that ensued Ursery stabbed Aiken to death with a Bowie knife.[4]

A few days later another tragedy occurred in Memphis, but of a different sort. One of the Memphians killed in the Cerro Gordo charge was Lieutenant Charles Gill. His father, Lyman Gill, not wanting his son's remains left in a foreign country, traveled to Mexico to retrieve the body and bring it home for burial. On his way back, the father became ill and also died. When the two corpses reached Mrs. Gill in Memphis, she planned a dual funeral for June 26. Before the burial, she requested that Charles's casket be opened so she could look at her son one last time, but her grief turned to horror when she discovered that it was not Charles. It is unclear how the mistake occurred, but Mrs. Gill's agony was debilitating until her son's remains finally made it home several months later.[5]

In the weeks following the Tennesseans' return home, the feud over the Cerro Gordo controversy raged in the press. At least seventeen officers, Whig and Democrat, accused Pillow of mismanagement, poor leadership, and worse, cowardice for running to the rear after receiving his arm wound.[6] Pillow's actions in Mexico merely added fuel to a political fire that had been burning back home since the previous year. While Tennessee's sons had been fighting and dying in Mexico, Democrats and Whigs had been fighting their own battles over President Polk's war policies, and Pillow's political appointment along with his apparent military incompetence served to stoke the flames of party politics. Closely contested elections had been a hallmark of Tennessee politics for a decade, but the war had exacerbated the ideological divide since its inception in May 1846. Polk's status as the most prominent Tennessean during the war and the primary agent of manifest destiny warrants further focus on his management of the conflict and the opposition it fostered.

Texas annexation and westward expansion had been a winning formula for Democrats, who sought to expand the fruits of republican government beyond the country's border. However, the controversy surrounding the declaration of war the previous year had alienated many Americans from the outset, and the president's personality and demeanor only intensified his opponents' suspicions. One historian described him as "stiffly formal," "dogmatic in his political views," "humorless," and "self righteous." These characteristics made for an unpleasant personality, but what Polk's political opponents feared most was his "penchant for disingenuousness, if not outright deception," and their opinion that the president was "underhanded and devious." In addition to being personally reserved, he was politically shrewd and determined—that is to say, he was uncompromising.[7] His political rise came in the 1830s during the Jackson revolt that resulted in the creation of the Whig Party in Tennessee. As noted earlier, the Whig challenge to Democrat hegemony in the state produced hotly contested political battles that had made Polk hypersensitive to opposition and fiercely determined to squash his opponents.[8]

Anti-war sentiment had been strong among Whigs from the beginning, and it revolved around questions concerning causes, the necessity of fighting, motives, and objectives. Because it was "Mr. Polk's war," much of the opposition centered on the president.[9] His personality and partisan nature, coupled with his heavy-handed methods, made it easy for the Whigs to mobilize opposition to his policies. Among his strongest detractors was former Whig congressman Meredith Gentry from Williamson County whose criticisms of Polk were so harsh that after the war he felt compelled to apologize to the president. Polk was unforgiving. But the outpouring of patriotism in the summer of 1846 sufficiently demonstrated to the Whigs that the war was popular with large segments of society, which put them in a political quandary. Also, they were cognizant of the fact that opposition to the War of 1812 had accelerated the demise of the Federalist Party thirty years earlier. So they walked a fine line in an effort not to appear unpatriotic.

Democrats knew history also and in 1846 began to refer to Whigs as Federalists so as to conjure the kind of unfavorable comparisons that Whigs hoped to avoid. During the course of the war, the Democratic press in Tennessee referred to Whigs as "The party which sustains the Mexican cause," and "Mexican Whigs," and "Whig Tories." The Whig press responded by pointing out that Tennesseans and Whigs had always fought for the honor of their state, as, for example, William Campbell, who "goes for his country . . . [but] does not bow to Executive dictation." Their opposition to the war clearly forced the Whigs to straddle the fence. While they condemned the war, they praised every battlefield victory and especially the Whig commanders who won them. Indeed, it was the Whig-saturated officer corps that most frustrated the president.[10]

And Polk knew history well enough to emulate Thomas Jefferson, who had confronted a similar problem regarding the composition of the army's command structure. When he became president in 1801, Jefferson faced an officer corps that was top-heavy with Federalists, whom the new president believed to be too aristocratic and anti-democratic. For Jefferson, it was essentially a political problem that he remedied with the creation of West Point in 1802—a school to educate good Jeffersonian-Republicans who would, over time, infuse the officer corps with a healthy dose of egalitarianism.[11] President Polk set out to solve his political/ military problem in much the same way—by remaking the officer corps.

One of Polk's greatest concerns was the creation of Whig military heroes who, upon their return home, would win political office. So, he took several steps in an attempt to remedy this potential problem, starting with the two top Whig generals in the army. Everyone knew that Winfield Scott, the commanding general, was a Whig, and also that he wanted to be president. Polk had hesitated sending him to Mexico at the outbreak of the conflict because of a war of words between them. Two years prior to the war, indeed before Polk's election, Scott had written that a country had "the highest moral obligation to treat national differences with temper, justice, and fairness; always to see that the cause of war is not only just but sufficient; [and] to be sure that we do not covet our neighbor's lands." And after the war began, he told the British Minister to the United States in a private conversation that he was "ashamed" of the war.[12] Scott was clearly in the Whig camp; that is, he was not in favor of going to war with Mexico, but as a soldier he was ready to do his duty.

His problem with Polk arose after the declaration of war when the president ordered him to Mexico to assume command of Taylor's army. Two weeks later, when Polk expressed concern that Scott was still in Washington, the general injudiciously responded that he needed to make sure all was ready for his departure so as to avoid "a fire upon my rear, from Washington" after he left. The short-tempered president angrily responded by removing Scott from field command and ordering him to remain in the capital. The shocked general sheepishly responded by apologizing and explaining that he had stepped out "to take a hasty plate of soup" when Polk's message arrived. In addition to denying the commanding general field command, the administration released Scott's "hasty plate of soup" statement to the press to ridicule and embarrass him, and it did. "A hasty plate of soup" became the punch line of jokes for months. It was only after Zachary Taylor had won impressive victories at Palo Alto, Resaca de la Palma, and Monterrey and was being discussed as a Whig presidential candidate that Polk returned to the notion of sending Scott to Mexico to de facto supersede Taylor with a new military campaign. The necessity of transferring half of Taylor's army to Scott three months after Monterrey forced Taylor to cease offensive operations, which, Polk hoped, would serve to throttle his rising star as a military hero. And then there was Gideon Pillow, first assigned to Taylor then transferred to Scott, the president's friend who conveniently kept a political eye on the top Whig brass. As one newspaper put it, the "Administration desired to sacrifice Scott and Taylor, in order to remove dangerous *political* rivals!"[13]

After reining in troublesome generals by humiliating Scott and supplanting Taylor, Polk pursued a plan to further defang the commanding general. In the fall of 1846, as he was reappointing Scott to field command and reminding him of the necessity of mutual trust and support, he was also going behind Scott's back and exploring the possibility of having Congress revive the rank of lieutenant general, which had not been held by an American officer since George Washington. The president's intent was to replace Scott with a loyal Democratic of higher rank. In a December meeting with a group of Democrat congressmen, Polk explained his "embarrassment . . . with the present officers" in an effort to enlist their support in passing a lieutenant general bill. The plan fell through when Congress failed to pass the necessary legislation, even though the attempt succeeded in driving a wedge deeper between the president and general. Weakening his top Whig generals and pushing for the reestablishment of the rank of lieutenant general constituted two parts of what historian John C. Pinheiro calls Polk's "tripartite strategy." The president's third approach was to "transform the command structure of the army . . . by appointing a solid Democratic cadre of volunteer generals." That process, begun in 1846, continued into 1847 as additional regiments were raised to meet manpower demands. During the course of the war, Polk appointed and Congress confirmed thirteen volunteer generals, all Democrats. Most of them had held political office before the war and two of them even ran for political office while serving in Mexico. They all brought their politics with them when they joined the army.[14]

Not content to appoint loyal party members as general officers, the administration hit on a way to extend executive patronage to inferior officer ranks in late 1846. In December, as General Scott was arriving in Mexico in preparation for his invasion at Veracruz, a Georgia Democrat introduced into the House of Representatives a bill to recruit and organize ten more badly needed regiments to send to Mexico. The Ten Regiment Bill, as it was called, was fraught with political implications. Traditionally, new volunteer units (companies and regiments) selected their own officers through elections. However, the Ten Regiment Bill would categorize the new units not as volunteers but as regulars, giving the president the prerogative of appointing officers down to company grade. The political benefit for Democrats was that it would ensure that Whigs would not be in positions of authority in the new regiments but rather loyal Democrats. The Ten Regiment Bill was a political tactic as much as a military one, and Whigs complained that it was yet another example of Polk's exercise of excessive executive power. The bill, warned Kentucky Senator John J. Crittenden, would concede to the president power that was "arbitrary, absolute, and unregulated." Even a few Democrats opposed the bill. Ultimately, military imperatives coupled with pressure exerted by the Democratic press resulted in Congress passing the bill on February 10, 1847.[15]

Did the president politicize the war as the Whigs contended? Polk asserted in his diary that he did not. Others did, his opponents did, but he declared that he "had never suffered politics to mingle with the conduct of the war." He was partially correct, for others had indeed brought politics into the conduct of the war, and he certainly wanted loyal generals who would not criticize the administration's handling of the war as Taylor had done. But after a career spent fighting intense political battles, Polk saw everything through the lens of politics, and because he was an ideologue he equated what was best for his party with what was best for the country. Pinheiro concludes in his book *Manifest Ambition* that Polk's political inclinations were nowhere more evident than in his selection of generals. "Substantial evidence exists to support the contention that Polk, in choosing his generals, ultimately valued party and nepotism over experience and professionalism." Historian Richard Bruce Winders drew a similar conclusion, writing, "Polk saw the army as a political battleground between Whig and Democratic officers and sent reinforcements, in the form of volunteer generals loyal to the Democratic Party, to aid his side."[16]

Even before the Lieutenant General Bill and the Ten Regiment Bill, another proposed piece of legislation provided fuel for the anti-Polk fire. In late summer 1846, Democrats sponsored the Two Million Bill to provide funds to facilitate the administration's peace negotiations. The president argued that the money was intended as a fair inducement to get the Mexican government to acknowledge the Rio Grande as the permanent border between the two countries, but critics quickly and accurately pointed out that the acquisition of additional Mexican territory, specifically New Mexico and Upper California, was the real purpose for the requested funds. Polk persisted in his contention that the war was not about territorial conquest, but nationally, Whigs opposed the bill, insisting that it was. Opposing the appropriation, however, once again put the Whigs in a conundrum. Just as their opposition to the war a few months earlier opened them to the criticism of being unpatriotic, now they found it difficult to oppose a funding bill that might hasten the end of the war.[17]

Then Congressman David Wilmot introduced his famous amendment to the bill that transformed what had been a party battle into a sectional debate. The Wilmot Proviso stipulated that the passage of the bill would not only appropriate the $2,000,000 but would also bar slavery from any territory acquired as a result of the war. Wilmot, a Pennsylvania Democrat, proposed the amendment for two reasons: first, to convince anti-slavery Whigs to cease their intransigence and second, to provide cover for Northern Democrats who were running for reelection against strong anti-slavery candidates. Thus, the proviso divided Northern and Southern Democrats as well as Northern and Southern Whigs and brought slavery to the forefront of the war debate. Likewise, the debate over appropriations, a peace treaty and possible land concessions by Mexico all served to render hollow the administration's claim that it had not pursued a war of conquest. The Wilmot Proviso did not pass, but some Tennessee Whigs were embarrassed by it; angry that the slavery issue had been injected into the war. Generally, however, the proviso drew little notice in the Tennessee press or among congressional candidates who were running for office in 1846. It was not until the war was over and the country was forced to make decisions regarding the 525,000 square miles of territory that it had gained from Mexico that the issue raised by Wilmot became such a divisive national dispute.[18]

Political rhetoric remained at a steady volume throughout the war's first year, in large part because of the mid-term elections. For much of the nineteenth century, states held their mid-term congressional elections at different times over a period of months, and the process was not standardized or uniform until an Act of Congress made it so in 1875. So, the elections for the Thirtieth Congress began in some states as early as August 1846 and lasted until all the states had voted in November 1847.

Tennessee's election was in September 1847. Thus, in the last half of 1846, Tennessee Whigs continued to hammer Polk on the war's controversial aspects: its questionable origins, expense, and officer appointment, all of which bespoke excessive executive power to Polk's adversaries. As historian Jonathan Atkins succinctly puts it, Whigs believed that Mr. Polk's war "revealed once again that the country faced the danger of a Democratic executive seeking to expand his power in order to subvert republican government" while promoting the interests of his party. Washington Barrow, a congressional candidate from Nashville, expressed the opinion that the president "was guilty of usurping power not given him by the constitution." In December 1846, Polk countered his critics by asserting in his annual message to Congress that those who were recklessly characterizing his actions as aggressive and unconstitutional gave "aid and comfort to the enemy."[19]

The Whig response to Polk's chastising was loud. The Nashville *Republican Banner* responded that the president was engaged in censorship by trying to "silence the press" and "stop freedom of discussion." In other editions, the same newspaper asserted that the press is the "last best bulwark against unlicensed power, and it is "time this censorship was overthrown at whatever cost or sacrifice."[20] Congressman Edwin H. Ewing from Nashville exclaimed in a speech, "What! Does this President hope to put down public discussion and free expression of opinion?" Criticism of the government in time of war may appear unpatriotic, Ewing explained, but "this is the price we pay for liberty; it is the mighty check upon domestic tyranny. And this should teach us that we were not made for distant wars of aggression and conquest."[21]

Both parties believed they had a winning issue leading up to the mid-term elections. Democrats believed the war was a popular issue, and they continued to label Whigs as unpatriotic and Federalists. Whigs too believed that they had the upper hand and that the coming election would be, as one Tennessee party member put it, "the easiest one for the Whigs since 1840. We have them on the defensive now." Indeed, by the end of 1846, the Democrats had lost over twenty seats in the House of Representatives with ninety seats still to be decided. The staggered voting dates made for rolling elections from state to state, and there appeared to be building momentum for the Whigs as 1847 began. Although they still held a majority of the House seats, it did not look good for the Democrats. When all the states had voted in fall 1847, the Whigs had gained thirty-eight seats in the House, giving them a five-seat majority, but Democrats retained control of the Senate. In Tennessee, Whigs won control of the state legislature (fifty-two to forty-eight) and the governor's chair. Tennessee's congressional delegation in Washington remained unchanged, with five Whigs and six Democrats.[22]

Tennessee's gubernatorial race was a referendum on the war and was essentially a microcosm of the national political debate. The Whig challenger, Neill S. Brown, criticized Polk for usurping Congressional authority and violating the constitution. Why had the president rushed to war if he was willing to negotiate a territorial settlement, he asked in a stump speech in Franklin. Incumbent Democratic governor Aaron V. Brown was formerly Polk's law partner, and he defended the president by arguing that Mexico refused to negotiate when it broke off diplomatic relations then started the war when its troops crossed the Rio Grande and attacked U.S. forces in an area traditionally claimed by Texas. While the sitting governor was hurt by the growing anti-slavery sentiment, he may also have lost some votes from the staunch supporters of the war who were still angry over his delay in calling for volunteers at the outset. The campaign was hard fought and the election was close but Neill Brown and the Whigs won by a thousand votes.[23]

One of the keys to Whig success in the 1846–1847 election was its paradoxical embrace of Zachary Taylor as the party's presidential candidate. Taylor had become an instant national hero following the Battles of Palo Alto and Resaca de la Palma in May 1846 when the call was just going out for volunteers. The sixty-two-year-old general had been an unremarkable officer in the army for thirty-eight years but had garnered moderate attention in the Seminole War a few years earlier. His name became a household word in the opening weeks of the war with Mexico. Two biographies of Old Rough and Ready were published within ninety days of those opening battles, and poems appeared, as did songs with titles like "General Taylor's Quick Step" and the "Rough and Ready Polka." The short, corpulent hero was compared to the likes of Frederick the Great, Napoleon, and George Washington. His instant fame in 1846 resulted in speculation about Taylor and the presidency, and the Whigs quickly embraced him as their standard bearer for the 1848 election. Promoting Taylor the war hero helped mask the anti-war element within the Whig Party and helped the party sustain its momentum in the congressional elections throughout 1847. However, Tennessee Whigs, as well as the national party, played a balancing act by blaming Polk for the irresponsible war but thumping their chests over victorious battles and the Whigs who won them. The hypocrisy did not go unnoticed. An editorial in *The National Union* called it "a ludicrous anomaly in politics" for the anti-war party to promote a man whose candidacy was made entirely by the war.[24]

Politics back home did not escape the notice of the soldiers in the field. Two months before leaving Mexico to return home, Lieutenant George Nixon's brother sent him a letter from Lawrenceburg in which he lamented that the "war is producing a great Division in the community[,] it has a great many opponents." He assured George that as long as the war lasts everyone agreed that the soldiers "must be secured & sustained" and the flag held high, but it was not just Whigs who opposed the war, some Democrats were getting war weary. Continuing his letter to George, he expressed the opinion that was likely shared by other Lawrence County residents that "the government ought immediately in any honorable & satisfactory manner bring this war to conclusion. . . . I believe that every reasonable effert should be made to put an end to this war."[25]

Another volunteer, Patrick Duffy, knew of the Whigs anti-war stance, and he wrote a letter from Jalapa to his brother in Gallatin condemning their brand of politics. His letter, riddled with misspelled words, highlights his own political passion. He disliked the "whigish way . . . of connecting the present war with politics like the northern blue lights instead of Sustsaining the governmint with their means and influance and flocking into the ranks of the army which is fighting for and Sustaining the honor and credit of our glorious governmint and its noble institutions." He went on to write about the "croaking course of the whigs," whose actions "disgraced the union." They reminded Duffy "of puppies that I have seen in the streets point a switch at them and they will tuck their tail and run." We will whip the Mexicans "in short order," he assured his brother, but all the soldiers ask is that the Whigs "not hollow so loud for the enemy."[26]

William Smart from Dekalb County and a member of the Mounted Regiment had seen a copy of a Nashville newspaper that angered him. The anti-war position that Whigs had adopted robs the Tennessee volunteers of "that glory so valiantly achieved upon the plains of Mexico." He went on to "Damn the man or set of men" who would turn people's hearts against those who are "fighting their country's batles."[27]

Political opposition to the war nationally tended to revolve around the slavery issue, but in Tennessee, executive power was the primary concern. However, a moral element to the opposition transcended slavery and politics. A nineteenth-century religious revivalism called the Second Great Awakening produced an evangelical fervor that served as a catalyst for an aggressive Abolitionist Movement in the northeast and was easy to couple with the anti-war sentiments. In the South, most religious groups generally supported the war, and Protestant preachers promoted the argument that the war was about freeing the oppressed Mexican people from the overbearing, anti-democratic Catholic church. Indeed, much of the Protestant pro-war rhetoric was rooted in religious views that were anti-Catholic, and that supported the notion that the war would further God's providential destiny for the country.[28]

The colorful East Tennessean, William "Parson" Brownlow, provides an interesting fence-straddling example of both support for and opposition to the war. He was an acerbic Whig and a Methodist preacher who would later become famous as the virulent anti-Confederate governor during Reconstruction. In 1846, the forty-one-year-old Brownlow was sufficiently in favor of the war that he became a lieutenant in a militia company, but the unit was never actually mustered into military service. Nevertheless, in that first summer of the war, he gave numerous speeches, often two hours or more in length, in which he encouraged young men to enlist in the war effort. He thought that Democrats, especially, should volunteer since it was a Democrat war. After speaking perhaps half an hour for the war, his speech shifted, and for the remainder of his lengthy orations he would condemn Polk and the war. The president, he argued, had unjustifiably incited the war, and worse, Polk had the audacity to appoint Catholic chaplains for the army. The nickname Brownlow's militia company assigned itself is telling: the "Protestant Invincibles."[29]

In the South, the Second Great Awakening also provided fuel for the Restoration Movement, which was a plea for Christians to return to the Bible as the only true guide for life. The Restoration Movement gave voice to a moral argument that was different from abolitionism. It advocated that Christians should be pacifists, and it called on God's people to shun involvement with secular government, especially wars that governments wage for secular gain. In the spring of 1847, clergyman James M. Arnell wrote a column for the *Lebanon Banner* entitled "Evils of War," in which he graphically described the horrors of combat. Battle can be seductive for man, he wrote, but after the smoke settles a ghastly sight appears. "Oh! What a scene for God and angels to look upon! . . . Dismembered limbs are scattered round like broken branches after a hurricane. . . . the shrieks and groans, and blasphemies that make the night horrible. . . . Oh! Shall we be so untrue to ourselves and to humanity as to fall down and worship the spirit of desolation."[30]

The most famous of the Restoration leaders was Alexander Campbell, a Scots-Irish immigrant who settled in Virginia in 1809. The Church of Christ, Disciples of Christ, and Christian Church all have their roots in the Restoration Movement, and the movement was particularly strong in Tennessee, Kentucky, and western Virginia, states in which Campbell traveled and preached extensively. His followers were sometimes referred to as Campbellites. By the 1830s, Campbell was a nationally known evangelist who enjoyed far-reaching influence—he was once invited to speak to a joint session of Congress, and he counted among his friends the likes of Henry Clay. Campbell founded and for three decades served as chief editor of *The Millenial Harbinger*, and in 1840 he founded Bethany College in Virginia to provide Biblical training to aspiring preachers. In the August 1846 issue of *The Millenial Harbinger*, Campbell wrote that he was opposed to "Christians volunteering to fight or kill, or to serve in the capacity of soldiers for their king, their political party, or their country." Three months later, he reminded his readers that Christians should not fight for earthly kingdoms and that Christ, the Prince of Peace, said "Blessed are the peacemakers." As Christians, he concluded, "may we not volunteer to fight and kill our neighbors for the good of the state!"[31]

Thomas Claiborne of the Mounted Rifle Regiment in the regular army had been attracted to Campbell's Gospel call, and briefly to a church affiliated with the Restoration plea. Years later, Claiborne's daughter, Mollie, wrote a memoir of her father based on stories he had told her, and in it she recounted how, as a young man, he was "deeply impressed with the christian faith," and for a while he was "a member of Alexander Campbell's Church." However, Claiborne "fell from grace" when he attended a horse race, which church goers frowned upon because of the gambling associated with such events. "For this dereliction, he was 'churched.'" Mollie's quotation marks around "churched" suggests that that was the word her father used when relating the story, and exactly what it means is unclear except to say that church members in some fashion condemned Claiborne's transgression. "This made him so mad that he never attended any church for years," even though he remained a believer and carried a Bible with him his entire life. There is, however, no evidence that he ever embraced the pacifism that Campbell preached.[32]

Another early convert was Dr. William D. Dorris, a surgeon in the First Tennessee Volunteers, who had grown up in the Baptist Church in Robertson County thirty miles north of Nashville. His grandfather Joseph had been a preacher and chaplain in Andrew Jackson's army in the War of 1812. When he was eighteen, Dorris moved with his parents to Nashville, began reading Campbell's writing, and tried to convert to the Christian Church there. It created a stir among his old brethren because his new church recently left the Baptist fellowship and had "gone over to Campbellism," and Dorris's membership there did not meet with their approval. Dorris's argument, that he was attending "the congregation which followed the Lamb of God the nearest!" did not arouse sympathy among his former brethren who viewed him as "a heathen man or a Publican," and who voted to expel him from their fellowship.[33] Again, in Dorris's case, there is no indication that he agreed with Campbell's teaching on war and pacifism. His service in the Mexican War twenty years later does not necessarily provide an answer because the churches that came out of the Restoration Movement have a rich history of conscientious objectors who served in noncombat roles in the military.

Campbell was also a mentor to many like-minded Christians who agreed with his nondenominational, "Christians only" approach, and one of his most ardent protégés was Nashville preacher and educator Tolbert Fanning. They met in Nashville in the 1830s, and twice Fanning had accompanied Campbell on the preaching circuit. Campbell was so impressed with Fanning that the older preacher described the Nashvillian as "devout," "ardent," and "gifted." Although the two men held differing views on other topics, they were at one regarding a Christian's requirement to shun war. Fanning's pacifism was not political, rather it was theological and therefore rooted in the belief that a Christian's first allegiance is to God's kingdom and not to any earthly kingdom. Fanning preached for Dr. Dorris's congregation in later years as did Fanning's protégé, David Lipscomb, who, in addition to preaching, was also an educator who founded Nashville Bible School in 1891, which eventually grew into Lipscomb University.[34]

Christian pacifism was not a major source of war opposition in Tennessee, and it is impossible to know how many young men declined to volunteer in 1846 for religious and moral reasons. From the above anecdotal examples, it appears that even though some were swayed by the Restoration plea of Campbell, Fanning, and others, they remained largely unconvinced when it came to the anti-war portion of their message. Some devoutly religious Tennesseans may have justified the war because of Mexico's state-sanctioned Catholic church. Even pacifists, it seems, placated their conscience by rationalizing that even though the war was, in their view, an immoral land grab, it was nonetheless a crusade against the Romish faith. Thus, citizens both for or against the war were held together by the consensus of anti-Catholicism.[35]

In West Tennessee during the war's second year, a moral argument seemed to sway opinions, but it was not a position rooted in religion, rather, it was espoused by a veteran. In the summer of 1847, the former colonel of the Second Tennessee, William Haskell from Jackson, ran for congress as a Whig critic of the war. The colonel's "extraordinary position

. . . upon the war question," wrote one correspondent, "has astonished men of both political parties." Haskell was a vocal and active supporter of the war a year earlier, but now he canvassed his district, calling the war "unjust and unconstitutional" and asserting that Americans should "acknowledge the error of our ways." He spoke publicly about "the horrors of that war, the dreadful pestilence and diseases incident to the climate of the country," and he chastised his opponent for painting an "eloquent picture" of the messy affair. Haskell spoke with the authority of someone who had been there and had returned disillusioned by his experience. Such is war. Another factor in Haskell's change of heart was likely his concurrent feud with Pillow. Perhaps Haskell's anger toward Pillow extended to Polk, Pillow's benefactor and, in like manner, stretched all the way to the war itself. On July 17, he concluded a campaign speech in Dresden, Tennessee by saying that he would not volunteer to return to Mexico—"I will not go unless *drafted*."[36] Again, it is difficult to know how many people were affected by Haskell's change of heart, but it is instructive to note that he won the election.

# Chapter Nine

# THE PILLOW FACTOR

By the time the three volunteer regiments got back home in June 1847 to receptions and banquets, there already had been melancholy gatherings and ceremonies for returning Tennesseans. On Wednesday, March 10, the steamer *Tennessee* arrived in Nashville and was tied to the wharf. Nearby, the Market House bell began to toll, and without prior notice, a crowd gathered on the river bank for the occasion. Soon coffins carrying the remains of William B. Allen, Robert W. Green, Peter H. Martin, Isaac Inman Elliott, and his cousin Julius C. Elliott, all killed at Monterrey, were taken off the vessel and carried into the city. The crowd formed a procession and followed the bodies to the home of Alexander Allison, the mayor of Nashville, whose son, James, had also died at Monterrey and had returned home two months earlier for burial. The repatriated bodies remained at the Allison home until the next morning when they were taken to the First Presbyterian Church for a somber funeral service, where family members and a large number of Nashvillians had gathered. According to the newspaper, "a mournful silence prevailed in the vast assembly."

After the volunteers were eulogized, their remains went to the appropriate locations for burial. Robert Green was interred at the City Cemetery on Nashville's south side. Julius Elliott's father had come to Nashville for the service, after which he took his son, nephew Inman, and Peter Martin back to their hometown, Gallatin, where they were buried side-by-side in the city cemetery. A dozen college students from Nashville and Franklin escorted William Allen's body back home to Lawrence County, where family members met the contingent. The family laid Allen to rest north of Lawrenceburg in a community cemetery, which today can be found on Andrew Jackson Highway (Hwy. 43). By nineteenth-century standards, each of these young men had died a glorious death and won an honorable grave. However, others, like Joseph Burkitt, were not exhumed and brought home. They were destined, as one author put it, to "sleep in their cold, bloody graves" on the battlefields of Mexico, but their distance from home did not diminish their honor in death nor their families pride in duty well done.[1]

In West Tennessee, the results of the Second Tennessee's Cerro Gordo disaster had a dampening effect on martial ardor for the remainder of the war—so much so that it made it difficult to enroll new recruits in spring and summer 1847. A regular army recruiting office on Union Street in Memphis had no enlistments in May, and by the end of the month it closed its doors and left the city. Anger aimed at Gideon Pillow persisted through the summer to the extent that some West Tennesseans lamented that their region's patriotic fervor had been "chilled by 'Pillowism.'"[2] The effort to entice young men to volunteer was further hampered by William Haskell's anti-war campaigning and his characterization of the war's unjust motives aimed at a weak and innocent opponent. No one knows how many returning veterans shared Haskell's revised attitude about the war, but John Reid McClanahan, a sergeant in the Second Tennessee, seemed to be one. He declined to reenlist, for as one author put it, "Cerro Gordo had shattered him."[3] And, as for Whig political gains in 1847, many Democrats blamed Pillow's poor performance at Cerro Gordo and the post-battle controversy it generated in newspapers across the state for their loss of seats in the state legislature.[4]

During the summer, there was a renewed push for a fresh round of volunteers to reinforce General Winfield Scott's army, which had been depleted by the departure of the three Tennessee regiments along with those from Alabama, Illinois, and Georgia in May. Two new recruiting stations were opened in Memphis and two more in nearby communities, but the response was disappointing. In August, the War Department sent an official call to Tennessee for additional regiments, and the original plan was to raise one new regiment from each of the three grand divisions of the state: west, middle, and east. The recruiting offices in and around Memphis had to combine their enrollees to come up with just one company. It became Company B of the Fourth Tennessee Volunteers, which was comprised of fifty-three Memphians and forty-two men from surrounding areas. West Tennessee could muster only three new companies. So tepid was the response from the western counties that six surplus companies were drawn from other parts of the state to flesh out the Fourth Tennessee (five from eastern counties and one from Middle Tennessee). The example of Richard Waterhouse proves that not all veterans had washed their hands of the war; after serving as a major in the Mounted Regiment, he volunteered again and was elected commanding colonel of the Fourth Tennessee.[5]

Benjamin Franklin Cheatham from Nashville serves as a similar example. Captain of Company E, the Nashville Blues, in the First Tennessee, Cheatham had been in the thick of it at Monterrey and had been slightly wounded when a musket ball grazed his back. But he was ready to return, and he played a key role in helping to organize the Third Tennessee Volunteers, then won election as the regimental colonel. Others who had already been to Mexico but who reenlisted in the Third included William Bate, Daniel Calgy, Perrin L. Solomon, and Robert Bruce Wynne, all from Sumner County. Middle Tennessee, the geographic birthplace of the "Bloody First," which had won success and fame, responded to the call for more troops by quickly raising eleven companies. Morale and support for the war remained considerably higher in this region of the state, which could boast of already having produced conquering heroes. Half a year after the Battle of Monterrey, newspapers still referred to the First Tennessee using words like "honorable," "daring," and "successful" and described the deeds of "individual heroism" that brought "glory" to the nation.[6] What twenty-year-old man would not hope for such praise?

Major military operations were over, and American forces occupied Mexico City before the Tennesseans even left home. Memphis was the rendezvous point for the new regiments. The Third Tennessee left Nashville on October 26 and arrived in Memphis three days later, taking on supplies before continuing its journey to New Orleans. The Fourth Tennessee followed a week later, and both regiments eventually made their way to Veracruz, the supply base for central Mexico. In August, General Scott's army had made its final push toward Mexico City and won four hard-fought victories at Contreras, Churubusco, Molino del Rey, and Chapultepec before capturing the capital on September 13. However, it took five additional months to negotiate the treaty that officially ended the war. Meanwhile, Scott's occupation force still needed supplies, and his army's umbilical cord stretched all the way back to Veracruz, 260 miles away. Bandits and guerrillas roamed the countryside and preyed on wagon trains traveling the road, necessitating military escorts.

Towns along the route also had to be garrisoned. During the final weeks of the Mexico City Campaign, Scott had cut his supply line to the coast and pulled in his troops to give his little army as much bulk as possible for the final stage of the operation. The only place at which he had left a sizeable contingent was Puebla, seventy-five miles east of the capital. Once he captured Mexico City, he reopened his supply line, which necessitated garrisons along the way to keep the roads open. As troops traveled inland from Veracruz, they passed through Jalapa, which was sixty-five miles from the coast and just beyond the Cerro Gordo battlefield. Another thirty miles beyond Jalapa was Perote, but the road between those two towns passed through guerrilla-infested regions like La Hoya and the Las Vigas mountain pass, sometimes called the Black Pass. From Perote, it was another eighty miles to Puebla. Given the situation in late 1847 and early 1848, the primary responsibility of the new Tennessee volunteer regiments was garrison and patrol.[7]

Sparse records provide little information about the late-war regiments, but the survival of some of Frank Cheatham's personal papers, augmented by a few more sources, thankfully provides a cursory outline of the activities of the Third Tennessee. The bulk of Cheatham's extant papers from this period consists of a partial diary that he kept—indicating that, unlike his year spent in the First Tennessee, this time he intended to document his experiences for posterity. After arriving in Veracruz in November, Cheatham received orders to march his regiment to Mexico City and join the occupation force there. He also learned that his men would be escorted by Thomas Claiborne and a troop of dragoons who had come over to Veracruz to pick up a shipment of ammunition and some Colt pistols.[8]

Escorting troops along central Mexico's dangerous roads was a task to which Claiborne was accustomed. His mounted regiment, along with Captain Samuel H. Walker's company, had been stationed at Perote all summer, guarding against guerrilla attacks and protecting the sick and wounded who were convalescing there in the weeks following the Battle of Cerro Gordo. The medical department had converted an eighteenth-century Spanish fortress called the Perote Castle into a hospital. It was made of dark lava rocks, had sixty-foot walls, and was surrounded by a deep moat; altogether an impressive and sinister looking bastion. Mexican forces had abandoned it instead of using it to defend the town and block the American advance in the spring of 1847. But the castle was filthy, and Claiborne called it a "vermin-infested Mexican stronghold," which helps to explain why, after its conversion to a hospital, so many Americans died there. The most significant action the Perote garrison had seen during the summer was a two-day battle in June with over a thousand guerrillas in an effort to clear the Las Vigas pass for a column of reinforcements and supplies headed for Scott's army. The two thousand–man column was commanded by General George Cadwalader and included George Maney and Chatham R. Wheat, two of Claiborne's former schoolmates from Tennessee.[9]

Now five months later, Claiborne began the long trek from Veracruz back to Mexico City with an entire regiment of Tennessee boys in tow. They made the march in November and December, and the lateness of the year, coupled with the high altitude from Jalapa westward, meant that they spent some cold nights camped along the road. Bruce Wynne wrote to his mother about Jalapa and his recollections of being in the town just seven months earlier as a member of the Bloody First. His brother, Bolivar, had also been a volunteer in the First Tennessee, but had been discharged due to illness at Camargo two weeks prior to the Battle of Monterrey and had not reenlisted in the Third. Bruce commented on the frigid temperatures in Jalapa, but his letter home was about more than just the Mexican scenery and weather, for it was also an earnest attempt to set the record straight. He had assured his parents when he first left home in May 1846 that he had reformed his youthful indiscretions with the bottle. Now eighteen months later and soon after arriving in Mexico for his second term of enlistment, he wrote home to counter gossip. It seems that acquaintances had spread stories asserting that Wynne had been seen indulging in alcoholic drinks in Nashville before the regiment boarded steamers for New Orleans. Wynne did not indicate how he had heard of the rumors, but he called them a "scounderly slander" and assured his parents that they still had "a son of Temperance." He concluded by telling his mother, "You have a sons voucher against all foul calumnies hurled against me by my enemies who are false friends to me and Father."[10]

Late in the day, after leaving Jalapa, they were marching through clouds before they stopped to camp at Las Vigas. Three months earlier when hostilities were still underway, this region was a hotbed of guerrilla activity, but now the region was pacified and docile. Although they were not bothered by hostile partisans in the Las Vigas Pass, they were troubled by plunging temperatures. It was "a very cold and disagreeable night," Cheatham recorded in his diary. But that was not the worst of it, for the night spent at San Martin twenty miles west of Puebla was "decidedly the coldest that I had ever saw in Mexico." The next day, bandits attacked the tail of the column and got away with twenty pack mules, but Cheatham and fourteen others pursued and retrieved the animals after a twelve-mile chase through the mountains.[11]

The Third Tennessee arrived in Mexico City near the beginning of 1848 and took quarters in Molino del Rey a short distance south of the capital. Sickness, though not as rampant as the previous year, remained a problem for the boys from Tennessee. For much of December and January only two hundred of his men were well enough to report for parade, and by February the number had improved to only about three hundred. On February 14, Cheatham signed discharge papers to send fifteen of his men home. Lieutenant John Brixy from Coffee County was too ill to travel, and he knew that he would not recover from his affliction because prior to dying he gave instructions that "he did not wish any one to go to any expense" to send his body back home.[12]

As spring approached, health improved considerably, but regardless of the condition of the regiment, there were no opportunities for the men to prove themselves in combat. Mounted troops went out on patrol or in search of rumored guerrilla bands, but for the hapless foot soldiers from Tennessee, the monotony of occupation duty was all they had. Regular military drills were intended to instill in them the discipline necessary in the event of combat, but alas, they never got the chance to translate their preparations onto the battlefield. Captain John W. Whitfield, a company commander, had seen service the year before in the First Tennessee and thus felt competent to assess the fighting spirit of his new unit. If the boys just had an opportunity to fight, he was confident that folks back in "Tennessee would have no right to complain" about their performance. Perhaps that was due, in part, to his low opinion of the fighting capabilities of Mexicans, because in the same letter he said, "I think that 50 American caps stuck on poles would be sufficient to take any town in Mexico."[13]

In February, Cheatham wrote to his father that peace rumors were floating about, and he feared that there was little or no fighting left to be done, "but if there is any honour to be had or glory to be won, I am in for a chance at any price." No such opportunities would present themselves to Cheatham and his men, for the peace rumors turned to reality when negotiators signed the Treaty of Guadalupe Hidalgo, officially ending hostilities that month. Nevertheless, General Joseph Lane, a Democrat politician from Indiana who had been commissioned a general by President Polk, thought he saw special qualities in Cheatham, who was also a Democrat. In mid-February, he pulled Cheatham aside and told him confidentially that he was resigning and going home with the next wagon train that left for the coast, and he said that with Cheatham's permission he would try to get the Tennessean appointed general to take his place. "I must confess that this took me considerably by surprise," wrote Cheatham, but the idea appealed to him. He asked Generals William O. Butler, Robert Patterson, and Gideon Pillow for letters of support to the president, and he asked his father, Leonard Pope Cheatham to use his influence back in Tennessee to help his cause. "[T]ake any steps you may think proper," he instructed.[14] But alas, Cheatham's generalship did not come until thirteen years later when he donned Confederate gray.

There were no battles involving the Third or Fourth Tennessee, nor were there any opportunities for glory afforded to the final regiment raised in the volunteer state. East Tennessee had also provided enough recruits to fill a regiment, and it would be designated the Fifth Tennessee Volunteers. It consisted of five companies from Knox County, three from McMinn County, two from Washington County, and one from Bradley County. However, it was not mustered in until December 1847, too late to play a significant role in the war. It arrived at Veracruz in February 1848, the same month the peace treaty was signed, and spent most of the spring patrolling the roads between the coast and Jalapa, being stationed, it appears, at the National Bridge halfway between the two. The Fifth Tennessee remained in Mexico until the final evacuation of American troops in the summer of 1848.

Although none of Tennessee's "late war" regiments participated in battles, individual Tennesseans made their mark late in the war; some positively and some negatively. William Trousdale, for example, contributed to Scott's effort to capture Mexico City in September 1847. At age fifty-seven, the Sumner County native was a veteran of combat before the war with Mexico. As a young man, he fought in Andrew Jackson's army in the War of 1812 and, in 1836, commanded Tennessee mounted volunteers in the Seminole War in Florida; in fact, on that occasion, he was William Campbell's commanding officer. In the twenty years prior to the Mexican War, Trousdale, a Gallatin attorney, successfully ran as a Democrat for city alderman and state senator, but he failed in five attempts at the United States Congress. In 1846, he received a commission as colonel in the regular army, and the following year when Scott's army fought several intense battles around the enemy capital, he commanded the Fourteenth U.S. Infantry and participated in the fighting at Churubusco on August 20, and three weeks later at Molino del Rey, where he was wounded in the shoulder. On September 13, he gallantly led his men in the Battle of Chapultepec for which he received a brevet promotion to brigadier general. After returning home, Trousdale was elected governor of Tennessee in 1849, and four years later President Franklin Pierce appointed him Minister to Brazil.[15]

In the fighting around Mexico City, no Tennessean garnered more fame, perhaps infamy is a more appropriate word, than Gideon Pillow. To complete the account of his role in the final months of the war, the narrative must to go back to the spring of 1847 and resume its chronological rendering to the war's end. He had returned to Tennessee in May to recuperate from his Cerro Gordo wound and to do battle with William Haskell in the press. Soon, however, he learned that Polk had promoted him to major general and assigned him to command regulars, a station that carried more prestige than commanding volunteers. So, Pillow did not tarry long at home before traveling back to Mexico to rejoin Scott's army. He arrived in U.S.-occupied Veracruz, the base of Scott's operations and the collection point for reinforcements who were preparing to march to Puebla 175 miles inland. On June 18, Pillow and a column of two thousand men marched out of Veracruz. Three weeks later, they arrived in Puebla, where the American army had been encamped all summer. Over the next two months, Pillow played a major role in the military operations that resulted in the capture of Mexico City; thereafter, he became the centerpiece of one of the major scandals of the war.[16]

Pillow's arrival at the army's Puebla encampment on July 8 coincided with a Mexican offer to open treaty negotiations in exchange for a million dollars. Pillow learned of the scheme from Nicholas Trist, the diplomat whom Polk had sent to Mexico to conduct peace talks when the opportunity arose. Trist was a loyal Democrat tapped to serve as the administration's direct spokesman on the scene, but his presence also represented the president's lack of trust in General Scott's negotiating prowess. The president had instructed Trist to freely consult with Pillow, and when the latter arrived, Trist did, informing him of the bribery scheme. Pillow sanctioned the idea. However, it was a shady deal, and Trist and Scott had already discussed the ethical dilemma of paying a million dollars under the table in return for a peace settlement. When Scott called a meeting with his high-ranking officers on July 17 to get their opinions, some offered mild approval while others were either skeptical or opposed to the idea. Pillow, however, spoke forcefully for the plan and even bragged that he had helped convince Trist to pursue this course. Ultimately, Scott made an initial $10,000 payment but that is where the cash for peace bribery scheme ended. No more money changed hands, and soon Scott resumed military operations.[17]

By August 7, reinforcements had brought the strength of the American army to 10,700, and on that day Scott began his exodus from Puebla, leaving behind 2,500 sick and wounded in the city's makeshift hospitals. One division departed the city each day through August 10 when Pillow's fourth and final division marched west. Preceding Pillow were divisions commanded by David Twiggs, William Worth, and John Quitman. Pillow's division of regulars was comprised of a total of six regiments: the Ninth, Eleventh, Twelfth, Fourteenth, Fifteenth Infantry and the Voltigeurs Regiment, all of which were organized into two brigades under Franklin Pierce and George Cadwalader.[18]

The first major action as Scott's army reached the outskirts of the capital was south of the city near the village of Contreras, where a two-mile-wide expanse of jagged lava rock blocked the advance. Scott chose to skirt the southern edge of the Pedregal, as the lava bed was called, and then turn north and approach Mexico City from the south. On August 19, he put Pillow in charge cutting a road for that purpose, but the commanding general had cautioned Pillow to beware of enemy troops in the area and to avoid a confrontation. Pillow's work parties made good progress all morning, but when he ascended a hill and observed Mexican soldiers hiding among the rocks several hundred yards ahead, he ignored Scott's orders and sent troops forward to clear the enemy. His actions initiated skirmishing that forced Scott's hand and led to the Battle of Contreras.

On the afternoon of the nineteenth, Scott ordered a turning movement and repositioned the bulk of Pillow's command in an isolated and vulnerable location across the Pedregal in preparation for a flank attack the following morning. Late in the day, Scott ordered Pillow to join his men, but in trying to cross the lava field after dark, Pillow got lost and returned to Scott's headquarters in the rear, where he was able to get a good night's sleep in a warm bed while his men spent a sleepless night in the rain. The next morning, an American attack routed an entrenched Mexican force in mere minutes, resulting in an all–day pursuit away from the Contreras battlefield and toward the capital. A well-rested Pillow rejoined his command during the pursuit, and the day ended with the bloody Battle of Churubusco, in which Pillow's command play an important role. At one point during the battle, Pillow encountered several Mexican officers who were galloping in his direction. Conflicting reports make it difficult to know whether the Mexicans were charging toward Pillow in an act of bravado or simply trying to escape from the battlefield—regardless, Pillow shot and killed one of them and the rest scattered.[19]

After Churubusco, the U.S. army was literally at the door of the capital, but rather than press his advantage, Scott agreed to Santa Anna's request for an armistice, which would ostensibly set the stage for peace talks. It was a ruse, and two weeks later (August 8), Scott attacked a collection of buildings south of the city that he thought housed a cannon foundry. The resulting Battle of Molino del Rey was one of the bloodiest of the war. Pillow had opposed the armistice and had written directly to Polk about Scott's bad judgment. He had also opposed the attack on the Molino, which, as it turned out did not house a foundry. In both cases, Pillow was correct in his judgment.[20] The armistice provided a lull during which time Pillow wrote or had someone to write the Leonidas letter that will be discussed later in this chapter.

By this late juncture in the campaign, Pillow felt quite self-assured. As a major-general, he was commanding regulars while maintaining a direct conduit of correspondence about military affairs with his friend in the White House, even though it was a flagrant breach of the chain of command. He had also participated in some of the campaign's most significant battles. In the five days between the disastrous Battle of Molino del Rey and the final climactic battle at Chapultepec on September 13, two episodes stand out. One illustrates how Pillow viewed himself and his position within Scott's army while the other demonstrates how other officers in the army viewed him.

Consider the latter example first. Lieutenant Daniel Harvey Hill, a West Point graduate and regular army officer, commanded a company in General Twiggs's division. When Hill's superior officer, Colonel Bennet Riley, ordered Hill to move his company to another location, Pillow countermanded the order and instructed Hill to remain where he was. Hill knew that neither his company nor Riley's brigade had been placed under Pillow's command, so the decision of which superior officer he should obey was an easy choice—he obeyed Riley's order to move his men. Hill's diary makes his lack of respect for Pillow obvious. Just two days earlier, he had penned an entry in which he referred to "the ass Pillow. . . . a pitiful fool calling himself a Major General of the Regular Army." In recording this event, he called Pillow "an ignorant puppy." For refusing to obey his order, Pillow reprimanded Hill using harsh and insulting language to which Hill responded by shaking his sword in Pillow's face and demanded that he retract his words. Pillow had him arrested, but later was persuaded to release him and forget the incident.[21] Hill's low opinion of Pillow was not only common, it was probably shared by most of the regular officers in the army.

The next episode occurred a few days later on September 12 at Scott's headquarters. The commander had summoned his generals on the eve of the attack at Chapultepec to give them their final instructions for the next morning. During the conference, Pillow had the audacity to propose his own plan of attack for the morrow. It was an egregious breach of etiquette that could only have resulted from either extreme naïveté or overweening arrogance. Being cautious not to appear confrontational with the president's factotum, Scott listened patiently to Pillow's "peculiar plan." Then, when his subordinate was finished, he laid out with precision and detail exactly what he expected each officer to do the next day. Apparently, Pillow's plan was not even considered, but that he would feel empowered to interject his own ideas on how to proceed and without solicitation from the commanding general evidences Pillow's sense of self-worth. He clearly had a high opinion of his own martial prowess, and, as would become evident soon after the battle, he fancied himself a military genius.[22]

Next day, Scott launched a two-pronged attack on the Chapultepec Castle, a hilltop fortress west of Mexico City. He ordered Pillow's division to attack from the west and Quitman's to attack from the south. Pillow (and he was not alone) did not like the plan and feared the consequences of assaulting such a strong enemy bastion, especially considering the fact that a successful outcome would still leave them outside the city walls. Following an artillery bombardment, the attack began at 8:00 a.m. Pillow had divided his force into three assault columns with his fellow Tennessean, William Trousdale, commanding one of them. When the columns began their attack, the Mexican defenders unleashed a devastating fire all across Pillow's front. Early in the battle, while commanding from horseback near the base of the hill, a ricocheting ball of grapeshot from the castle guns struck him on the ankle, breaking the bone. Captain Robert E. Lee was nearby and had Pillow carried to a spot behind a cypress tree and out of the line of fire where the general turned over command to George Cadwalader. To the left, Trousdale's column was hit hard by artillery and musketry, and the fighting was so intense that one of Trousdale's men, James Elderkin, who also fought in the Civil War, remembered years later that Chapultepec was "the hottest engagement I ever experienced."[23]

The advance up the steep incline and the capture of Chapultepec took about an hour-and-a-half, and as exultant Americans gathered around the castle at the summit, Pillow, having compelled some of his men to carry him up the hill, arrived amid the celebration. Looking at a soldier who stood nearby, Pillow asked to which unit he belonged. It was Sergeant Thomas Barclay of the Second Pennsylvania, which had been in Pillow's brigade at the disastrous Cerro Gordo attack. Barclay's bold response revealed that he had not forgotten who Pillow was and that he still held a grudge: "this is the 2nd Pa. Regt., the men who you said waved at Cerro Gordo." Pillow's demeanor quickly changed from pleasant to angry as he shot back, "I think you have a damn sight of impudence for a sergeant." The fighting continued through the afternoon as the Americans pushed on to the gates of the city and claimed possession of the enemy capital.[24]

When Pillow returned to Mexico a few weeks earlier, his military reputation was on the line. At Chapultepec, he had acquitted himself admirably, using good judgment and determined aggression to achieve his objective. He also received his second wound of the campaign, which always counted as a badge of honor in nineteenth-century culture. He had done enough to go back home with pride. But Pillow was both arrogant and ambitious, and, as unfolding events would demonstrate, he could not leave well enough alone.

Pillow called the Battle of Chapultepec "one of the most brilliant fields known to the American Arms." Others agreed that the battle and the subsequent capture of Mexico City was a significant accomplishment, and Scott's officers wanted to be sure that their contributions were fully acknowledged and that due credit came to them. Pillow was chief among the glory seekers. When he submitted his battle report, he characterized himself as the general who was in control of the army's movements in the fighting around Mexico City even when he was merely forwarding orders he had received from General Scott. He often did this by inserting the first-person pronoun "I" as in: "I ordered all the batteries silenced and the command to advance" when referring to the bombardment that preceded the attack on Chapultepec, and having captured the castle but being unable to carry on with his division due to his wound he continued, "I ordered it forward under Generals Quitman and Worth." When Scott read his report, he registered his displeasure with Pillow's "inaccuracies" and instructed him to correct it. "[Y]our report . . . is unjust to me, and seems . . . to make you control the operations of the whole army, including my own views and acts," wrote the commanding general. Pillow apologized and changed most of the objectionable statements, but not all.[25]

Soon after, in a letter to his wife, Pillow informed her that she was married to the "Hero of Chapultepec," a title "I have won . . . by the *glorious charge upon that powerful fortification. It was daring & glorious.*" But Pillow was not content with telling his wife of his exploits (both real and imagined), he wanted the public back home to share his lofty view of himself, and he attempted to portray himself as a hero in two ways. One was by commissioning a painting that featured him in the Battle of Chapultepec; the other was by providing newspapers with an account of Contreras and Churubusco that portrayed him as the principle agent of American success, the one who had planned and executed the attack at Contreras.[26]

First the painting. James Walker, an English immigrant to the United States, had been teaching drawing in Mexico for some time when the war began. In the latter stages of the Mexico City Campaign, he had offered his services to the American army as an interpreter, and in that capacity, he had witnessed the fighting around Mexico City. After the capital's surrender, he established a studio in the city and went to work painting battle scenes. It was an avocation in which he held considerable talent, and one in which the twenty-seven-year-old artist would garner notoriety over the years. For instance, modern-day visitors to Point Park in Chattanooga, Tennessee, will remember Walker's 13' × 30' mural of the "Battle of Lookout Mountain," which has been on display in the visitor's center since 1986. It depicts the 1863 Civil War battle and was commissioned by General Joseph Hooker, and as a result, features Hooker on horseback near the center of the painting.[27]

With his studio set up, Walker began to paint a depiction of the attack on Chapultepec. The painting was intended to be of the south face of the castle, thus featuring General Quitman and his storming party. When Pillow learned of Walker's work, he visited the young painter and offered him a hundred dollars to change the angle of his intended work so as to feature Pillow's division attacking from the west and, of course, to also feature a mounted Pillow leading the assault. Walker refused to alter his original intent, so when he completed the painting, he accepted Pillow's money to paint a second rendering that featured the Tennessean. Pillow was very pleased with the finished product and immediately sent it to Polk for display in Washington, where "it may be seen by the *world*." In a letter to his wife, Pillow expressed satisfaction that "I am placed in my proper position in the painting." He expected that the painting would help solidify his military legacy.[28]

The other thing Pillow did—and this was actually just after the Battles of Contreras and Churubusco back on August 19 and 20—was to produce a narrative account of those battles, which characterized him as the hero of the army. The account made Pillow the intellectual architect of the army's movements and the driving force behind the successful battles south of Mexico City. Pillow's version of the engagements appeared in two New Orleans newspapers in the second week of September under the pseudonym Leonidas, and it was only a short time until the army in Mexico City received copies. According to the Leonidas letter, the army was in a gloomy state and a desperate situation as it approached Mexico City, whereupon General Scott turned to Pillow to rescue the army from its predicament. Leonidas compared Pillow to Napoleon and went on to explain how the Tennessean's *"masterly military genius and profound knowledge of the science of war . . . astonished so much the mere martinets of the profession."* Leonidas put forward the fictional idea that Pillow was commanding virtually the entire army during the Contreras and Churubusco battles and that he was primarily responsible for the successful outcome. "The victory was most brilliant," concluded Leonidas. This new version even gave an exaggerated account of Pillow's chance encounter and his shooting of a Mexican officer at Churubusco, describing it as two enemy officers who squared off in a test of mortal, one-on-one combat.[29]

Although the laudatory letter was signed "Leonidas," most readers quickly surmised that Leonidas and Pillow were the same person, or at least that Pillow was involved in the letter's composition. Lieutenant A. P. Hill of the regular army said, "I saw that some fool, supposed to be the gentleman himself, endeavoured to give Pillow the credit and glory of the whole affair." Lieutenant John D. Wilkins wrote a letter home in which he described the "sycophantic manner in which everything is told," by Leonidas. The episode demonstrated colossal temerity on Pillow's part, and the account of the battles was so panegyric that it made him look foolish and even comical to the army rank and file. Pillow's biographers, Nat Hughes and Roy Stonesifer, tend to be fair-minded and even-handed in their portrayal of their subject, but even they called the Leonidas account "outrageous."[30]

Pillow's post-campaign grab for glory caused his relations with Scott and other high-ranking officers to deteriorate rapidly. He did not attend a farewell dinner that Scott hosted to honor General David Twiggs, and in October when the Aztec Club was formed as a fraternity of American officers, Pillow did not join. Then, too, there was the issue of the two Mexican howitzers that had been taken as prizes and placed in Pillow's baggage wagon by two staff officers on the day of the Chapultepec battle, September 13. Pillow likely wanted to take them home and display them as trophies at his Columbia plantation, Clifton. After all, William Haskell of the Second Tennessee had returned to Tennessee with a captured cannon. However, in the days that followed, the missing howitzers became an issue. Pillow claimed that he ordered them removed from his wagon and he thought that they had been, but they had not, and the Tennessean apparently forgot them. Pillow wrote to Scott on October 9, stating that the howitzers had been returned, but the commanding general did not accept his explanation. First it was Pillow's self-aggrandizing battle reports, then the Leonidas account surfaced, and now Scott viewed the missing howitzers as strike three.[31]

A testy Pillow assumed the role of victim and demanded a court of inquiry. In a letter to his wife, Pillow contended that he had been a loyal subordinate, had been given "all the *hard jobs & dangerous work*," and had not provoked Scott in any way. But now the commanding general, envious of Pillow's prestige, turned on him. The Tennessean, however, believed that his standing with the president put him "above his [Scott's] reach." The court convened two weeks later, and after several days of testimony placed most of the blame on the staff officers who had loaded the howitzers in Pillow's wagon, faulting Pillow only for knowing that the trophies had not been removed from his baggage. It was a mild rebuke, and others thought that Pillow had gotten off light by transferring blame to his staff.

Controversy within the army's high command continued to pile one on top of another in a cascading effect that eventually and collectively paralyzed the army officer corps with so much recrimination that the president got involved. Soon after the appearance of the Leonidas letter, another letter was published under the name "Veritas," and it praised General William Worth and Colonel James Duncan for saving Scott from potentially costly mistakes in the approach to Mexico City. A livid Scott issued a scathing order, reminding officers that it was a violation of army regulations to write accounts of military operations for publication, and the commanding general used phrases like "scandalous letters" and "false credit." Although Scott did not name Worth in his reprimand, the latter correctly assumed that the order was aimed at him. In an act of vengeance, Pillow had earlier written directly to Polk to inform the president of his perceived mistreatment at Scott's hands and specifically to inform him of the secret bribery scheme that Scott had considered back in the summer. (In his letter, Pillow lied to Polk by telling him that after initially offering tepid support for the plan, he changed his mind and strenuously opposed it.) Now following Pillow's example, Worth went over Scott's head by writing directly to Washington complaining of Scott's "malicious and gross injustice." When Scott learned that Pillow and Worth had broken the chain of command by writing directly to the president, he had them both arrested, and when he discovered that Colonel Duncan was the author of the Veritas letter, he arrested him also.[32]

As 1847 turned to 1848, Pillow, because of his personal relationship with Polk, succeeded in having the shoe put on the other foot. In December, the president received Pillow's and Worth's letters, and soon after, an additional letter from Pillow informing the president of the three officers' arrest. In early January, Polk sent instructions addressing the state of affairs in Mexico City. He demanded the release of Pillow, Worth, and Duncan, he relieved Scott of command, replacing him with a loyal Democrat, William O. Butler, and he ordered a court of inquiry to investigate Scott's conduct. Pillow now had the advantage—he knew it and was confident that the investigation "will show a degree of *malignity* in Scott, as *black* and *atrocious* as ever *disgraced* a fiend."[33]

The rest of the army was indignant, and the Third, Fourth, and Fifth Tennessee Volunteers, arriving as they did in late 1847 and early 1848, had front-row seats to the army's contentious wrangling. Especially angry were the West Point trained regular officers. Robert E. Lee thought that Scott had been sacrificed for Pillow's gain, and he expressed the hope that Pillow and Worth would "be held up in the light they deserved." Daniel Harvey Hill thought that Scott's situation had resulted from "the intrigues of that arch-scoundrel Pillow. He has very great influence with our weak, childish President." He went on to assert that Butler was "a creature of Mr. Polk's appointment and of course a fool." Theodore Laidley believed that presidential politics were at the root of Scott's recall and that his removal from command was "the greatest misfortune that could possibly happen to the Army." Finally, Romeyn B. Ayres wrote that removing such a successful general from command and bringing him before a court to face charges brought by a subordinate who was himself under charges for unethical conduct was "A most anomolous affair!" It was primarily the work of two Tennesseans, Pillow and Polk, that had the occupying army so hamstrung.[34]

The court convened in Mexico City in March, but soon adjourned and relocated to Frederick, Maryland, where it reconvened in June. The inquiry evolved basically into a showdown between Scott and Pillow, and it took on the tone of an inquisition against Scott. The results of the court were anticlimactic. It focused largely on the bribery scheme with Pillow, fallaciously claiming that he had opposed it, but the court concluded that there was inadequate evidence to condemn Scott. It did, however, offer mild condemnation of Pillow, whom it found had actively tried to claim more credit than was due him. Ultimately, Polk decided to drop the matter, and the court disbanded in early July. But the ultimate purpose had been served, which was to knock Scott, a politically ambitious Whig, out of presidential contention in 1848. In addition, Pillow believed that he had been vindicated, and he took pride in the role he had played in cutting Scott down to size. However, his primary accomplishment was in creating a totally dysfunctional army high-command that lasted more than six months.[35]

The Third Tennessee had arrived in Mexico City just as these events were coming to a head in December 1847. Although members of the regiment did not record their opinions, they certainly would have been aware of army gossip, as this unflattering episode unfolded at the end of the war. Nicholas Trist and his Mexican counterparts signed the Treaty of Guadalupe Hidalgo on February 2, 1848, ceding over half a million square miles of territory to the United States and recognizing the Rio Grande as the permanent boundary in exchange for $18.25 million for American claims and war damages. The treaty arrived in Washington on February 19, and the Senate approved it the following month, officially ending the conflict. Three months later, the occupation phase ended and all U.S. troops returned home.[36]

Throughout the war, Tennesseans had been at the forefront. A staggering turnout of volunteers in May 1846 set a standard that no other state matched. During the twenty-two-month conflict nearly 5,500

Tennessee volunteers served in a total of six regiments: five infantry and one mounted. Tennesseans played a prominent role at Monterrey, they played an important but disappointing role at Cerro Gordo, and two Tennesseans, Pillow and Polk, were central players in, even instigators of, the army turmoil that dominated the final months of the conflict. Indeed, Tennesseans made their mark, for good or ill.

*Chapter Ten*

# MEXICAN WAR LEGACIES

"No country likes to part with a good earnest war. It likes to talk about the war, write its history, fight its battles over and over again, and build monument after monument to commemorate its glories." So wrote a Confederate soldier several years after the Civil War. Holding true to that principle, the country appears to have been well on its way to memorializing the war with Mexico in the years that immediately followed until the magnitude of the Civil War derailed such efforts. When the guns fell silent and the volunteers returned home, Tennesseans wanted to remember and memorialize this episode in the state's history. The national significance of the event was a major reason to remember. The war had given the United States control of the entire continent all the way to the Pacific Ocean. It had been the largest military operation in the country's brief history and, other than brief incursions into Canada, it was the country's first foreign war. When it ended, many Americans believed that it would constitute a great chapter in history, and those who had served and survived were proud to have participated in writing that chapter. Two quotations from regular army officers perhaps best encapsulate the feelings of returning veterans. One surmised that what the American forces had accomplished in Mexico would "astound the world," while another concluded that U.S. military operations "will be written—blazoned—as the great event—the epoch—of the 19th century: and not surpassed by any military achievement in all previous history."[1]

The cost of victory provided another strong motivation to remember. Tennessee lost 695 of its volunteers in Mexico, with a staggering

646 or 92 percent of its deaths resulting from disease. The numbers from Sumner County are illustrative of how losses affected localities. Of the 265 who volunteered from that county, fifty-four died: eight in combat and forty-six from disease. The average age of Sumner County's dead was twenty-three. One of that county's veterans stated what was obviously a common feeling: those who died had "won a glorious grave, and died a glorious death." Samuel Lauderdale, another Sumner Countian, wrote before his death at Cerro Gordo that the accolades that Tennesseans had received (he was thinking about Monterrey) were "blood bought honors." But where was the glory and honor for those who died in the Third, Fourth, and Fifth Tennessee Volunteers? Those three regiments got to Mexico too late to participate in any of the battles, and yet 429 of them died; all from disease.[2]

Part of remembrance was to rename American towns for Mexican War battles and heroes as well as Mexican towns that American troops had occupied. So, in the years immediately following the war, the names Cerro Gordo, Saltillo, Jalapa, and Molino began to appear on the map of Tennessee, and add to that the town of Winfield which is the seat of Scott County, Tennessee. And the volunteer state was not the only one to memorialize the war in such a manner. The town of Ringgold is situated in north Georgia and was named for Samuel Ringgold, the first U.S. officer killed in the war. Georgia also has Resaca (named for the Battle of Resaca de la Palma), Buena Vista, Quitman, and Cerro Gordo (later renamed Bowdon). North Carolina and Illinois also have towns named Cerro Gordo, and Alabama has towns named Ringgold, Victoria, and Monterey and also a Gordo, which is supposedly a shortened version of the Mexican War battle. Six counties in Iowa are named for Mexican War battles and heroes (Cerro Gordo, Buena Vista, Palo Alto, Ringgold, Taylor, and Scott). Pennsylvania has Buena Vista, Ringgold, and Saltillo, and there is a section of Pittsburgh that was developed after the war, and when the streets were laid out, they were all given Mexican War names. Today that area of the city is still known as "Mexican War Streets." Clearly, Tennesseans were not the only Americans who believed that the war deserved a lasting legacy. But, of course, no one at that time could have imagined that only a dozen years later a far more significant and costly conflict would come along and ultimately cast such a large shadow that it completely obscured the war with Mexico.

Polk, too, had his name affixed to counties in eight states and to miscellaneous townships across the country. Unfortunately for the former president, Polk did not live long enough to help shape his own legacy. He purchased a house in Nashville that had been owned by Felix Grundy, where he and Sarah intended to live the remainder of their years. Polk Place was the name he gave his new estate, and he looked forward to overseeing renovations when he left Washington. Sarah would live there for more than four decades, but James for barely three months. He died of cholera at Polk Place in June 1849. Cholera is an intestinal infection that produces agonizing diarrhea and vomiting, ironically, some of the same symptoms of diseases that killed so many American soldiers in Mexico—Montezuma's revenge, indeed.

Periodically during the twentieth century, when historians ranked presidents, Polk has always been listed relatively high. In assessing the effectiveness of presidents, adjudicators typically have used five rating categories: great, near great, average, below average, and failure—Polk is always judged to be one of the "near greats." His primary deficit was his acerbic personality. He was just not likeable, and that translated into an inability to inspire, which is one of the considerations ranking presidents. However, concrete accomplishments are another way of measuring success, and in that regard, the eleventh president excelled. His objectives may have been questionable but not his ability to get things done.[3]

While many Americans in the twenty-first century may not know much about Polk, he was, more so than any other president, the one responsible for expanding the country's reach across the entire continent. Polk's legacy was land, or to put it differently, geography. Geography was that all important factor that turned the Atlantic and Pacific Oceans into giant moats, protecting the United States from foreign invasion for a century, until it was strong enough to take its place among the super powers of the world. As one foreign policy expert adeptly notes, "The militarism and pragmatism of continental Europe through the mid-twentieth century, to which the Americans always felt superior, was the result of geography." Ironically, the provincial man who rarely ventured out of Tennessee and Washington, and who never traveled to other countries laid the foundation for the United States to become a global power. And one more irony attaches to the eleventh president. He was a nationalist and the chief agent of Manifest Destiny's nationalistic goals, and yet, in the words of historian Tom Chaffin, he "ultimately sectionalized the nation's politics, creating a geographical fracturing that soon led to civil war."[4]

But those Polk legacies were not apparent to Mexican War veterans in the 1840s who simply wanted to be remembered as patriots who did their duty. In November 1846, fifteen months before the end of the war, Nashvillians met to discuss the proposal to erect a monument to honor Tennessee's Monterrey dead, and residents from surrounding counties were invited to attend. Hickman, Marshall, Smith, and Sumner were among those counties represented. Nothing came of the Nashville/Davidson County monument idea, but two communities did commission such memorials to commemorate their fallen, and those two monuments still stand today. One is prominently located on the town square in Lawrenceburg, conspicuously memorializing Lawrence County's Mexican War dead. It was erected in 1849. In November 1863, after defeating a small contingent of Confederates in Lawrenceburg, the Fourteenth Michigan occupied the town, and its commander, Major Thomas Fitzgibbon, agreed not to burn the Lawrence County courthouse in order to spare the nearby Mexican War monument from potential damage. The other one is a twenty-four-feet tall monument that stands in the Gallatin City Cemetery. The names of all of Sumner County's dead are etched on its sides and it marks the place where several Mexican War dead are buried, including Julius Elliott and Hynds Martin, friends who died together on the streets of Monterrey.[5] Both monuments commemorate members of the First Tennessee. There are no such memorials to members of the Second Tennessee.

Veterans of the war went on to a variety of activities in both public and private life. Some went to California for the gold rush. Robert Farquharson, a native of Scotland and an officer in the Bloody First, was one of them. He had immigrated to Middle Tennessee in 1827, worked as a farmer, businessman, and lawyer in Lincoln County before being elected to the state legislature. As a prominent citizen in Fayetteville, it was natural that he was elected to serve as major in the First Tennessee. Because he had been ordered to stay behind at Camargo to help care for the sick in September 1846, he missed the Battle of Monterrey; so, to be "fair," he was attached to the Second Tennessee at Cerro Gordo, where he was wounded during its ill-fated attack. In early 1849, Farquharson was the leader of a group of thirty-seven people organized in Fayetteville for the purpose of going to California. However, like many forty-niners, he returned home without striking it rich, then a few years later he fought for the Confederacy as colonel of the Forty-first Tennessee Regiment and had the misfortune of being among those captured when Fort Donelson surrendered in early 1862.[6]

James C. Cooper, who had served in Company C of the Tennessee Mounted Regiment, also led a group to California in 1849, as did John T. O'Brien of Company L, Fifth Tennessee, and George V. Hebb of Company G, First Tennessee. Ephraim Willey, Company A, First Tennessee, and two of his friends made an agreement that they would go to California. They each committed to pay the other two $100 if they backed out. Willey got cold feet and backed out, but his friends did not make him pay.[7]

Perhaps the most interesting experience among Tennessee's forty-niners was that of Benjamin Franklin Cheatham, who led a group of fourteen Nashvillians to the gold fields in the fall of 1849. They traveled by steamer to New Orleans then down to the isthmus, where they crossed Central America and caught another steamer to San Francisco. Having delivered his companions, Cheatham made his way to Stockton where, rather than panning for gold in the rivers and streams, he established a general store to sell supplies to the miners. The following year he opened the Hotel de Mexico, which was described as a hangout for "gamblers and the headquarters of intriguing politicians." Cheatham became active in Stockton's politics, and from his "headquarters," he emerged as a leader in what was referred to as the Southern wing of the Democratic Party. According to one source, he not only "ran the politics" of Stockton but also gained a reputation for being a "corrupt politician," lending his support to fellow Tennessean William M. Gwin, who had recently traveled to the new state to run for the United States Senate. Before returning home in 1852, Cheatham assumed a leading role in the lynching of Jim Hill, a local trouble-maker and habitual thief. He remained active in Democratic politics after returning to Nashville and was offered, but declined, a diplomatic post by President James Buchanan.[8] It is perhaps fortunate for Cheatham that his later Civil War experience overshadowed this period of his life.

Numerous Tennessee volunteers who got their first taste of combat in Mexico offered their services again when the Civil War began. George Maney, who was discharged from the First Tennessee for medical reasons and who then returned to Mexico with a commission in the Third Dragoons, later served as an officer in Cheatham's Division in the Confederate army. For gallantry at Shiloh, Maney received promotion to brigadier general and was given command of a brigade. He was wounded at Missionary Ridge in 1863, and while recuperating in Atlanta he fought a duel with an army surgeon who questioned his bravery. After the Civil War, he became a railroad president and staunch Republican. Maney was a gifted orator and, according to one source, "a brilliant conversationalist." His talents apparently opened political doors. Maney lost a bid for governor in 1876, but later was elected to the state senate and periodically held diplomatic posts in Colombia and Uruguay before his death in Washington, DC, in 1901.[9]

Lawrence County native George Nixon, who took command of Company M after William Allen's death at Monterrey, entered politics prior to serving in the Civil War. He first sought a diplomatic post in South America, but despite letters to the State Department attesting to his good "character & reputation," he failed. Nixon's "gallant bearing upon the bloody field of Monterey," and his "courage and conduct" served him well as he jockeyed for command in the state militia and ran for a seat in the state legislature.[10] As a member of the state legislature in the 1850s, Nixon sought ways to improve his hometown, including efforts to entice railroad investment and establish a college. He later served the Confederacy as a colonel for the duration of the Civil War, first commanding the Forty-Eighth Tennessee Infantry and later the Twenty-Second Tennessee Cavalry.[11]

José María Jesús Carvajal and Roberdeau "Bob" Wheat both had colorful post–Mexican War experiences even though their connections to Tennessee were tenuous. Carvajal had grown up in the borderlands of northern Mexico and advocated northern Mexico's separation from the rest of the country. Stephen F. Austin took Carvajal under his wing when he was a teenager in the 1820s and sent him east to learn a trade and get an education. In the process, he became acquainted with Alexander Campbell, the Restoration minister and pacifist mentioned in chapter 8. Campbell liked the young man, converted him away from Catholicism, and allowed Carvajal to live in his home for several years. Carvajal attended Campbell's seminary, which came to be known as Bethany College, became quite spiritually minded and on one occasion sought funding to distribute Bibles back in colonial Texas. The irony of this part of the story is that after living with and studying under such an ardent pacifist in the 1820s, Carvajal went on to have a distinctive military career. He returned home and participated in the Texas Revolution in 1836.[12]

Wheat was from Louisiana, but his father, John Thomas Wheat, became Rector of Christ Church in Nashville in 1837, so the family moved to Tennessee, where Bob attended the University of Nashville. In 1846, Bob joined the Tennessee Mounted Regiment. After the war, he became a traveling mercenary, first joining Carvajal in a revolt against the Mexican government, and becoming a general in Carvajal's army. Later, Wheat was involved in an attempt to seize Cuba, then later joined another Nashvillian, William Walker, in his famous filibustering activities in Central America. Wheat found his next dose of military adventure when he traveled to Italy, joined the forces of Giuseppe Garibaldi, and participated in several battles of Italian unification. When the Civil War began, the charismatic leader returned to his native Louisiana and raised a company of Zouaves that fought in Virginia. At First Bull Run, he ran into his old Nashville friend and fellow Mexican War veteran, Thomas Claiborne, who once referred to Wheat's "vagabond and adventurous life." After recovering from a chest wound received at Bull Run, Wheat went on to participate in Stonewall Jackson's Valley Campaign before being killed a few weeks later at Gaines Mill.[13]

Other Tennessee Mexican War veterans served prominently in the Civil War. Thomas Claiborne was among them, serving as a colonel in the cavalry under both Nathan Bedford Forrest and Joseph Wheeler. The First Tennessee's second in command, Lieutenant Colonel Samuel R. Anderson, went into banking after the war until his appointment as postmaster of Nashville in 1853. Later, he saw brief service as a Confederate general commanding a brigade of Tennesseans in Virginia before resigning in spring 1862 due to either bad health or deficient leadership ability, depending on the source. However, he was back in the army in 1864 in charge of the Confederate conscription service. Henry B. Davidson from Shelbyville joined the First Tennessee volunteers at age sixteen, was promoted to sergeant for bravery at Monterrey, and then went to West Point after Mexico. Later, he served on the staff of several Confederate generals, and by 1864 he commanded a brigade in Joseph Wheeler's cavalry. After the Civil War, Davidson became a sheriff in New Orleans before moving on to California, where he died in 1899. John W. Whitfield was born in Williamson County in 1818 and served as a captain in the Bloody First. Later he led pro-slavery elements during the "Bleeding Kansas" episode, then in the Civil War commanded Texas cavalry. Another Tennessean, Cadmus M. Wilcox, graduated from West Point in 1846 before fighting with the regular army in the Mexico City Campaign. He went on to be general in the Confederacy. Many others with Tennessee roots served in both the Mexican War and Civil War, like John C. Vaughn, John P. McCown, and Bushrod Johnson. Still other Mexican War veterans from Tennessee fought on the Union side, for example, David Farragut and Samuel P. Carter, both from East Tennessee.[14]

And, of course, there was Gideon Pillow, who fancied himself a military hero, and who ended his lackluster Mexican War service with the Leonidas controversy. He tried unsuccessfully to parlay his military exploits into political gain by running for the Senate in 1857, but he found his Mexican War record more of a liability than an asset. The aged Winfield Scott wrote publicly to debunk him, and Nashville newcomer Simon Bolivar Buckner, a West Point graduate and veteran of Scott's army, wrote several scathing editorials lampooning Pillow. Referring to Pillow's excoriation by Buckner, Nashville Mayor Randal McGavock penned in his diary, "Poor Pillow—he is in a made fix."[15]

Although Pillow played a role in the Civil War, he is best remembered for his premature departure from Fort Donelson just prior to its surrender to Ulysses S. Grant. In February 1862, Pillow, a brigadier general in the Confederate army, found himself commanding troops at the Dover, Tennessee fort on the Cumberland River near the Kentucky border, and other generals present included John B. Floyd and the Mexican War veteran Buckner. Following a sharp battle with Grant's Federals outside the fort, the three Southern generals made the controversial decision to surrender their force to Grant rather than attempt a breakout. After deciding to leave Buckner to parley with Grant (Buckner willingly accepted the role of martyr), Pillow and Floyd ingloriously slipped away to safety the night before the surrender. It was a decision that forever sealed the fate of Pillow's reputation as a military novice. The days leading up to the surrender had been marred by a lack of cooperation between Pillow and Buckner, and their fractious meeting the night before the surrender did not heal old wounds. As he was departing Dover in the dead of night, Pillow was overheard telling Floyd, "This thing began at the court martial in Mexico." And just like in Mexico, Pillow's battle report, written a month later, placed himself in the most favorable light. "It was all Pillow," wrote McGavock. After the fort's surrender, Grant met with his old friend Buckner, and as they talked, their conversation turned to Pillow. When the Union general asked about Pillow's whereabouts, Buckner responded that he had left because "he thought you'd rather get hold of him than any other man in the Southern Confederacy." Grant broke in and said that if he had captured Pillow, he would turn him loose because "He will do us more good commanding you fellows." Both men broke out laughing.[16]

One of the most significant contributors to the Confederate cause was John Reid McClanahan, a veteran of the Second Tennessee Regiment in Mexico. His service, however, was not on the battlefield but rather in print media, for McClanahan was owner of the *Memphis Daily Appeal*. The paper staunchly and unapologetically defended the Southern cause, and as Federal troops occupied Tennessee in 1862, and later pushed farther south, McClanahan moved his printing operation from Memphis to Mississippi, then to Alabama and finally to Georgia. It became the country's most famous traveling newspaper and was soon known as the *Moving Appeal*. The *Appeal* never halted publication, and it became famous not just among Confederate soldiers but among Federals as well. While the owner always kept it just out of reach of advancing Yankee forces, many copies found their way into the Federal lines. When the war ended, McClanahan returned to Memphis with plans to resume operations, but in January 1866, he was beaten to death in an alley behind the Gayoso Hotel.[17]

An examination of the pension files of members of the Bloody First speaks to the war's long-term legacy of pain and suffering. While service pensions were not available until 1887, disability and survivors' pensions were. Disabled veterans and family members of those killed in action could submit applications with accompanying testimonials from physicians, eyewitnesses and the like. The following examples of some of the Monterrey wounded are representative. John Vining was wounded by musket balls in the foot and hip. In the 1880s when he sought an increase in his disability pension, he reported that his chronic pain had caused him to be bedridden for several years. Charles Talley was only slightly wounded at Monterrey, but at Tampico in early 1847 he began to suffer from dysentery. Frequent bouts of diarrhea persisted for two years, and for the twenty years that followed, he experienced a variety of health problems that he blamed on his war service. Twenty-three-year-old Richard C. Locke received a wound when a musket ball entered his left thigh near the hip joint. He remained in the hospital nearly four months before being discharged with a surgeon's certificate stating that he was "totally disabled." He died of his wound in 1853, but not before marrying and fathering four children. Marshall Watson suffered from a thigh wound for decades after the war, and in 1885 wrote that his leg had "all most rotted off" and "smelled badly." Finally, Lycurgus G. Stewart received a wound when a musket ball entered his right hand between the thumb and forefinger, shattering his carpal bones in his wrist and breaking his ulna before exiting his forearm. His 1879 request for an increase in his disability pension included affidavits confirming his loyalty during the Civil War-he served as an orderly sergeant in the Tenth Tennessee U.S. Infantry. Although Stewart was known to be a regular drinker and a daily visitor in bars and saloons, one testimonial humorously wrote to assure the pension office that Stewart was never seen drunk. "He has a stumbling gait," but his disability "was not caused by vicious habits."[18]

The most poignant legacy of the Mexican War lies in a comparative examination of the post-war careers of William Campbell and William Haskell. There is perhaps no better example of the repercussions that can accompany battlefield success or failure. For Campbell, part of the motivation for going to Mexico had been to maintain family honor and to prove to himself, if to no one else, that he was worthy of his family name. Apparently, he believed that his election to the state legislature and the U.S. Congress, along with his military service during the Seminole War in Florida, was inadequate for that aspiration. However, his experience in Mexico, especially Monterrey, more than made up for any perceived shortcomings. Before he even returned home in the summer of 1847, several prominent Tennesseans wrote urging him to consider a run for governor. Despite his reluctance to seek public office, he was elected a circuit judge in 1847, and four years later he succumbed to the pressure and ran for governor as a Whig.[19]

His opponent was incumbent Democratic governor William Trousdale from Gallatin, a veteran of battlefields both political and military. Trousdale's military experience played no small role in his being elected governor in 1849, but it was during Trousdale's governorship that the aftermath of the war began to tear at the fabric of the Union. The territorial acquisition from Mexico placed the slavery question at the center of the national stage. The debate over the Compromise of 1850 was long and heated, and when it finally passed, rather than settle disputes, it ushered in one of the most tumultuous decades in American history. And Tennessee had its own role in the unfolding events. In the middle of the turmoil, delegates from nine Southern states met in Nashville in June 1850 as a show of unity against any attack on slavery. A full 176 delegates met at the Nashville Convention, as it was called, but instead of producing broad support for concerted action—to include the threat of secession if necessary—the convention demonstrated that in 1850 the South was more inclined toward unity than to separation.[20]

In this volatile atmosphere observers began to associate Governor Trousdale with the more radical secessionist elements of the Democratic Party, which led some people to turn to the forty-four-year-old Campbell as a more moderate voice for Tennesseans. Campbell was a loyal Southerner and a bona fide military hero, but he was also a staunch unionist who, like most Tennesseans, supported the Compromise of 1850. In endorsing him for governor, one newspaper referred to him as the "hero of Monterrey," and his campaign slogan was "Boys, follow me!" which is supposedly what he shouted to his men during the bloody dash to Fort Tenería five years earlier, and which was also intended to blunt the impact of Trousdale's martial experience. Campbell won the election by just over 1,600 votes. During his tenure, he closely adhered to the Whig principles of internal improvements and education, but growing increasingly disenchanted with politics, he chose not to seek reelection. Rather, he retired to private life briefly working as a cotton merchant in New Orleans before settling in as president of the Bank of Middle Tennessee.[21]

But Campbell's life of service was not over. He returned to the public arena as a circuit judge in the late 1850s, then he supported the moderate Constitutional Union candidate and fellow Tennessean John Bell for president in 1860. After Abraham Lincoln's election, Campbell spoke out against secession. In the spring of 1861, former members of the now defunct Whig Party, along with pro-Union Democrats, turned to Campbell with entreaties that he run for governor in an effort to steer the state away from secession. According to one source, Campbell's "martial image" and unionist stand attracted bipartisan support across the state, and a letter from at least one correspondent seemed to bear that out. Rolf Saunders wrote to Campbell that if he ran, his Mexican War reputation alone would assure him of carrying Davidson County by a two-to-one margin. But alas, Campbell's disgust with party politics caused him to decline this golden political opportunity.[22]

After Tennessee joined the Confederacy in the summer of 1861, both sides sought Campbell's loyalty and services. Not knowing which side Campbell would take, one writer urged him to make his position known, because "quiet thousands [are] turned to you in hope." Many Tennesseans wanted Campbell to accept the reality of what had happened and join the Confederate cause. Gideon Pillow and others tried to persuade him to accept a general's commission in the Confederate army, but Campbell remained silent and seemed almost lethargic in his unwillingness to get involved. His sister, Margaret, described him as a "sad and silent man." When he did get involved, however, it was to accept a commission as brigadier general in the Union army.[23]

Being offered a military commission was actually more of a consolation prize. Soon after Federal troops occupied portions of the state in 1862, Campbell was considered for appointment as Military Governor of Tennessee, but the post went to East Tennessee Democrat Andrew Johnson. Conservative unionists thought that Campbell would have been a better choice because even though Johnson had remained loyal, it was his party that had taken the state out of the Union, making him less acceptable to Union sympathizers in Tennessee. Soon after, however, Campbell accepted the commission of general, but because of poor health, he never assumed field command and he resigned the commission after only a few months. In 1863, Tennesseans turned to him again in an abortive effort to get him elected governor of the state. After the war, they showed their abiding respect and admiration for the Mexican War hero by electing him to Congress in 1866, one year before his death.[24]

While Campbell remained a popular public figure and a symbol of unity even as his party disintegrated in the 1850s, William Haskell's postwar years were different. His regiment's failed attack at Cerro Gordo led to a disappointing wartime experience, which was compounded by the deaths of numerous people close to him. He had appointed his sister's beau, Wiley Hale, as his adjutant in order to see to the boy's safety, only to have him mortally wounded at Cerro Gordo, and at least seven others from Haskell's hometown were killed. As their commanding officer, Haskell felt responsible. But his wartime losses were not limited to men in his regiment. Haskell's childhood friend Tom Ewell had died at Cerro Gordo, adding weight to the melancholy burden that he felt. In addition, his brother-in-law, who was serving in another unit, died on his way home after contracting a disease in Mexico.

The price of war had been high for Haskell, and according to one acquaintance, "he came home with his constitution wrecked." It is bad enough to suffer such losses in the attainment of great and memorable success, but to lose so much only to return from Mexico with a sense of failure and without achieving battlefield glory proved to be a permanent and heavy burden for Haskell. If battlefield triumph brought honor to self, family, and community, then failure brought the opposite—shame.[25] That he would return home in 1847 and immediately run for Congress as an anti-war candidate indicates that Haskell was deeply conflicted about his military experience. In his campaign speeches, he repeated the assertion that the war was "unjust," which causes one to wonder if he believed his own sense of personal injustice was compounded by the injustice of the war in general. Perhaps his condemnation of the war was Haskell's way of rationalizing his failed experience, and if his Cerro Gordo experience had been a success, one wonders if he would have adopted his anti-war position.

Before the war, Haskell enjoyed a promising political future in the Whig Party. In addition to practicing law, he was a poet and a brilliant orator who, at the age of twenty-two, had been elected to the Tennessee House of Representatives. During his foray into state politics in the early 1840s, his speeches won him notoriety. According to one source, "He had every grace and gift of the orator and unlimited flow of purest and strongest words, the finest fancy, the richest imagination, . . . [and] a voice of unequalled beauty." He possessed "extraordinary natural gifts, . . . [and] acquired certain things without effort." His grandiose oratorical style merged eloquence and genius, and elicited comparisons to the great Daniel Webster.[26]

Upon his return from Mexico, he quickly won a seat in the U.S. Congress, once again displaying his mesmerizing style at the podium, only now he was preaching his new-found opposition to the war. He quit politics after only one term, but he did not completely disappear from public life. The service he had rendered to his country in Mexico and his brief prewar and postwar stints in politics had garnered him a considerable reservoir of respect, and in the 1850s he was still regarded as a Whig leader in West Tennessee. In 1852, he put his oratorical skills to good use, campaigning across the state for presidential candidate Winfield Scott.[27]

However, Haskell was never the same after coming home from war. He fought a physical war in Mexico in 1846–1847, but in the years that followed, he fought a psychological war with himself. He increasingly slipped into idleness and seclusion, which helps to explain his abrupt departure from political office. Soon after his return from the war, he began to drink heavily, and along with his isolation, he began to sink into depression and despondency. Apparently, his drinking was a problem at times while he was canvassing the state for the Scott campaign. On one occasion after a speech in East Tennessee, he boarded the Knoxville-to-Nashville stagecoach near Crossville looking "worn, slovenly, [and] soiled," and he was cursing as he entered the coach. But he recognized one of the travelers as an old acquaintance and immediately apologized for his language. In fact, Haskell reminded the man that they used to be members of the same church and that his wife (Haskell's) was a good Christian woman. Late in the evening it began to rain and the driver told the passengers that he would go no farther on the slippery mountain road unless two men got out and held the lead horses. Haskell volunteered for the task and insisted on taking the horse on the more dangerous precipice side of the road, because, he said, his life was worth less than the others.

Alcohol became a growing problem. At the time, newspaper editors shied away from stories about public intoxication if it involved a noted member of society, but that kind of information gets out. At some point in the 1850s, Haskell apparently gave up drinking, because he became a speaker in the Temperance Movement. His oratorical excellence was once again on full display as he traveled across Tennessee professing the evils of alcohol and preaching the need for social reform. At one moment, he would have his audience laughing and at the next crying. However, in his own personal struggle Haskell eventually succumbed to temptation and returned to the bottle—if he ever really left it. Friends tried to save him from his demons, but his bouts with depression and alcohol grew in tandem. The sad irony is that this renowned temperance speaker became an alcoholic, and his erratic behavior caused some people to question his sanity.[28]

Haskell was exhibiting symptoms of Post-Traumatic Stress Disorder (PTSD), a medical condition undiagnosed in the nineteenth century, but one that has received considerable attention in the late twentieth and early twenty-first centuries. Combat-related PTSD can be brought on by traumatic events or the loss of comrades, and is sometimes associated with remorse over deaths that resulted from battlefield errors or feelings of anger because of leaders who betrayed expectations. All of these factors were part of Haskell's Mexican War experience. Survivors sometimes feel shame because of mistakes or they feel guilt because others died while they survived, and these emotional feelings can last for years and lead to "a downward spiral into depression." Combat veterans who suffer such emotions often become socially withdrawn. As their depression deepens, they become anxious and find it increasingly difficult to cope with life, and their condition "can lead to destructive behaviours, such as substance abuse." One modern study found that 73 percent of those who exhibit PTSD had increased alcohol consumption. In extreme cases, PTSD can be mentally debilitating.[29]

Evidence indicates that Haskell suffered from "survivor guilt," and he displayed most, if not all, of the characteristics described above. He continued to display flashes of oratorical brilliance in the 1850s as he maintained a level of involvement in politics. After the demise of the Whigs in the early part of the decade, he became involved in the American Party, often referred to as the Know-Nothing Party, and in 1856 he tested the political waters again by expressing an interest in that party's nomination for governor. Diarist and, at that time, future Nashville mayor Randal McGavock recorded his opinion that Haskell "made a most eloquent speech" on September 3, but the following day at another campaign event the results were not so positive. "Haskell was the orator of the day," McGavock wrote, and he spent four-and-a-half hours on the stand addressing issues and answering questions, but often the discussion was "entirely irrelevant." Furthermore, Haskell "was drunk while speaking and I think did his cause more injury than good." His candidacy did not go very far.[30]

Haskell became mentally unstable, and his decline in the late 1850s was difficult to watch. The author of an early twentieth-century biographical sketch struggled to describe Haskell's increasingly irrational behavior. He asserted that Haskell had "excessive nervous strain" and that "the irregularities of his life, finally subverted his nervous system. . . . His mind never recovered its balance." Another writer who knew Haskell described him as "amazingly eloquent, frail, and unfortunate." Fifteen months after his abortive gubernatorial bid, McGavock saw Haskell in Nashville and penned this curt entry in his diary; "He still appears crazy." Indeed, in 1857 and 1858, Haskell was a patient at the Eastern Kentucky Asylum for the Insane in Lexington. He had gone to Kentucky to stay with family members who lived there. At the asylum, he was registered as patient number 237 and the reason listed for his admission was "Intemperance." While there he became attached and indebted to one of the matrons at the institution, Louisa Rice, who offered kind and tender-hearted care for the troubled patient. In late 1857, Haskell wrote a poem, probably his last, which he dedicated to Rice with a note thanking her for her "ministering care when the pathway of life was very dark." Part one of the composition describes the storms of life that surrounded Haskell; it consists of half of the poem's six verses. The first two verses are published below, and they suffice in conveying insights into Haskell's strained psychological state and his agonizing thoughts.[31]

> I'm adrift on life's ocean, and wildly I sweep,
> Aimless and helmless, its fathomless deep;
> The wild winds assail me, it threateningly storms,
> The clouds roll around me in hideous forms;
> I drift to a lee shore! I strike! Am aground!
> The mad waters whelm me! I drown! Oh, I drown!
> Mercy! Oh, mercy! Oh, Lord set me free,
> And take me, Oh, take me, to Heaven and Thee.

I wander life's desert—lone, desolate, sad!
Faint, reeling, and weary; I'm mad! Oh, I'm mad!
No glad waters greet me, no streams flowing free;
I perish! I perish! Rain, rain! Give me rain!
Let the stream of deliverance flow gently to me,
And drift me, Oh drift me, to Heaven and Thee.

The tone changes in the final three verses (Part II) as Haskell writes about finding peace in death. For the writer, death not only provides peace, but also offers hope and victory from life's pain. The last verse is representative.

Joy! Joy! Oh, anguish and sorrow no more
Shall lead me its victim of life's crumbling shore.
The winds waft me gently, I perish no more;
I thirst not—the war of Life's crumblin is o'er
Hope beckons me on, with the sweet whispering tale,
To walk through, all hopefully, Life's pleasant vale;
And I come to Thee, Lord! Unprisoned and free,
And I bless Thee! Ah! bless Thee! for mercy to me![32]

William Haskell died in 1859 at the age of forty. Records state that he died of "consumption," but in truth he was yet another casualty of the Mexican War.

*Chapter Eleven*

# THE QUEST FOR
# RECOGNITION AND RESPECT

As the years passed, aging Mexican War veterans saw that their service was not as highly esteemed nor their legacy as firmly fixed in public memory as those who had fought in the Civil War. A manifestation of what many interpreted as a lack of respect seemed obvious from Congress's failure to pass a pension provision for veterans in the twenty-five years following the war. A few veterans ascribed Congress's inaction and the public's seeming indifference to the fact that no Mexican War veteran organizations existed, which was not the case for Civil War veterans, whose varied organizations had a range of activities that kept the memory of that war constantly in the public eye. But a change occurred in the early 1870s when veterans began to organize and push for recognition and remembrance.[1]

Several men played prominent roles in trying to attain the recognition that Mexican War veterans deserved, and two of them merit notice here. One was James S. Negley from Pittsburgh, Pennsylvania, a graduate of the University of Western Pennsylvania, and a general in the Federal army during the Civil War. In 1862, Negley was the post commander in Union-occupied Nashville, where he oversaw the construction of a series of fortifications around the city designed to thwart any Confederate effort to retake it. The largest of these fortifications, indeed the largest inland stone fort on the continent, was dubbed Fort Negley, and its remains can still be visited just south of downtown Nashville today. But Negley had another connection to Tennessee that predated the Civil War. In 1846, he served in the First Pennsylvania Volunteers, the regiment that was supposed to attack alongside Haskell's Second Tennessee at Cerro Gordo but that was out of position and too late to join the assault. Because Negley resigned from the Union army under a cloud of controversy after the Battle of Chickamauga in 1863, he perhaps felt greater nostalgia for his Mexican War service, for in 1873, while serving as a Pennsylvania Congressman, Negley presented to Congress a petition requesting that Mexican War veterans be granted a pension.[2]

The other man who worked to focus more of the nation's attention on Mexican War veterans was Alexander Kenaday, a veteran from Virginia who had relocated to California during the Gold Rush. He started a local Mexican War veterans association in San Francisco in 1866 and led the effort to start a national organization in the 1860s and 1870s. Kenaday and several other veterans met in Washington, DC, in February 1873, where they decided to band together and attend Ulysses S. Grant's second inaugural as a group the following month in order to focus attention on Mexican War veterans. Subsequently, the group formed the Associated Veterans of 1846, and called for Mexican War veterans from across the country to gather in Washington the following January to participate in framing a memorial to Congress requesting a pension. They advocated for the same pension rate that veterans of the War of 1812 received.[3]

Thirty-three states sent delegates to the Washington meeting in January 1874, and among the attendees were several veterans who had gone on to serve as generals in the Civil War. Tennessee's delegation included Joseph Cooper (Mounted Regiment), Richard J. Hays (Second Tennessee), George McPherson (Fifth Tennessee), and Nathaniel S. Reneau (Mounted Regiment). Gideon Pillow was selected to attend but he declined. He did, however, send a letter that was read to the gathering. In it he struck a note of post–Civil War reconciliation: "we knew no North, no South" in 1846, he wrote. All "were patriots and brothers, . . . ready to sacrifice our lives for the good of the country." At this meeting, the Associated Veterans of 1846 officially formed the National

Association of Veterans of the Mexican War (NAVMW), whose primary mission was to promote the idea of a pension. In choosing officers for the new organization, those present elected Pillow, in absentia, as one of its vice-presidents, demonstrating that despite his checkered performance in Mexico and the Civil War, many people still held a favorable impression of him. Over the years, however, Pillow played no active role in the association, because its formation coincided with a period of his life in which he was busily engaged in a futile effort to stave off his approaching financial ruin.[4]

Negley addressed the convention and, in his speech, he returned to the concept of honor as the central force in the conflict. The Mexican War had been a "historical achievement" attained by men who "fell into line to defend the honor . . . [of their] government in its third great war." He referred to the "Grand . . . fulfillment" of the country's destiny and then went on to echo many of the themes that had practically become clichés in the 1840s. In speaking to his former comrades in arms, Negley portrayed the Mexican adventure as "the triumphs of truth, christianity, and universal liberty, since you eventuated the first page of the biography of the armies that forced an insolvent and treacherous government to salute with respect the Stars and Stripes." Their "heroic deeds and humble valor [is] now dimmed by the sweep of years," but, he concluded, the martial exploits of that war "will always be famous in history." It was an auspicious beginning for NAVMW, which would spawn affiliated organizations in thirteen states, including Tennessee, and which collectively would boast of more than five thousand members by the end of the 1870s along with a monthly newsletter called *The Vedette*, which had a circulation of ten thousand through the 1880s.[5]

An additional objective of members of NAVMW was to push for more national commemoration of the Mexican War in the form of monuments. They had witnessed an outpouring of honors bestowed on Civil War veterans after 1865, and they believed that their achievements were equally commendable. However, it proved difficult to rally support for a proposed monument in the nation's capital. The only thing resembling such was an equestrian statue of General Winfield Scott located where 16th Street, Massachusetts Avenue, and Rhode Island Avenue intersect.

It was dedicated in the same year that NAVMW was formed as a part of a series of similar statues intended to honor the commanders of U.S. forces from the Revolution to the Civil War. The statue contains no mention of the war with Mexico, and veterans of that war would get no such commemorative monument.[6]

As soon as the Washington convention adjourned, Senator John A. Logan and Congressman James Negley submitted a pension bill to their respective houses requesting an eight-dollar-per-month service pension. At the time of the bill's submission, J. H. Baker, the Commissioner of Pensions, estimated that there remained in 1874 approximately thirty-nine thousand living Mexican War veterans. Thus began a thirteen-year battle to get Congress to pass a pension bill. Consistent opposition came from Republicans, who did not want to see service pensions go to Southerners who might also have fought for the Confederacy. Indeed, it would violate the law they argued, because of an 1862 statute that forbade federal assistance to ex-Confederates. While some Republicans saw a Mexican War pension as a surreptitious way of bestowing monthly payments to former secessionists, veterans of Mexico thought it was simply a benefit they had earned just like participants of other wars. The party's anti-pension stand drove some of its members away, and the national association endorsed Democrat Winfield Scott Hancock for president in 1880 because of the Republicans' refusal to support the pension. Ironically, endorsing a presidential candidate contradicted NAVMW's intended goal of non-partisanship.[7]

Several pension bills faltered in Congress over the years. One passed the House in the early 1880s, but when it arrived in the Senate, Republicans loaded it with so many amendments it was unacceptable. The Tennessee General Assembly passed a resolution calling on Congress to pass the amendment-laden version, but that stirred the emotions of Tennessee veterans who viewed the bill as an insult to those who gave Tennessee the name "The Volunteer State." It dishonors "the brave Pillow, Campbell, Haskell and others." Numerous members of the Tennessee Association of Mexican War Veterans signed an open letter that was published in a Nashville newspaper protesting the bill in its current corrupted state.[8]

Meanwhile, soon after NAVMW was formed, some members of the organization tried to focus attention on the Americans who had died in the conflict and were buried in obscure graves in Mexico. That sentiment led a veteran named A. G. Carothers to travel to Monterrey in 1875 to visit the burial sites of soldiers who died in that battle. North of the city, numerous Americans killed in that battle had been buried at Walnut Spring, the camp site of Zachary Taylor's army in September 1846. The site had become a makeshift American cemetery. An unknown number of Tennesseans were buried there, but with certainty, it was the resting place of Joseph Burkitt, who had been wounded in the charge on Fort Tenería and was carried back to camp by his brother James. Those buried had been carefully identified with stone markers before Taylor's army moved on, but the land was never purchased by the United States. After the war, the Mexican owner sold the headstones and plowed the cemetery to grow corn. When Carothers visited three decades later and discovered how the graves had been desecrated, he petitioned the War Department to purchase the field and erect a monument to memorialize the sacrifices made by American soldiers at that location. No action was taken.[9]

One way that the national and state veterans' organizations stayed active and kept Mexican War issues before the public was by holding periodic reunions. The national association met periodically, and it choose Nashville for its 1882 meeting location. The three-day event began on September 13, and between four hundred and five hundred veterans attended, not counting family members. Tennessee's state association hosted the reunion and raised money to pay expenses. A week before registrants began to arrive, *The Daily American* newspaper published a story about Thomas Claiborne's fund-raising efforts and his need for an additional $350 to cover entertainment expenses.[10]

Veterans from across the country traveled to Nashville for the reunion, and as they arrived they were given badges to distinguish them from others in the hotels and on the streets. Various artifacts from the war were on display at reunion headquarters on College Street, including a Mexican escopeta and the piece of coral that Henry Hart had taken from San Juan de Ullua in the Veracruz harbor. For veterans of the

Bloody First, the most memorable event came on September 13, the opening day of the reunion. Although not a part of the general program, locals had arranged for members of the First Tennessee to gather at 4:00 p.m. and march together to the old Nashville Female Academy grounds, where the regiment had participated in a ceremony and flag presentation in 1846. On that occasion, academy president Dr. C. D. Elliott had spoken to the young men as they prepared to go to war. On this occasion, thirty-six years later, Elliott was again there, and he spoke to the aging veterans, but not so much about Mexico, rather more about the effects of the more recent sectional conflict, "the late war" as it was often called in the nineteenth century. He spoke of his desire to see the Southern states restored to a status of equality with the Northern states, and then he talked about what he really hoped would be the lasting impact of such reunions. He hoped that they would help bring healing to a nation still struggling to reconstruct itself after the bloody Civil War, and indeed, what better way to foster reconciliation than to bring Northerners and Southerners together to reminiscence about a time when they fought together under the same flag. While the North's victory had reunified the country politically, there had not yet been emotional reconciliation between North and South. Elliott's desire was that such reunions might be "instrumental in bringing about a more perfect union in sentiment between the States."[11]

Others also spoke. John H. Savage, a congressman from Dekalb County, Tennessee, had fought in the war's latter stages. In 1847, he had received a commission in the Fourteenth United States Infantry, arriving in time to participate in the final battles around Mexico City. He was also a colonel in the Sixteenth Tennessee Infantry in the Confederate army, and was twice wounded (Perryville and Stones River) before resigning his commission out of frustration over not being promoted. Addressing the crowd after Elliott's opening speech, Savage said that he had grown to hate war. He said that he did not wish those present to interpret his comments as denigrating to "the glory of conquest," but he nevertheless asked all present to pray for the end of war. The audience responded with loud applause. Frank Cheatham then spoke briefly, a band played Dixie and the group disbanded.[12]

September 14 was the first full day of reunion activities. At 9:00 a.m., all the veterans formed behind a band and marched in unison to the capital building, then inside to the house chamber, where a crowd of spectators filled the galleries. On the walls hung portraits of Polk, Campbell, Pillow, Haskell, and Trousdale, and between columns were the words Monterrey, Veracruz, Cerro Gordo, Chapultepec, and other famous battles of the war. As president of the Tennessee Association of Mexican War Veterans, Thomas Claiborne's duty was to begin the day's events with a welcome address. When he rose to speak, he stood behind a podium draped with the flags of the various Tennessee regiments. "God bless you; we are glad to see you; our hearts are open to receive you; make yourselves at home," he began. When he went on to chastise members of Congress "who know how to squander the public Treasury" but who have "not yet pensioned the old veterans of the Mexican war," the hall erupted with applause. Continuing his talk, Claiborne guided his listeners in a "retrospective glance" back to Mexico where he saw "the mystic form of Gen. Scott, . . . [and] the grim old warrior, Gen. Taylor." His speech also carried a tone of reconciliation when he mentioned "our beloved Colonel, Wm. B. Campbell," who had died fifteen years earlier, but who had remained fiercely loyal to the Union. He closed his address with a reference to "our glorious country and its flag," and with his wish that Mexican War veterans always "be held in reverence and honor by every true-hearted son of America as long as one remains ready to die for his country."

Among the speakers that day was Nashvillian Andrew J. Caldwell, a congressional candidate whose talk no doubt struck a positive nerve with his audience. "Our late civil war, which made a continent a battle-field, has dwarfed, by its tremendous strategy and terrible battles, all preceding history"—a common lament that resonated with the crowd. The Civil War, he continued, "has laid under the smouldering ashes of sectional hate a coal of distraction and disdain for the services of the gallant men who bore the American eagle to unbroken victory. . . . You, veterans of Mexico, enabled the young Hercules . . . to bestride the continent like a Colossus." Caldwell's point was to cajole the federal government into action on the pension issue, but the meaning of his statement was greater than that. The Mexican War had brought a continent together while the Civil War had torn it apart.

Another speaker on the fourteenth was William B. Bate, a veteran of Mexico who went on to be elected to the Tennessee House of Representatives before serving as a general in the Confederate army. He too was running for office and so garnered political benefit from speaking at the event. The following year, he would be elected governor of the state and after two terms (1883–1887) he served the remaining eighteen years of his life as senator (1887–1905), dying of pneumonia a few days after attending Theodore Roosevelt's inauguration. In his speech, Bate cited great Mexican War battles and compared America's spread across the continent to the victories of Alexander the Great, Hannibal, and Napoleon. Making such a lofty comparison probably indicates that after almost four decades Mexican War veterans still wanted respect for their accomplishments. It is also interesting and perhaps telling that this Civil War general did not compare battles in Mexico to Gettysburg, Shiloh, or any other battle of the war that had obscured 1846–1847 in a giant shadow. Bate only mentioned the Civil War once, and that was when he lamented the fact that Revolutionary War, War of 1812, and Civil War veterans all received service pensions but not veterans of Mexico. "We honor our country for her liberality to the soldiers of her wars," he said, and with the country paying a hundred million a year in veteran pensions, it is time to give the few thousand remaining Mexican War veterans, who are old and needy, a pension also. The house chamber erupted in enthusiastic applause.

One other time in his speech, Bate alluded to the Civil War but did not mention that conflict by name, and that was when he articulated, perhaps better than anyone else, the conciliatory value of Mexican War memory. There is "a broad and enlarged patriotism in the brotherhood of the surviving soldiers of the Mexican war. This brotherhood had no partisan feeling, no sectional hate. Its spirit is abroad with healing and binding sentiments." A pension and post–Civil War reconciliation were the two dominant themes in the various speeches on September 14. One historian asserted that the national Mexican War veterans reunions were a force for unity because they brought Northerners and Southerners together in celebration of a common cause. Over the years, NAVMW met in cities like Norfolk, Virginia, Columbus, Ohio, and Indianapolis, Indiana; thus the effort to keep Mexican War memory alive continued.[13]

After the morning speeches, an entourage went to Polk Place two blocks from the capitol to pay respects to Sarah Polk. The seventy-nine-year-old former first lady had been, in 1882, widowed for thirty-three years. Although she had relatives fighting for the Confederacy, her home had been protected as neutral turf during the Union occupation of the city, and during the Civil War she had received several visits from Union generals. On this day, Sarah greeted her visitors dressed in black and wearing a likeness of her husband around her neck, her daily attire for the forty-two years she lived following James's death.[14]

The reunion turned festive in the afternoon when the crowd traveled a short distance southwest of town to the Belle Meade Plantation for a barbecue. The original itinerary called for a banquet at the Maxwell House Hotel, but it could not accommodate the number of attendees who came to the reunion. Belle Meade, an opulent Greek Revival mansion, was a 1,200-acre estate built by John Harding, which, after the Civil War and at the time of the reunion, had become one of the world's premier breeding farms for thoroughbred race horses. The setting was (and remains today) beautiful, and the hospitality of the Harding family was impeccable. One source indicated that a thousand people attended the barbecue, a number that included not only veterans but also accompanying family members. Attendees enjoyed a free lemonade and cigar stand, but the most popular station at the event appears to have been the champagne bar. The large crowd consumed plenty of barbecue and imbibed in liberal amounts of champagne.[15]

On the following day, the fifteenth, 2,500 veterans, family, and other visitors gathered at the Nashville Fair Grounds, where the itinerary called for a military demonstration by the Porter Rifles and the Burns Tennessee Light Artillery, and following that a bicycle race. Then, in mid-afternoon, most of the veterans left the Fair Grounds and made their way to the nearby Melrose Estate, home of Cynthia Pillow Brown. She was the sister of Gideon Pillow but more importantly she was the widow of Aaron V. Brown, who had been governor of Tennessee in 1846 when the call for volunteers went out. Cynthia had invited the veterans to a reception at her home where she and her daughter, Narcissa, were exquisite hosts, serving every imaginable "delicacy." There, William Bate, ever the politician, spoke again as did other dignitaries.[16] After renewing old friendships and reliving past glory, the three-day event ended and the attendees departed.

The care for ageing veterans remained an active issue and was, no doubt, buoyed by the reunion, and thanks to the work of men like William B. Walton, the public was not allowed to forget veterans. Walton was active in the Tennessee Mexican War Veterans Association through the turn of the twentieth century, serving in leadership posts including president of the organization. He was from a prominent family in the town of Carthage in Smith County, where Company H of the Bloody First had been raised. Walton had been the principle organizer and financier of the company, and fittingly enough, the men then elected him as their captain and company commander. He was one of the men, along with Henry Hart, who had ventured out to the fortress of San Juan de Ullua in the harbor at Veracruz and brought back a chunk of coral as a souvenir. After Mexico, William married Emily Donelson Brodie, a member of the famous Donelson clan of Nashville. In 1863, they moved to the capital city (moving to the Union-occupied city in the middle of the Civil War is a curiosity indeed), and in 1870 the family moved to a beautiful estate called Glen Echo just northeast of Nashville.[17]

A surviving Minute Book kept by Walton indicates that local veterans met in Nashville regularly through much of the 1880s, with the typical attendance ranging from ten to fifteen. Burrill G. Wood was president of the state association for much of the decade, and the small but consistent gathering usually took place in his office on Front Street next to the Cumberland River. In 1884, the group selected Narcissa Pillow Brown Saunders to go to the national veterans reunion in St. Louis as the state's official representative. The following year, Walton drafted, and the state association endorsed, a petition to the state's general assembly requesting "relief funds for 'unfortunate and destitute veterans.'" Apparently Mexican War veterans increasingly felt the pinch of financial hardship as they grew older, because also in 1885 Walton endorsed the idea to convert Andrew Jackson's Hermitage into a home for disabled veterans. Gallatin Senator J. W. Blackmore had submitted the proposal to the state legislature, and others, like Chattanooga Senator H. B. Case, supported it.[18]

Their mutual support of the Hermitage plan prompted an exchange of letters between Walton and Case with one from the latter that focused on a reconciliation theme. In addition to reiterating his support for the proposal, Case went a step further, stating that the Hermitage should be used "for all destitute Mexican War Veterans first," only opening its doors for veterans of other wars later. Case continued, stating that Mexican War veterans who also fought for the Confederacy should not be discriminated against in matters related to old-age care, and withholding assistance to such men was wrong. The "late war" was a mistake, Case wrote, but many people did not realize it at the time. Are we not all Americans? "Let us lay aside this bitterness—we are but brothers that were estranged but now are reconciled." The country should take care of its "destitute ex soldiers without regard to how they manifested American valor," thought Case.[19] The state senate adopted the Hermitage resolution but nothing came of it.

A faithful handful of Tennessee's old Mexican War boys continued to meet as, for instance, when they came together in August and September 1885 to discuss the upcoming national reunion in Indianapolis and to secure special railroad rates for Tennesseans who planned to attend. But more could be counted on to turn out for important events. When Frank Cheatham died in 1886, this prominent Nashvillian and renowned Confederate general was fondly remembered by his old Mexican War comrades. Thousands of citizens turned out at the First Presbyterian Church downtown for what was the largest funeral in Nashville to date, and mourners included Governor William Bate and George Maney, two of his closest Civil War compatriots but whose service alongside ole Frank went all the way back to Mexico. At least twenty veterans of the Bloody First attended as a group, and they carried with them the blue eagle flag of the First Tennessee.[20]

The persistence of the pension advocates finally paid off in 1887. In January of that year, Congress approved a service pension for Mexican

War veterans and their widows. Eligible applicants received $8 a month until the turn of the century when the amount was increased to $12 then $20 a month. Out of seventy-five thousand volunteers who enlisted nationwide to fight in Mexico, there were probably no more than six thousand veterans still alive in the 1880s. Soon after the pension bill passed, the president of the Tennessee Veterans Association, Burrill Wood, estimated that there were forty-four living Mexican War veterans in Davidson County and perhaps three hundred statewide.[21] Most of those eligible applied within three years, but applications were accepted until the 1920s.

In October 1887, the president who signed the pension bill into law, Grover Cleveland, visited Nashville during a good-will tour, and a contingent of Mexican War veterans gathered on the seventeenth to meet him. Cleveland visited Sarah Polk at Polk Place and later went to the state capitol to meet with Governor Robert L. Taylor. According to prearranged plans, thirty-three veterans met at the equestrian statue of Andrew Jackson on the capitol grounds to wait for the president and governor to conclude their meeting inside. At the appointed time, Cleveland exited onto the grounds and each of the thirty-three men shook his hand after being introduced individually. While a majority of the group consisted of members of the First Tennessee, other units and states were represented. Three members of the Tennessee Mounted Regiment were on hand as were three from the Third Tennessee. In addition, there were five members of regular army units present, a veteran of the United States Navy, and representatives from volunteer units from the following states: Alabama, Illinois, Kentucky, Mississippi, North Carolina, Ohio, Pennsylvania, and Texas. The regimental flag of the Second Tennessee was also on display at the event; presumably brought by the lone member of that regiment to attend.[22]

Several months later, on the afternoon of March 28, 1888, a newspaper reporter went to President Burrill Wood's office on Front Street adjacent to the river in downtown Nashville. When he entered the office, he found three gray-haired men engaged in lively and animated conversation, but they stopped and looked up as the reporter entered. He noted that their eyes were intense; "their faces were flushed and their gestures were full of expression." One of them spoke up: "We were talking about Vera Cruz," said Henry Hart a veteran of the Bloody First. The three men, Wood, Hart, and B. F. Harrison, were talking about the surrender of Veracruz, which had occurred forty-one years ago that month. Their tone was not boastful, remembered the reporter, but "cheery and glowing . . . as comes a natural compensation from memory to heroes who have won more than they have received." Hart had been "telling the 'boys'" the story about when he and William Walton got permission from Colonel Campbell to go to the fortress of San Juan de Ullua in the harbor "to secure a relic" and came back with two large pieces of coral. They got the largest pieces that they could comfortably handle and carried them for the remainder of their service, then back to Tennessee. Hart bragged that he still had his piece of coral at his house, and he speculated that Walton, who still lived at Glen Echo a few miles away, had his also. The reporter was there to do a story on the capture of Veracruz and on the dwindling number of Mexican War survivors.[23] In 1888, the veterans had recently won their battle for a pension, but they were still fighting old battles from Mexico, at least in stories. As illustrated by the meeting with a reporter, they still had their memory and they continued to try to shape the way their legacies would be remembered.

Passage of the Mexican War pension meant that the primary issue that had provided focus and purpose for thirteen years was gone. After 1887, memory, nostalgia, and fraternity collectively served as the primary reason for the existence of veterans organizations, and perhaps shaping memory was its most important function. The NAVMW tried to foster a positive memory of 1846–1848, and one of its means was stressing the unity and brotherhood that existed prior to the Civil War. This had been one of the tactics employed to argue for a pension and to assert the opinion that even Southern veterans of Mexico deserved it. The 1882 reunion in Nashville was an example of this conciliatory approach. However, historians are divided on the success of veterans organizations in shaping Mexican War memory. The tendency of the Civil War to overshadow what happened in Mexico was a source of frustration, and one of the goals of NAVMW was to elevate the memory of the earlier conflict, but, as one recent study indicates, doing so had an unintended consequence. Shining a brighter light on the Mexican War actually fostered a broader historical context for the Civil War, which caused many Americans to focus on the former conflict as a major cause for the latter. Remembering the war with Mexico meant remembering the antebellum years of slavery and sectionalism, as well as the divisiveness that resulted from territorial expansion. Remembering Mexico seems to have had a greater unifying effect among those who fought there than within the general population, but even among veterans, Southerners tended to view the war more favorably than did Northerners. This is perhaps owing to the fact that Southern veterans were more interested in being viewed as worthy of a pension.[24]

Regardless of the rest of the country, Tennesseans remembered their volunteers favorably. Fifty years after the First Tennessee's return from Mexico and thirty years after Campbell's death, *The Nashville American* newspaper did a retrospective look at the regiment and its commander. "No officer in the American army in the Mexican war enjoyed in a higher degree the respect and confidence of his associates than Col. Campbell. The memory of the Bloody First and its gallant commander will always be honored by the people of Tennessee." After fifty years, the article held firmly to the state's claim that Tennesseans were the first to reach Fort Tenería on the Monterrey battlefield, and it went on to assert that in no other war have Tennesseans done more to honor the state. Such sentiments echo what a Campbell relative wrote in a biographical sketch of the colonel. "Perhaps no charge in the history of American wars has contributed so much to render the gallantry of Tennessee's citizen soldiery illustrious as that which was led by Col. Campbell at Monterey."[25]

These were lofty accolades, which certainly reflected with accuracy the way some people remembered a war that most people had forgotten. Such praise provided great satisfaction for those who chose to remember. William Walton was one of them, and he hoped that others would also choose to remember. He had carefully recorded the monthly meetings of Nashville veterans in his Minute Book until 1888, when such entries ceased. The Tennessee Association of Mexican War Veterans appears to have become less active after the pension bill passed in 1887, but one might expect as much since that was the primary reason why such organizations had been established fifteen years earlier. It did not, however, cease to exist, and Walton continued to be an active member. For example, as association president, he helped plan a reception for the First Tennessee Infantry when it returned from the Philippines in 1899. Also, he still had the names of all of his old Company H comrades and continued to correspond with them over the years. As time passed, he tried to keep up with those who died and he made a note of each death in his Minute Book.[26]

Late in life, Walton tried to reach out to members of other First Tennessee companies in order to collect accurate lists of all of their members. As he accumulated company rosters, he copied them in the back of his Minute Book in an effort to compile a list of all those who joined the Bloody First in 1846. In 1906, at the age of eighty-two, Walton wrote to Moscow Carter, a fellow veteran who had been a member of Company B. Following the war with Mexico, Carter had served as lieutenant colonel in the Twentieth Tennessee in the Confederate army. He had been captured at the Battle of Mills Spring in January 1862, and several months later had been paroled and sent home to Franklin, Tennessee. He was faithful to his parole and remained a noncombatant even as the 1864 Battle of Franklin swirled around his family's house. He did not even venture out of the safety of his home's basement until after the battle ended, and then only to retrieve his mortally wounded brother Todd, whose body lay on the family estate.

Walton's 1906 letter asked if Carter still had a roster of his old Mexican War company. The ninety-one-year-old Carter responded with apologies that he no longer had any company rosters, for they had been "carried off by the Yankees when pillaging my house" during the Civil War. Reminiscing with his correspondent, Carter speculated that he was the only surviving member of Company B; they were all dead, he informed his old friend. He continued his letter in a light-hearted manner, bragging that he was still able to work in his garden and was in no hurry to go and meet his old comrades in arms. Then, expressing the kind of tranquility that had evaded other Mexican War veterans, Carter concluded that he had "lived a model life, my sleep is sweet and refreshing—so much for a clear conscience." He lived in peace until 1913.[27]

# EPILOGUE:
# FINAL DISPOSITIONS

The war ended 170 years ago, and memory of the conflict had lain dormant for decades until recently. Skeletons from the past have brought to the forefront the memory of the Mexican-American conflict—at least for Tennesseans. Two issues from the 1840s have figuratively, perhaps one could even say literally, risen from the grave to take Tennesseans back to a near-forgotten time. Those issues pertain to the final resting place for several men who were participants in the conflict. The Merriam-Webster Dictionary defines "disposition" as a final arrangement or settlement or the transfer of care to another, and all of these meanings are appropriate for a final word regarding these two war-related topics. One issue appertains to the skeletal remains mentioned in the Prologue that were discovered in Monterrey, Nuevo León, Mexico in recent years. They are believed to be U.S. casualties of the battle fought there in September 1846. The other issue relates to the little-known proposal to remove James and Sarah Polk's remains from Nashville and take them to Polk's hometown of Columbia, Tennessee. First, a summary of the "Monterrey Remains Project."

Periodically during the first dozen years of the twenty-first century, construction projects in Monterrey, Mexico, uncovered human skeletal remains. The burial sites were unmarked, but as time passed, the number of graves grew as did the total number of bones. Each time, the construction halted as Mexican anthropologists and archeologists conducted a careful dig to preserve the remains. There was no clothing, it had turned to dust, and if wooden coffins were used, they too had deteriorated. All that remained, other than bones, were some coins and buttons. The coins were U.S. and the buttons were American military, items that quickly led to the conclusion that the remains were of United States soldiers who had died during the Battle of Monterrey. There was nothing else to identify the people or even the units to which the supposed soldiers belonged—just the logical supposition that they were U.S. soldiers.

Captain Jim Page was historian for the 101st Airborne Division at Fort Campbell near the Tennessee-Kentucky line, and when he heard of the discovery of the remains he took a special interest. He noted that the burial sites had been located near what was, in the mid-nineteenth century, the northeast corner of Monterrey, where a Mexican fort called Tenería had stood during the battle. The fort, of course, had been captured by the First Tennessee and the First Mississippi volunteer regiments on September 21, 1846. Other units fought in that vicinity, including Marylanders and members of the First, Third, and Fourth U.S. Infantry Regiments, but more members of the First Tennessee died in taking Fort Tenería than from any other unit. While the artifacts found with the bones had led to the conclusion that they were American soldiers, the location of the burial sites led Page, and others, to speculate that some of the remains might belong to Tennessee volunteers. Regardless of the fact that no one knew to whom the remains belonged, Page's overriding concern was that American soldiers found in unmarked graves needed to be brought home. And he was, no doubt, buoyed by the fact that his base, Fort Campbell, had been named for William Campbell, the colonel of the First Tennessee. So, he began a campaign to bring back the remains by contacting members of Congress and the appropriate offices in the Department of Defense like, for instance, the POW/MIA Accounting Agency. Meanwhile, he sought to raise public awareness, especially in Tennessee, by sharing what he knew at a variety of civic and history organizations. It was the author's chance attendance at one of his presentations that sparked an interest in the topic, and that spark grew into a desire to tell the story of the Tennessee volunteers in Mexico. Research for this book ran on a parallel course with the effort to repatriate the skeletal remains.

Over time, as the story of the bones circulated, others became involved in the effort to bring them home. John O'Brien of the Pratt Museum at Fort Campbell, Fred Prouty at the Tennessee Wars Commission, Patrick McIntyre at the Tennessee Historical Commission, Derek Frisby, a historian at Middle Tennessee State University, and Tennessee State Representative Steve McDaniel all took an early interest in the project. So did Hugh Berryman, a forensic anthropologist and Director of the Forensic Institute for Research and Education at MTSU, who saw the potential of what could be learned from studying the bones. Berryman's extensive connections within the government and the military proved to be a significant asset in pushing the project forward. Tennessee's congressional delegation also got involved, especially Congresswoman Diane Black, and several years of negotiations began to pay off. Unfortunately, Captain Page passed away unexpectedly in 2013, before the mission he put in motion was completed. However, by that time, enough people had taken an interest in the project that it did not die with the captain, and gradual but consistent prodding and pressure finally bore fruit.

A hundred and seventy years to the month after they died, the remains returned to U.S. soil in September 2016. The author was privileged to be with a contingent of Tennesseans who welcomed the soldiers home at Dover Air Force Base in Delaware, where the military mortuary is located. In a ceremony called a "Dignified Transfer," the remains received all the honors befitting fallen warriors. At the writing of this Epilogue in 2018, the bones are still held at Dover pending an ongoing effort to identify the individuals. In a unique collaborative effort, military officials granted permission to Berryman and his team of forensic scientists to study the bones in an effort to glean whatever can be learned about the circumstances surrounding each subject's death. Meanwhile, the two historians on the project, Frisby and the author, assist with historical research. Through genealogy analysis, done primarily by Frisby, the goal is to identify living maternal descendants of the twenty-one

Tennesseans known to have been killed and buried at Monterrey in order to facilitate DNA testing. As this book goes to press, the process continues, but hope remains that the bones still contain enough clues to yield their identity.

The issue regarding the Polk burial site is even more recent. The eleventh president left detailed instructions regarding his final wishes. He wanted to be buried at Polk Place in Nashville in a manner reminiscent of Andrew Jackson, who is buried at the Hermitage, and George Washington at Mt. Vernon. However, Polk died during a cholera epidemic and as stipulated by city ordinance, Sarah had him buried within twenty-four hours in the city cemetery outside of town. A year later, after fear of the spread of the disease had subsided, Sarah had his body exhumed and reburied at Polk Place in keeping with his wishes. In 1891, Sarah was laid to rest beside him. According to Polk's will, the house was to go to the state of Tennessee with the governor appointing a deserving family member to live in the house as a caretaker. Numerous relatives came forward seeking to live in the house, and the subsequent property dispute led to a lawsuit and a judge declaring the will null and void. Ultimately, the Polks were moved to the state capitol grounds two blocks away, and a developer purchased Polk Place, tore it down in 1901, and built apartments in its place. Because of this, the only extant home that James K. Polk ever lived in, other than the White House, is in his hometown of Columbia.

The Polk Home, where James lived as a young man, is owned by the James K. Polk Memorial Association, a nonprofit organization that runs the historic site. The Polk Home in Columbia has interpreted Polk's legacy since 1929. Many of the furnishings that were at Polk Place in Nashville are preserved at this site. In recent years, private citizens, along with members of the Polk Memorial Association, started a campaign to move the Polks' tomb to the Columbia property. The impetus of the reinterment movement stemmed primarily from two arguments. One is that the president ultimately did not get what he requested as a final resting place and the Polk Home in Columbia would more closely resemble where he wished to be buried. The other contention is that the current location of the tomb is not prominently located, which offers limited opportunities to interpret the story of Polk's presidency to a broad audience. The story, like the tomb, gets lost. An equestrian statue of Andrew Jackson as well as a statue of World War I hero Alvin C. York enjoy greater visibility than the Polk tomb. So, like Polk's war, which was obscured by a larger conflict, Polk's tomb has been overshadowed by other more prominent memorials to famous Tennesseans.

Moving the remains of a former president and first lady is not an easy undertaking. Historic preservationists and others in the Nashville community make their own compelling case for leaving the burial site alone. They contend that moving Polk to Columbia would create a false sense of history since he did not live there after he rose to national prominence. And moving him to Columbia would simply be taking him to yet another location that he did not specify. Besides, Polk's current resting place provides the nation's only example of a president buried on the grounds of a state capitol, making it a truly unique location. In addition, moving the tomb would be expensive, and the money would have to be raised through private donations.

The controversy generated by the project has not deterred the Association or other supporters. A proposal to move the Polks was introduced in the Tennessee General Assembly in 2017, and it passed the Senate but not the House. In 2018 supporters again introduced the proposal. It too failed, but in a surprise move was reintroduced a month later (April) when it passed by a slim margin. However, even with a nod from the state legislature, the undertaking will not proceed without approval from other entities, including the Tennessee Historical Commission, Capitol Commission, and Chancery Court. So, at the time of this writing, Polk's fate remains unclear, but the debate continues.

Thus, the final chapter of Tennessee's Mexican War legacy is yet to be written. The story, long thought to be dead, continues to live through the bones of the deceased.

# NOTES

PROLOGUE

1.  Christopher D. Dishman, *A Perfect Gibraltar: The Battle for Monterrey, Mexico, 1846* (Norman: University of Oklahoma Press, 2010); Richard Bruce Winders, *Panting for Glory: The Mississippi Rifles in the Mexican War* (College Station: Texas A&M University Press, 2016); Randy W. Hackenburg, *Pennsylvania in the War with Mexico* (Shippensburg, PA: White Mane Publishing Company, 1992); Robert E. Corlew, *Tennessee: A Short History* (Knoxville: University of Tennessee Press, 1981); Paul H. Bergeron, Stephen V. Ash, and Jeanette Keith, *Tennesseans and Their History* (Knoxville: University of Tennessee Press, 1999); *Nashville Daily American*, September 15, 1882.

2.  William Dusinberre effectively argues that land and slave property were strong incentives for Polk's expansionist policies. William Dusinberre, *Slavemaster President: The Double Career of James Polk* (New York: Oxford University Press, 2003) (especially chapter 11); Jonathan Atkins, *Parties, Politics and the Sectional Conflict in Tennessee, 1832–1861* (Knoxville: University of Tennessee Press, 1997), 7–8.

3.  Atkins, *Parties, Politics*, 8–10.

4.  Amy S. Greenberg, *Manifest Manhood, and the Antebellum American Empire* (New York: Cambridge University Press, 2005), 9. Greenberg's compelling study argues that during the period of Manifest Destiny, there were two "preeminent and dueling" types of masculinity: restrained manhood, which was more disciplined, moral, and inclined toward the Whig Party, and martial manhood, which placed greater value on physical dominance, aggression, and violence, and tended toward those who were Democrats. See 11–12 for discussion.

5.  Bertram Wyatt-Brown, *Southern Honor: Ethics and Behavior in the Old South* (New York: Oxford University Press, 1982), vii, 14.

6.  Winders, *Panting for Glory*, ix–x.

7.  Quoted in Tom Kanon, *Tennesseans at War, 1812–1815: Andrew Jackson,*

the *Creek War, and the Battle of New Orleans* (Tuscaloosa: University of Alabama Press, 2014), 25.

8. Cave Johnson to William B. Campbell, June 27, 1846, Campbell Papers, Duke.

9. Kanon, *Tennesseans at War*, 26; McClanahan to Sarah McClanahan, October 25, 1846, McClanahan and Taylor Papers; *The National Union*, May 26, 1847; Adolphus Heiman, "Concise Description of the Services on the First Regiment of Tennessee Volunteers" (unpublished), 1.

10. McClanahan to Sarah McClanahan (sister), September 14, 1846, McClanahan and Taylor Family Papers; Wyatt-Brown, *Southern Honor*, 4.

11. Kanon, *Tennesseans at War*, 1–3.

12. James M. McCaffrey, *Army of Manifest Destiny: The American Soldier in the Mexican War 1846–1848* (New York: New York University Press, 2002), 31.

13. Tallying the names on Cox's rosters in *Foot Volunteers* (Brent A. Cox, *Foot Volunteers: Tennesseans in the Mexican-American War 1845–1848* [Sons of the South Publications, 1986]), one arrives at a total of 5,483 volunteers from Tennessee; Gentry R. McGee, *A History of Tennessee from 1663 to 1930* (Nashville, TN: Charles Elder, 1930), 167–68; W. J. Cash, *The Mind of the South* (New York: Knopf, 1941), 46. Eighty-two years later, when the state's last known Mexican War veteran died, the newspaper account of his death praised him for, among other things, the fact that he "avenged the Alamo." *Sumner County News*, January 19, 1928.

14. Paul H. Bergeron, *Antebellum Politics in Tennessee* (Lexington: The University Press of Kentucky, 1982); Atkins, *Parties, Politics*.

15. Tom Chaffin, *Met His Every Goal? James K. Polk and the Legends of Manifest Destiny* (Knoxville: University of Tennessee Press, 2014), 24, 45–46; Both quotations in the paragraph found in Robert W. Merry, *A Country of Vast Designs: James K. Polk, the Mexican War and the Conquest of the American Continent* (New York: Simon & Schuster, Inc., 2009), 471–72.

16. B. H. Gilley, "Tennessee Whigs and the Mexican War," *Tennessee Historical Quarterly* 40 (Spring 1981): 46; quotation in Randal W. McGavock, *Pen and Sword: The Life and Journals of Randal W. McGavock*, eds. Jack Allen and Hershel Gower (Nashville: Tennessee Historical Commission, 1959), 48.

17. Robert Remini, *Andrew Jackson and the Course of American Democracy, 1833–1845* (New York: Harper & Row Publishers, 1984), 352–55.

18. John Hoyt Williams, *Sam Houston: A Biography of the Father of Texas* (New York: Simon & Schuster, 1993), 116; Gregg Cantrell, *Stephen F. Austin: Empresario of Texas* (New Haven, CT: Yale University Press, 1999), 199, 232–33; Elijah Embree Hoss and William B. Reese, *History of Nashville, Tenn* (Nashville, TN: Publishing House of the Methodist Episcopal Church, 1890), 170; the most comprehensive collection of documents related to the Texas Association is Malcolm McLean, ed., *Papers Concerning Robertson's Colony in Texas*, 19 vols. (Arlington: University of Texas at Arlington Press), 1974–93 ; Crockett quotations found in James Wakefield Burke, *David Crockett, The Man Behind the Myth* (Austin, TX: Eakin Press, 1984), 195, and Robert Morgan, *Lions of the West: Heroes and Villains of the Westward Expansion* (Chapel Hill, NC: Algonquin Books, 2011), 139; Mary French Caldwell, *Tennessee: The Dangerous Example* (Nashville, TN: Aurora Publishers, 1974), 319–20; Robert Bruce Winders, *Crisis in the Southwest: The United States, Mexico, and the Struggle over Texas* (Wilmington, DE: Scholarly Resources, Inc., 2002), 33.

19. Joel H. Silbey, *Storm Over Texas: The Annexation Controversy and the Road to Civil War* (New York: Oxford University Press, 2005), 13–14. The article, "Tennessee, Mother State of Texas: The Montgomery County Texas Connection," by Robin Montgomery appeared in *The Courier of Montgomery County* in 2014, and has since been republished in Robin Montgomery, *Transformation of the Miracle City: A History of Conroe and Montgomery County as Told Through Selected Columns of Robin Montgomery, as They Appeared in the The Courier of Montgomery County* (San Antonio, TX: Historical Publishing Network, 2014), 161–62.


CHAPTER ONE  *Background: Politics and Texas*

1. Atkins, *Parties, Politics,* 2.
2. Ibid., 1; Corlew, *Tennessee,* 178–79.
3. Thomas M. Leonard, *James K. Polk: A Clear and Unquestionable Destiny* (Wilmington, DE: Scholarly Resources, Inc., 2001), 21–22; Robert E. Corlew, Stanley J. Folmsbee, and Enoch L. Mitchell, *History of Tennessee,* vol. 1 (New York: Lewis Historical Publishing Company, Inc., 1960), 314; Atkins, *Parties, Politics,* 34; Jonathan Atkins, "Politicians, Parties,

and Slavery: The Second Party System and the Decision for Disunion in Tennessee," in *Tennessee History: The Land, the People, and the Culture,* ed. Carroll Van West (Knoxville: University of Tennessee Press, 1998), 129. For Jackson's use of the veto, see Gerhard Peters, "Presidential Vetoes," in *The American Presidency Project,* ed. John T. Woolley and Gerhard Peters (Santa Barbara: University of California, 1999–2017). He was destined to use the veto power more often than all of his predecessors combined.

4. Remini, *Andrew Jackson,* 99–103.

5. Mark R. Cheathem, *Andrew Jackson: Southerner* (Baton Rouge: Louisiana State University Press, 2013), 168–69.

6. Atkins, "Politicians, Parties, and Slavery," 129; Phillip Langsdon, *Tennessee: A Political History* (Franklin, OH: Hillsboro Press, 2000), 86–90; Corlew, Folmsbee, and Mitchell, *Tennessee,* 1:309; Cheathem, *Andrew Jackson,* 168.

7. Quoted in Atkins, *Parties, Politics,* 2–3.

8. William Groneman, *David Crockett, Hero of the Common Man* (New York: Tom Doherty Associates, 2005), 90–97, 127–28; Charles Grier Sellers, *James K. Polk, Jacksonian 1795–1843* (Princeton, NJ: Princeton University Press, 1957), 123–26.

9. Corlew, Folmsbee, and Mitchell, *Tennessee,* 1:309–10; H. W. Brands, *Andrew Jackson: His Life and Times* (New York: Doubleday, 2005), 530.

10. Walter Durham, *Balie Peyton of Tennessee: Nineteenth Century Politics and Thoroughbreds* (Franklin, TN: Hillsboro Press, 2004), ix, 101.

11. Corlew, *Tennessee,* 184; Ibid., 20.

12. Langsdon, *Tennessee,* 89; Corlew, *Tennessee,* 183; Corlew, Folmsbee, and Mitchell, *Tennessee,* 1:315; Gilley, "Tennessee Whigs," 47; Atkins, *Parties, Politics,* 35; Bob Holladay, "Ideas Have Consequences: Whig Party Politics in Williamson County, Tennessee, and the Road to Disunion," *Tennessee Historical Quarterly* 63 (Fall 2004): 156; Cheathem, *Andrew Jackson,* 169.

13. Corlew, Folmsbee, and Mitchell, *Tennessee,* 1:319; Atkins, *Parties, Politics,* 39–53; Corlew, *Tennessee,* 189–90.

14. Atkins, *Parties, Politics,* 72–73.

15. Corlew, *Tennessee,* 195, 257; Atkins, "Politicians, Parties, and Slavery," 129.

16. Corlew, *Tennessee,* 257–58.

17. Bergeron, Ash, and Keith, *Tennesseans,* 101–2; Corlew, *Tennessee,* 195, 259. Even after the slavery issue began to break down the two-party system in

the 1850s, party competition continued in Tennessee. Atkins, "Politicians, Parties, and Slavery," 129.

18. Bergeron, Ash, and Keith, *Tennesseans*, 101; Corlew, *Tennessee*, 261.

19. David M. Pletcher, *Diplomacy of Annexation: Texas, Oregon, and the Mexican War* (Columbia: University of Missouri Press, 1973), 29, 56–57.

20. McLean, *Papers Concerning Robertson's Colony*, I:xlii–lvi.

21. Winders, *Crisis*, 34–39, 50–51.

22. Elijah Embree Hoss and William B. Reese, *History of Nashville, Tenn.* (Nashville: Publishing House of the Methodist Episcopal Church, 1890), 170. Atkins, *Parties, Politics*, 127, 128, 132; quotation found in Corlew, *Tennessee*, 268.

23. Pletcher, *Diplomacy of Annexation*, chapter 1, esp. 10, 30.

24. Durham, *Balie Peyton*, 95.

25. Atkins, *Parties, Politics*, 126.

26. Hoss and Reese, *History of Nashville*, 171.

27. Sam W. Haynes, *James K. Polk and the Expansionist Impulse* (New York: Longman, Inc., 2002), 59.

28. Ibid., 64–65, quotation on 65; Nathaniel Cheairs Hughes Jr. and Roy P. Stonesifer Jr., *The Life and Wars of Gideon J. Pillow* (Chapel Hill: University of North Carolina Press, 1993), 31–34.

29. Atkins, *Parties, Politics*, 132–33; Clay quotations found in Merrill D. Peterson, *The Great Triumvirate: Webster, Clay, and Calhoun* (New York: Oxford University Press, 1987), 360.

30. Peterson, *Great Triumvirate*, 361.

31. Haynes, *Polk*, 61; Atkins, *Parties, Politics*, 131; Lawrence Frederick, *The Politics of Individualism: Parties and the American Character in the Jacksonian Era* (New York: Oxford University Press, 1989), 133–34.

32. Bergeron, Ash, and Keith, *Tennesseans*, 101.

33. Ibid., 104; Atkins, *Parties, Politics*, 136; Durham, *Balie Peyton*, 100.

34. McGavock, *Pen and Sword*, 31; Atkins, *Parties, Politics*, 129; Allan Nevins, ed., *Polk: The Diary of a President, 1845–1849* (New York: Longmans, Green and Co., 1929), 8.

35. Durham, *Balie Peyton*, 96; Atkins, *Parties, Politics*, 138–39; Norma Lois Peterson, *The Presidencies of William Henry Harrison and John Tyler* (Lawrence: University Press of Kansas, 1989), 255–56.

36. Gilley, "Tennessee Whigs," 62.

37. Haynes, *Polk,* 122–26; quotation found on 140; Ibid., 48; Pletcher, *Diplomacy of Annexation,* 382–84; Kanon, *Tennesseans at War,* 30.

38. Gilley, "Tennessee Whigs," 46, 48–50, 67.

39. Lee to Mary Custis Lee, May 12, 1846, quoted in Richard McCaslin, *Lee in the Shadow of Washington* (Baton Rouge, LA: LSU Press, 2004), 51; Ulysses S. Grant, *Personal Memoirs of U.S. Grant* (Lincoln: University of Nebraska Press, 1996), 37.

40. Hoss and Reese, *History of Nashville,* 172; Gilley, "Tennessee Whigs," 48, 52.


CHAPTER TWO  *Tennessee Volunteers*

1.  *Lincoln Journal,* Dec. 11, 1845; John Blount Robertson, *Reminiscences of a Campaign in Mexico by a Member of "The Bloody First"* (Nashville, TN: John York and Co., Publishers, 1849), 58.

2.  Campbell speech, June 1847, Campbell Collection.

3.  Keating, *Memphis,* I:261; J. M. Keating, *History of the City of Memphis and Shelby County Tennessee* (Syracuse, NY: D. Mason & Company, Publishers, 1888). Quotation found in Robertson, *Reminiscences,* 58.

4.  Robertson, *Reminiscences,* 58; *Lincoln Journal,* May 21 and 28, 1846.

5.  *Lincoln Journal,* May 21, 1846; Hoss and Reese, *History of Nashville,* 172–73.

6.  Bobby Alford, "History of Lawrence County Tennessee." Lawrence County Archives (Leoma, TN), 59; Walter T. Durham, *Old Sumner: A History of Sumner County, Tennessee from 1805 to 1861* (Nashville, TN: Parthenon Press, 1972), 357; Jay Guy Cisco, *Historic Sumner County, Tennessee* (Nashville, TN: Jay Guy Cisco, 1909), 42, 46. Militia and volunteers were not the same. A 1792 act of Congress required every able-bodied white male between eighteen and forty-five to serve in the militia, which would serve as emergency military units to augment the army in times of crisis, like internal rebellions or invasions. Militia units were under state jurisdiction and regulation, and except under extreme circumstances they could not operate outside the borders of their home state. Volunteers, on the other hand, were called up by the War Department and they remained under federal authority. Richard Bruce Winders, *Mr. Polk's Army: The*

*American Military Experience in the Mexican War* (College Station: Texas A&M University Press, 1997), 67–68.

7. This story from the *Nashville Banner* is recounted in Kanon, *Tennesseans at War*, 1.

8. White to Bradley, May 24, 1846, Misc. Mexican War Papers.

9. Turner J. Fakes, "Memphis and the Mexican War," *West Tennessee Historical Society Papers* 11 (1948): 119–44.

10. Hoss and Reese, *History of Nashville*, 172–73; *Lincoln Journal*, May 21, 1846. In actual practice, the companies that organized to go to Mexico contained approximately ninety to 100 privates.

11. Hoss and Reese, *History of Nashville*, 172–75; *Lebanon Banner of Peace and Cumberland and Presbyterian Advocate*, May 22, 1846.

12. Corlew, *Tennessee*, 269; quotations found in Robertson, *Reminiscences*, 59–61, and George C. Furber, *The Twelve Months Volunteer: Journal of a Private, in the Tennessee Regiment of Cavalry, in the Campaign, in Mexico, 1846-7* (Cincinnati: U. P. James, 1857), 43, 45.

13. Fakes, "Memphis," 123–24. The six companies accepted from West Tennessee were as follows: Infantry—Memphis Rifle Guards, Shelby County; Gaines Guards, Shelby County; The Avengers, Madison County; The Tennessee Guards, Carroll County: Cavalry—Eagle Guards, Shelby County; Fayette Cavalry, Fayette County. The four infantry companies became part of the Second Tennessee Regiment and the two cavalry companies were part of the Tennessee Mounted Regiment.

14. Winders, *Mr. Polk's Army*, 82–85.

15. From an article printed in the *New Orleans Delta* and reprinted in the *Knoxville Tribune*, June 9, 1847.

16. *The National Union*, May 26, 1847; Corlew, *Tennessee*, 270.

17. *Lebanon Banner*, May 29, 1846.

18. This list is from Cox, *Foot Volunteers*, and was compiled from National Archives records. The county of origin for Company F is sometimes incorrectly given as Trousdale. That county, however, was named for Colonel William Trousdale of Sumner County, who had fought in the War of 1812 and the Seminole War in Florida prior to commanding the 14th Infantry of regulars in Mexico. Trousdale did not become a county until

1870, when it was broken off from Sumner and other adjoining counties. Durham, *Old Sumner*, 357.

19. Lowell Hagewood, "The Road to Fratricide: William Bowen Campbell and the Secessionist Crisis in Tennessee" (PhD diss., Middle Tennessee University, 1995), 33; Spencer Tucker, ed., *Encyclopedia of the Mexican-American War: Political, Social, and Military History*, 3 vols. (Santa Barbara: ABC-CLIO, 2013), I:114; William Campbell to Adolphus Heiman, June 4, 1846, THS Misc. Mss File; Carroll Van West, *The Tennessee Encyclopedia of History & Culture*. (Nashville: Rutledge Hill Press, 1998), 416–17.

20. Hagewood, "Road to Fratricide," 33, 59; William Campbell to David Campbell June 4, 1846; St. George L. Sioussant, ed., *Mexican War Letters of Col. William Bowen Campbell of Tennessee, Written to Governor David Campbell of Virginia, 1846–1847* (Granville, PA: Wert Bookbinding, 1989), 134. Pamphlet reprint from the Tennessee Historical Magazine, June 1913. Owing to a quirk of marriage, David Campbell was both the cousin and uncle of William.

21. W. Jerome D. Spence and David L. Spence, *A History of Hickman County Tennessee* (Nashville, TN: Gospel Advocate Publishing Co., 1900), 27, 31–32, 34, 55, 69.

22. Robertson, *Reminiscences*, 60.

23. Walter T. Durham, "Mexican War Letters to Wynnewood," *Tennessee Historical Quarterly* 33 (Winter 1974): 389–90; June 10, 2017, Kevin Smith, interview.

24. Cox, *Foot Soldiers*, 1.

25. *Daily American*, January 12, 1882.

26. Ibid.

27. Keating, *Memphis*, II: 67; R. A. Young, "Haskell," *Christian Advocate*, April 28, 1859; McClanahan quoted in Hughes and Stonesifer, *Pillow*, 71.

28. Fakes, "Memphis," 123.

29. Caswell to wife, June 14, 1846, Caswell Papers. There is a source indicating that General William Brazelton, the militia general in charge of organizing the East Tennessee companies, had a son named James, but the author cannot substantiate if this is him.

30. Cox, *Foot Soldiers*, 1.

31. William Campbell to David Campbell, June 4, 1846, Sioussant, ed., *Mexican War Letters*, 134.

32. Alford, "Lawrence County," 60–61; Robertson, *Reminiscences*, 64–65; *The Academist*, June 10, 1846. *The Academist* article indicates that Campbell's comments were "too inaudible . . . for but a few to hear."

33. Campbell Speech, June 1847, Campbell Collection; Robertson, *Reminiscences*, 65–66.

34. Robertson, *Reminiscences*, 68–69, quotation on 66; Hoss and Reese, *History of Nashville*, 175.

35. Fakes, "Memphis," 125; quotation found in Blackstone McDannel to Elizabeth McDannel, September 19, 1847, McDannel Family Papers. Blackstone McDannel was a civilian contractor who traveled to Mexico with a later volunteer unit from Tennessee. He provided supplies to the army and spent the final months of the war working out of Jalapa, Mexico.

36. Fakes, "Memphis," 121–22.

37. B. G. Ellis, *The Moving Appeal: Mr. McClanahan, Mrs. Dill, and the Civil War's Great Newspaper Run* (Macon, GA: Mercer University Press, 2003), 59.

38. Emma Inman Williams, *Historic Madison: The Story of Jackson and Madison County Tennessee* (Jackson, MI: Jackson Service League, 1972), 112–13; *West Tennessee Whig*, June 5, 1846.

39. Williams, *Historic Madison*, 112–13; John McClanahan to Sarah McClanahan, August 15, 1846, McClanahan and Taylor Family Papers. The author was unable to document a relationship between Wiley Hale and Caroline Haskell, but a lifelong Jackson resident, Charles Richards, who has been collecting material on William Haskell and the Second Tennessee for decades told the author (August 6, 2016) that it was known in the community that the two were destined to be married.

40. Zella Armstrong, *The History of Hamilton County and Chattanooga Tennessee*. Vol.1 (Johnson City: The Overmountain Press, 1931), 191, 375; The Chattanoogan.com, March 7, 2006; Fakes, "Memphis," 125. The Read House, which later passed to John Read's son Samuel, remained in business in downtown Chattanooga in 2017.

41. Fakes, "Memphis," 128–29; Francis Heitman, *Register and Dictionary of the United States Army*, vol. 1 (Baltimore, MD: Genealogical Publishing,

1994*)*, 516; *Tennesseans in the Civil War*. Vol. 1 (Nashville, TN: Civil War Centennial Commission, 1964), 188–90.

42. Pillow to Polk, January 22, 1846, quoted in Hughes and Stonesifer, *Pillow*, 41.

43. Hughes and Stonesifer, *Pillow*, 40–42; Walter R. Borneman, *Polk: The Man Who Transformed the Presidency and America* (New York: Random House, 2008),14; West, *Tennessee Encyclopedia*, 92.

44. Hughes and Stonesifer, *Pillow*, 42; Winders, *Mr. Polk's Army*, 73–79.

45. Carl R. Coe, "Politics and Assassination: The Story of General Levin Hudson Coe," *Tennessee Historical Quarterly* 54 (1995), 33–34; *Memphis Eagle*, July 11, 1846.

46. David Campbell to William Campbell, July 10, 1846, Campbell Papers, Duke. Chapter three of Winders, *Mr. Polk's Army* is particularly effective in demonstrating the political nature of officer election and appointment during the Mexican War.

47. William Campbell to David Campbell, June 4 and July 3, 1846; Sioussant, ed., *Mexican War Letters*, 134–35.

48. Pillow's reference to Caswell is from a July 19 letter quoted in Hughes and Stonesifer, *Pillow*, 42; Caswell to wife, July 21, 1846, Caswell Papers.

49. Hughes and Stonesifer, *Pillow*, 43; Caswell to wife, July 21 and August 7, 1846, Caswell Papers.


CHAPTER THREE  *From Tennessee to the Rio Grande*

1.  Robertson, *Reminiscences*, 70–71.

2.  Foster to mother, June 16, 1846, Foster-Woods Papers; William Campbell to David Campbell, June 14, 1846, Sioussant, ed., *Mexican War Letters*, 134–35; Robert B. Wynne to Alfred R. Wynne, June 14, 1846, Wynne Family Papers.

3.  Daniel King to Sarah King, July 1, 1846, King Letters; Robertson, *Reminiscences*, 72–75.

4.  Robertson, *Reminiscences*, 76–79; Nimrod D. Smith to Alfred R. Wynne, July 2, 1846, Wynne Family Papers; W. E. Blackburn to Henrietta Blackburn (wife), June 11, 1846, Blackburn Papers, Filson.

5. Justin H. Smith, *The War with Mexico* (New York: Houghton Mifflin, 1919), I:205, 227.

6. Nimrod D. Smith postscript in R. Bruce Wynne to Alfred R. Wynne, July 2 and 30, 1846, Wynne Family Papers; Blatti, ed., *Pickett's Journal*, p. 77.

7. McClellan, *Diary*, p. 36; Blatti, ed., *Pickett's Journal*, 76; Daniel King to Sarah King, July 1, 1846, King Letters; William Campbell to David Campbell, July 3, 1846, Sioussat, ed., *Mexican War Letters*, 135.

8. Robertson, *Reminiscences*, 81–82; Anonymous Diary, TSLA.

9. Hale to mother, July 26, 1846, Hale Papers; Robertson, *Reminiscences*, 82, 101–2.

10. William Campbell to David Campbell, July 11, 1846, Sioussat, ed., *Mexican War Letters*, 136; Robertson, *Reminiscences*, 87–90; Nimrod D. Smith to Col. Alfred R. Wynne, July 2, 1846, Wynne Family Papers; *Western Weekly Review*, August 14, 1846.

11. Bruce Wynne to father (Alfred), August 7, 1846, Wynne Family Papers.

12. R. B. Alexander to Francis Duffy, August 14, 1846, Duffy Papers.

13. Hoss and Reese, *History of Nashville*, 175; Anonymous Diary, TSLA; Alford, "Lawrence County," 62; Henry L. Burkitt, *A Concise History of the Kehukee Baptist Association* (Philadelphia, PA: Lippincott, Grambo and Co., 1850), 333, 335. Dr. Daniel McPhail was a native of Inverness, Scotland, and he had studied at the University of Edinburgh. He had lived in Williamson County, Tennessee, for twenty years at the time of his death on July 13, 1846. Just before the war began, he had dissolved a partnership in a medical practice in Franklin, but he remained indebted to his former partner, Daniel B. Cliff. When McPhail entered the army, he agreed to send Cliff half of his army pay to apply toward the debt, but his death left his widow, Sarah, to settle his financial issues. McPhail is buried in the city cemetery in Franklin. According to Williamson County Historian, Rick Warwick, McPhail's comrades preserved his body for the trip back home by pickling it in a barrel of whiskey. *Western Weekly Review*, 38; see a copy of the legal complaint against Sarah McPhail dated March 22, 1847 in Daniel McPhail Papers, Williamson County Archives.

14. McClanahan to Sarah McClanahan, October 25, 1846, McClanahan and Taylor Papers.

15. Nimrod Smith to Alfred R. Wynne, July 2, 1846, Wynne Family Papers.

16. Park Marshall, *A Life of William B. Bate: Citizen, Soldier and Statesman* (Nashville, TN: The Cumberland Press, 1908), 28–29.

17. Ibid.; Kent Barnett Germany, "Patriotism and Protest: Louisiana and General Edmund Pendleton Gaines's Army of Mexican-American War Volunteers, 1845–1847," *Louisiana History: The Journal of the Louisiana Historical Association* 37 (Summer 1996): 328–29, 333; Madison Mills Diary, July 22–23, 1846.

18. Durham, *Balie Peyton*, 99, 101–2; *Biographical Memoirs of Louisiana*, vol. 1, 74.

19. Durham, *Balie Peyton*, 102–3.

20. Mollie M. Claiborne, typescript "Rescued Records and Memoirs," 2–3.

21. Claiborne, "Memoirs," 3–5.

22. Claiborne, "Reminiscences," 4–6; slogan quoted in Fakes, "Memphis," 126.

23. Fakes, "Memphis," 125.

24. Wiley Hale to mother, July 26 and August 17, 1846, Hale Papers.

25. Robertson, *Reminiscences*, 98–99; Heiman, "Concise Description," 3; Hughes and Stonesifer, *Pillow*, 74–75.

26. Quoted in Hughes and Stonesifer, *Pillow*, 44.

27. Heiman, "Concise Description," 3; R. B. Alexander to Francis Duffy, August 14, 1846, Duffy Papers.

28. William Campbell to David Campbell, August 28, 1846, quoted in Hughes and Stonesifer, *Pillow*, 44; Taylor quoted in Felice Flanery Lewis, *Trailing Clouds of Glory: Zachary Taylor's Mexican War Campaign and His Emerging Civil War Leaders* (Tuscaloosa: The University of Alabama Press, 2010), 108.

29. Robertson, *Reminiscences*, 108; J. Hugh LeBaron, *Perry Volunteers in the Mexican War: First Regiment of Alabama Volunteers, 1846–1847 and the Mexican War Diary of Captain William G. Coleman* (Bowie, MD: Heritage Books, Inc., 2002), 43.

30. Wiley Hale to mother, September 1, 1846, Hale Papers; Caswell to wife, August 28, 1846, Caswell Papers; Robertson, *Reminiscences*, 108.

31. H. Grady Howell, ed., *A Southern Lacrimosa: The Mexican War Journal of Dr. Thomas Neely Love, Surgeon, Second Regiment Mississippi Volunteer Infantry, U.S.A.* (Chickasaw, MI: Bayou Press, 1995), 111.

32. K. Jack. Bauer, *The Mexican War, Zachary Taylor: Soldier, Planter, Statesman of the Old Southwest* (Baton Rouge: Louisiana State University Press, 1985), 88–89; William Campbell to David Campbell, August 28, 1846, Sioussant, ed., *Mexican War Letters*, 140; John McClanahan to Sarah McClanahan, August 15, 1846, McClanahan and Taylor Papers; Lewis, *Trailing Clouds,* 109; Robertson, *Reminiscences*, 109; Patrick Duffy to Francis Duffy, September 5, 1846, Duffy Papers; Heiman, "Concise Description," 3; Durham, "Mexican War Letters," 396.

33. Frank Cheatham to F. R. Cheatham, September 3, 1846, Cheatham Papers; Ezra J. Warner, *Generals in Gray: Lives of the Confederate Commanders* (Baton Rouge: Louisiana State University Press, 1959), 131.

34. Durham, "Mexican War Letters," 390, 396.

35. Lewis, *Trailing Clouds,* 107; William Caswell to Uncle Ephraim, September 19, 1846, Caswell Letters, UNC.

36. Bauer, *Mexican War*, 89–90; Lewis, *Trailing Clouds,* 107.

37. Smith, *War*, I:229; Anonymous Diary, TSLA; Robertson, *Reminiscences*, 122.

38. Robertson, *Reminiscences*, 121, 124; Patrick Duffy to Francis Duffy, November 20, 1846, Duffy Papers; Anonymous Diary, TSLA; Heiman, "Concise Description," 4.

CHAPTER FOUR  *Fandango in Monterrey*

1. Lewis, *Trailing Clouds,* 127; Bauer, *Mexican War*, 91–92; Robertson, *Reminiscences*, 127.

2. Dishman, *Perfect Gibraltar*, 94–97.

3. Bauer, *Mexican War*, 92–93; Dishman, *Perfect Gibraltar*, 32–34; Smith, *War*, I:230–32, 239–40; George Nixon to Sarah Nixon, September 29, 1846, Nixon Letters, TSLA; Robertson, *Reminiscences*, 127.

4. Dishman, *Perfect Gibraltar*, 60.

5. Lewis, *Trailing Clouds*, 129; Bauer, *Taylor*, 178. Bauer asserts that Worth's flank attack was not characteristic of Zachary Taylor and was likely suggested by a staff officer or perhaps Worth himself.

6. James Kimmins Greer, *Texas Ranger: Jack Hays in the Frontier Southwest* (College Station: Texas A&M University Press, 1993), 15; Dishman, *Perfect*

*Gibraltar*, 49; Durham, *Balie Peyton*, 104, 268 n. 49; Lewis, *Trailing Clouds*, 142.

7. Heiman, "Concise Description," 4; Robertson, *Reminiscences*, 134; Dishman, *Perfect Gibraltar*, 101.

8. Robertson, *Reminiscences*, 134; Dishman, *Perfect Gibraltar*, 101–2; quotation found in Heiman, "Concise Description," 4–5.

9. Dishman, *Perfect Gilbraltar*, 107–8; N. S. Jarvis, "Abstract of Letter Written by U. S. Army Surgeon at Monterrey, October 1846," *New York Journal of Medicine* (March 1847): 151.

10. Jarvis, "Letter by Army Surgeon," 152; Grant, *Memoirs*, 69; Bauer, *Mexican War*, 95–96; Dishman, *Perfect Gilbraltar*, 113–15.

11. Robertson, *Reminiscences*, 138.

12. Unidentified soldier to mother, September 25, 1846, TSLA.

13. James Burkitt to brother, October 1, 1846, published in Burkitt, *Concise History*, 336; Durham, *Old Sumner*, 361; Hoss, *History of Nashville*, 176; Robertson, *Reminiscences*, 138. A column formation is narrow across the front, perhaps four soldiers abreast, and deep, front to back. This alignment allows for more rapid movement, but the units have to be realigned into linear formation to attack, so as to provide a broad front and mass musketry.

14. Bauer, *Mexican War*, 92, 95; Lewis, *Trailing Clouds*, 127; Smith, *War*, I:249–52. A surgeon reported that, from long range, most of the wounds were to the feet and legs and were most often inflicted by cannon shot, but from short range, musket shots from the waist up were most common. The longer range of cannon makes this unsurprising, but that a number of the cannon wounds were to the lower extremities suggests that the cannonballs were near the end of their trajectory or perhaps were skipping across the ground. Jarvis, "Letter by Army Surgeon," 152.

15. Durham, *Old Sumner*, 361; George Nixon to Sarah Nixon, September 29, 1846, Nixon Letters, TSLA; Campbell's battle report, September 27, 1846, 30th Cong., 1st Sess., House Exec. Doc. No. 17, 24; Burkitt, *Concise History*, 336. The Mississippian was John S. Holt from General John Quitman's staff. Holt's journal is quoted in Francis Hamtramack Claiborne, *Life and*

*Correspondence of John A. Quitman,* 2 vols. (New York: Harper & Brothers, 1860), I:227.

16. Campbell's battle report, September 27, 1846, 30th Cong., 1st Sess., House Exec. Doc. No. 17, 24; Cheatham to Medora Riggs, October 16, 1846, Cheatham Papers; Unidentified soldier to mother, September 25, 1846, Unknown Soldier Letter, TSLA.

17. Unidentified soldier to mother, September 25, 1846, Unidentified Soldier Letter, TSLA; Robertson, *Reminiscences,* 139–40; W. P. Rowles, *Life of William Bethel Allen* (Printed by W. P. Rowles, 1850). Copy in Lawrence County Archives, 11, 15–16, 90.

18. *The Tennessean,* April 23, 1888.

19. Campbell's battle report, September 27, 1846, 30th Cong., 1st Sess., House Ex. Doc. No. 17, 25; West, ed., *Tennessee Encyclopedia,* 417; Heiman, "Concise Description," 5.

20. Anderson letter quoted in Durham, *Old Sumner,* 361; Cheatham to Medora Riggs (sister), October 16, 1846, Cheatham Papers.

21. Unknown soldier to mother, September 25, 1846, unidentified soldier letter, TSLA; Robertson, *Reminiscences,* 140.

22. Patrick Duffy to Francis Duffy, November 20, 1846, Duffy Papers, TSLA; George Nixon to Sarah Nixon, October 18, 1846, Nixon Letters, TSLA; Frank Cheatham to Medora Riggs, October 16, 1846, Cheatham Papers, TSLA.

23. Robertson, *Reminiscences,* 140; Anonymous Diary, TSLA; George Nixon to Sarah Nixon, October 18, 1846, Nixon Papers.

24. Anonymous Diary, TSLA; William C. Davis, *Jefferson Davis, The Man and His Hour* (New York: HarperCollins, 1991), 144–45; Bauer, *Mexican War,* 95–96. Conflicting reports make it difficult to chronicle with precision the order of events at the moment the fort fell, as well as the exact number and location of fortified buildings adjacent to and near Fort Tenería. Contrary to some sources, Bauer asserts that Captain Electus Backus's company of the First Infantry Regiment had actually cleared all the enemy-defended buildings behind Tenería before the Tennesseans and Mississippians reached the fort. In addition to Bauer, see Robert E.

May, *John A. Quitman: Old South Crusader* (Baton Rouge: Louisiana State University Press, 1985), 157–58.

25. Patrick Duffy to Francis Duffy, November 20, 1846, Duffy Papers, TSLA; George Nixon to Sarah Nixon, September 29 and October 18, 1846, Nixon Letters; Hoss and Reese, *History of Nashville*, 177.

26. James Burkitt to Henry Burkitt, October 1, 1846, published in Burkitt, *Concise History*, 337.

27. Dishman, *Perfect Gibraltar*, 132–35.

28. Patrick Duffy to Francis Duffy, November 20, 1846, Duffy Papers.

29. William Blackmore's letter recounting the incident is published in Durham, *Old Sumner*, 368–70.

30. Robertson, *Reminiscences*, 124, 143.

31. Unidentified soldier to mother, September 25, 1846, Durham, *Old Sumner*, 368–70. Their bodies were later returned to Gallatin for reburial.

32. Anonymous Diary, TSLA; Madison Mills Diary, Filson; Robertson, *Reminiscences*, 145.

33. Robert Selph Henry, *The Story of the Mexican War* (New York: Da Capo Press, 1950), 147–48; Durham, *Balie Peyton*, 104–5; Henry, *Story of the Mexican War*, 147.

34. Robertson, *Reminiscences*, 146–47; Heiman, "Concise Description," 6.

35. Chamberlain quoted in Dishman, *Perfect Gibralter*, 140–41. The Third Infantry surgeon, Dr. Jarvis reported that a total of twenty-eight amputations were performed in the army, with the most, fourteen, occurring in the volunteer division. Twenty of the amputations took place "on the field, or on the following morning, in camp," while the remaining eight occurred from one to three weeks after the battle. Twelve of the amputees, or 43%, ultimately died. Jarvis, "Letter by Army Surgeon," 157. Jarvis also describes how the stumps of amputated limbs became infested with maggots—something the doctors had not anticipated; see 153.

36. Heiman, "Concise Description," 6; Lewis, *Trailing Clouds*, 151–53.

37. Lewis, *Trailing Clouds*, 153–55.

38. Patrick Duffy to Francis Duffy, November 20, 1846, Duffy Papers; Taylor quoted in Lewis, *Trailing Clouds*, 155–56; Jonathan A. Beall, "The United States Army and Urban Combat in the Nineteenth Century," *War in History* 16, no. 2 (April 2009): 167–68.

39. Bauer, *Mexican War*, 99–101; Tucker, ed., *Encyclopedia of the Mexican-American War*, 441–42; Beall, "United States Army," 167–68.

40. Robertson, *Reminiscences*, 161.

41. Bauer, *Mexican War*, 100; letter from an unknown Lawrence County soldier with no date seems, from the context, to have been written within days of the battle, Nixon Papers; Bennett quoted in Durham, *Old Sumner*, 364. First Tennessee killed—William B. Allen (Lawrence County), S. M. Putnam (Davidson County), John B. Porter (Dickson County), William H. Robinson (Dickson County), James York (Dickson County), John A. Hill (Warren County), B. F. Coffee (Warren County), E. W. Thomas (Davidson County), Brooker H. Dalton (Sumner County), Julius Elliott (Sumner County), Peter H. Martin (Sumner County), Edward Prior (Sumner County), John Raphile (Sumner County), Benjamin Soaper (Sumner County), Henry Collins (Smith County), James Allison (Davidson County), James H. Johnson (Sumner County), James B. Turner (Sumner County), Richard D. Willis (Davidson County), Joseph B. Burkitt (Bedford County), J. M. L. Campbell (Davidson County), Andrew J. Eaton (Lincoln County), Andrew J. Gibson (Lincoln County), Finley Glover (Davidson County), Andrew J. Pratt (Lincoln County), William Rhodes (Davidson County), John W. Sanders (Lincoln County), G. W. Wilson (Davidson County), W. D. Cabler (Davidson County). *Niles Register*, November 21, 1846.

42. Jarvis, "Letter by Army Surgeon," 157.

43. Richard Gifford Pension File, National Archives.

44. Cheatham to Louisa Cheatham, October 6, 1846, Cheatham Papers; Patrick Duffy to Francis Duffy, November 20, 1846, Duffy Papers.

45. Patrick Duffy to Francis Duffy, November 20, 1846, Duffy Papers.

46. Lebanon *Banner*, October 16 and 23, 1846; Claiborne, *Life and Correspondence,* I: 249. Anderson's letter quoted in Durham, *Old Sumner*, 362; *National Union*, April 28, 1847.

47. William Campbell to David Campbell September 28, 1846, Sioussant, ed., *Mexican War Letters*, 144; Campbell's battle report, September 27, 1846, 30th Cong., 1st Sess., House Ex. Doc. No. 17, 25.

48. Winders, *Panting for Glory*, 37; Davis to John Jenkins, November 16, 1846, in Rowland, ed., *Davis Constitutionalist*, vol. 1, 62.

49. Joseph E. Chance, *Jefferson Davis's Mexican War Regiment* (Jackson: University Press of Mississippi, 1991), 62; Davis to John Jenkins, November 16, 1846, in Rowland, ed., *Davis Constitutionalist*, vol. 1, 63.

50. Cheatham to Medora Riggs, October 16, 1846, Cheatham Papers; McDaniel letter was published in the *Nashville Whig*, November 7, 1846; Robertson, *Reminiscences*, 167.

51. Durham, *Bailie Peyton*, 104–8; Meade letter to his wife quoted in Lewis, *Trailing Clouds*, 150.

52. Hoss and Reese, *History of Nashville*, 176.

53. Campbell to David Campbell February 19, 1846, Sioussant, ed., *Mexican War Letters*, 154; Mississippi Whig quote found in Durham, *Bailie Peyton*, 108; Cooper, *Jefferson Davis*, 154.

54. Quoted in May, *Quitman*, 160.

55. Robertson, *Reminiscences*, 168. Forty-seven-year-old Alexander Blackburn Bradford from Jackson, Tennessee, was elected to the state senate, fought in the Creek War in 1836, and served as major general in the Tennessee militia prior to moving to Holly Springs, Mississippi in 1839. While practicing law there, he was elected to the Mississippi legislature before joining the First Mississippi Rifles at the outset of the war. After the war, he invested in Bradford Place, a plantation in Bolivar County and continued in Mississippi state politics through the Civil War. Ezra J. Warner and W. Buck Yearns, *Biographical Register of the Confederate Congress* (Baton Rouge: Louisiana State University Press, 1975), 28–29.

CHAPTER FIVE  *Caught in the Idleness of War*

1. Blatti, ed., *Pickett's Journal*, 100, 102; McClanahan to Sarah McClanahan, October 25, 1846, McClanahan and Taylor Papers.

2. Hughes and Stonesifer, *Pillow*, 45; Caswell to Uncle Ephraim, September 19, 1846, Caswell Letters, UNC.

3. Hale to mother, September 1 and October 3, 1846, Hale Papers.

4. Caswell to Uncle Ephraim, September 19, 1846, Caswell Letters, UNC; Letter from a Second Tennessee volunteer published in *Lincoln Journal*, October 15, 1846.

5. In 1980, Hurricane Allen caused flooding that unearthed some of the Americans buried there. LeBaron, *Perry Volunteers*, 42–43, n. 95.

6. Wiley Hale to mother, October 3, 1846, Hale Papers; Caswell to Uncle Ephraim, September 19, 1846, Caswell Letters, UNC; LeBaron, *Perry Volunteers*, 46.

7. Hughes and Stonesifer, *Pillow*, 46.

8. LeBaron, *Perry Volunteers*, 52.

9. Hughes and Stonesifer, *Pillow*, 47–48.

10. Winfield Scott to William L. Marcy, January 16, 1847, Marcy Papers; Anderson, *Artillery Officer*, 46.

11. Daniel Harvey Hill, *A Fighter From Way Back: The Mexican War Diary of Lt. Daniel Harvey Hill*, ed. by Nathaniel Cheairs Hughes and Timothy D. Johnson (Kent, OH: Kent State University Press, 2002), 28, 47, 58; LeBaron, *Perry Volunteers*, 52.

12. Unidentified correspondent, September 23, 1846, Benham Papers; Hill, *Diary*, 62.

13. Anonymous Diary, TSLA.

14. Cheatham to Louisa Cheatham, October 6, 1846, and Cheatham to Medora Riggs, October 16, 1846, Cheatham Papers.

15. Cheatham to Aunt Fanny, December 4, 1846, Cheatham Papers.

16. Patrick Duffy to Francis Duffy, November 20, 1846, Duffy Papers; Cheatham to Louise Cheatham, October 6, 1846, Cheatham Papers; Madison Mills Diary, July 25, 1846; William Campbell to David Campbell, November 9, 1846, Sioussant, ed., *Mexican War Letters*, 148.

17. George Nixon to Sarah, October 18, 1846, Nixon Letters; Robertson, *Reminiscences*, 174–80.

18. Robertson, *Reminiscences*, 174, 178–79.

19. Nixon to Sarah, October 18 and November 8, 1846, Nixon Letters.

20. Hoss and Reese, *History of Nashville*, 177; Bergeron, *Antebellum Politics*, 94–95; Atkins, *Parties*, 143, 149.

21. Wesley Nixon to George Nixon, January 7, 1847, Nixon Papers; Brother to George Nixon, March 29, 1847, Nixon Papers.

22. *Republican Banner*, November 30, 1846.

23. *National Union*, April 28, 1847.

24. Wesley Nixon to George Nixon, January 7 and January 15, 1847; George Nixon to Wesley Nixon, February 24, 1847, Nixon Papers.

25. Robert W. Johannsen, *To the Halls of the Montezumas: The Mexican War in the American Imagination* (New York: Oxford University Press, 1985), 118; Bauer, *Taylor*, 216.

26. Nevin, ed., *Polk Diary*, 144, 148, 155–56, 166–67.

27. Timothy D. Johnson, *A Gallant Little Army: The Mexico City Campaign* (Lawrence: University Press of Kansas, 2007), 14–15; quotation found in Scott to Duncan Clinch, July 10, 1846, Anderson Papers.

28. Smith, *War with Mexico*, I, 362; Henry, *Story of the Mexican War*, 199.

29. Hale to mother, December 28, 1846, Hale Papers.

30. Furber, *Twelve Months Volunteer*, 69–74, 141–42, 167; Bauer, *Mexican War*, 146; Tucker, ed., *Encyclopedia of Mexican-American War*, 736.

31. Furber, *Twelve Months Volunteer*, 167–68; 179–81. There were two Smiths in Company I, both privates: Christopher H. Smith and Elijah M. Smith. Cox, *Foot Soldiers*, 14.

32. Furber, *Twelve Months Volunteer*, 368, 141.

33. Anonymous Diary, TSLA; Ibid., 286, 288, 338–40.

34. Robertson, *Reminiscences*, 197; Furber, *Twelve Months Volunteer*, 324–25.

35. Grant, *Memoirs*, 84–85.

36. Furber, *Twelve Months Volunteer*, 330–31, 339–40.

37. Robertson, *Reminiscences*, 197; Furber, *Twelve Months Volunteer*, 337; George Nixon to Sarah Nixon, January 15, 1847, Nixon Papers.

38. Smith, *War with Mexico*, I, 366; Bauer, *Mexican War*, 204–5; Furber, *Twelve Months Volunteer*, 343–48, quotations on 343 and 348.

39. Adolphus Heiman to Mrs. Ephriam H. Foster, February 28, 1847, Adolphus Heiman Letter, TSLA; quotations found in Hughes and Stonesifer, *Pillow*, 82–83.

40. Madison Mills Diary, January 25, 1847; Furber, *Twelve Months Volunteer*, 391; Nashvillian quotation from Robertson, *Reminiscences*, 208–9; West Tennessean quotation in John McClanahan to Sarah McClanahan, February 20, 1847, McClanahan and Taylor Papers.

41. Furber, *Twelve Months Volunteer*, 402–4.

42. Robertson, *Reminiscences*, 491.

43. Madison Mills Diary, January 24, 1847; Furber, *Twelve Months Volunteer*, 435; Tom Duffy to parents, January 12, 1847, Duffy Papers; William Walton to Timothy Walton, February 25, 1847, Walton Papers.

CHAPTER SIX  *Mexico's Gibraltar*

1. Johnson, *Gallant Little Army*, 11, 15.
2. William Walton to Timothy Walton, February 25, 1847, Walter Papers; Smith to George Wynne, March 7, 1847, Wynne Family Papers.
3. K. Jack Bauer, *Surfboats and Horse Marines: U.S. Naval Operations in the Mexican War, 1846–48* (Annapolis: U.S. Naval Institution Press, 1969), 78–79; Uncapher Diary, UT Arlington; Johnson, *Gallant Little Army*, 9–11; Robertson, *Reminiscences*, 218–19; S. R. Anderson to G. F. Crocket and A. R. Wynne, March 18, 1847, Wynne Family Papers.
4. Heiman, "Concise Description," 9; Robertson, *Reminiscences*, 220.
5. Robertson, *Reminiscences*, 222.
6. Robertson, *Reminiscences*, 222–23; S. R. Anderson to G. F. Crocket and A. R. Wynne, March 18, 1847, Wynne Family Papers; Wiley Hale to mother, March 18, 1847, Hale Papers; Hughes and Stonesifer, *Pillow*, 57–58; Hill, *Fighter From Way Back*, 76–77.
7. Samuel Anderson to G. F. Crocket and A. R. Wynne, March 18, 1847, Wynne Family Papers; Hackenburg, *Pennsylvania*, 27; Bauer, *Mexican War*, 245–47; Johnson, *Gallant Little Army*, 26–27.
8. Alfred Hoyt Bill, *Rehearsal for Conflict: The War with Mexico, 1846–1848* (New York: Alfred A. Knopf, 1947), 213. Anonymous Diary, TSLA; quote found in Samuel Anderson to G. F. Crocket and A. R. Wynne, March 18, 1847, Wynne Family Papers.
9. Henry, *Mexican War*, 267–68; Johnson, *Gallant Little Army*, 38–44; Hughes and Stonesifer, *Pillow*, 59–60; Bill, *Rehearsal for Conflict*, 214.
10. Hughes and Stonesifer, *Pillow*, 54, 60.
11. Furber, *Twelve Months*, 497–503; Cooper Diary, Albert Gallatin Cooper Papers.
12. Hale to mother, March 18, 1847, Hale Papers. Hale obviously misdated his letter since the bombardment had not yet started on the eighteenth. Robertson, *Reminiscences*, 228–29.

13. Samuel Anderson to G. F. Crocket and A. R. Wynne, March 18, 1847, Wynne Family Papers; Christopher Losson, *Tennessee's Forgotten Warriors: Frank Cheatham and His Confederate Division* (Knoxville: University of Tennessee Press, 1989), 15–16.

14. Robertson, *Reminiscences*, 231–32; Furber, *Twelve Months*, 542–43; quotation found in Hughes and Stonesifer, *Pillow*, 60. About a half dozen Tennesseans were wounded in this engagement, including Hugh Gavin (Lincoln County), William P. Ayles (Knox County), Mark Fox (Knox County), Daniel Vann (Knox County), Green Woodlee (Hamilton County), and Thomas Young (Sumner County).

15. Patterson quoted in Furber, *Twelve Months*, 543.

16. Losson, *Tennessee's Forgotten Warriors*, 16.

17. Furber, *Twelve Months*, 543; Chauncey Forward Sargent, *Gathering Laurels in Mexico: The Diary of an American Soldier in the Mexican American War*, ed. Ann Brown Janes (Lincoln, MA: The Cottage Press, 1990), 7.

18. George Winston and Charles Smith, *Chronicles of the Gringos* (Albuquerque: University of New Mexico Press, 1968), 194; Johnson, *Gallant Little Army*, 48.

19. William Campbell to David Campbell, March 28, 1847, Sioussat, ed., *Mexican War Letters*, 160; Samuel Lauderdale to James Lauderdale, April 2, 1847, Lauderdale Papers; Jackson quoted in James I. Robertson Jr., *Stonewall Jackson: The Man, the Soldier the Legend* (New York: Macmillan Publishing, 1997), 54, 58.

20. Campbell to David Campbell, March 29, 1847, Sioussat, ed., *Mexican War Letters*, 161; Hughes and Stonesifer, *Pillow*, 65; *Nashville Daily Union*, April 23, 1847.

21. Campbell to David Campbell, March 28 and 29, 1847, Sioussat, ed., *Mexican War Letters*, 160–61.

22. Furber, *Twelve Months*, 544, 559, 561; Caswell to Thomas Hord, April 4, 1847, Caswell Letters, UNC.

23. Unknown newspaper article entitled, "Mexican Veterans: Only Forty-four Known in Davidson County," March 29, 1888, found in Walton Papers.

24. Fitzgerald to William Blackburn, July 10, 1847, Blackburn Family Papers; Furber, *Twelve Months*, 578; Caswell to Elizabeth Caswell, April 24, 1847, Caswell Papers; Johnson, *Gallant Little Army*, 66.

1. Claiborne, "Reminiscences," 18; Robert E. Lee to Mary Custis Lee, April 12, 1847, George Bolling Lee Papers; Antonio López Santa Anna, *The Eagle: The Autobiography of Santa Anna*, ed. Ann Fears Crawford (Austin, TX: Pemberton Press, 1967), 96.; Albert Ramsey, ed. and trans., *The Other Side; or, Notes for the History of the War Between Mexico and the United States* (New York: John Wiley, 1850), 200; Johnson, *Gallant Little Army*, 68–73.

2. Allan Peskin, *Volunteers: The Mexican War Journals of Private Richard Coulter and Sergeant Thomas Barclay, Company E. Second Pennsylvania Infantry* (Kent, OH: Kent State University Press, 1991), 74; Sargent, *Gathering Laurels*, 8–9; Thomas D. Tennery, *The Mexican War Diary of Thomas D. Tennery*, ed. D. E. Livingston-Little (Norman: University of Oklahoma Press, 1970), 80; Tipton, "Journal," TSLA; Anonymous, "Tennessee Cavalry Journal."

3. Claiborne, "Reminiscences," 19.

4. Johnson, *Gallant Little Army*, 84, 88–89; Pillow's Statement, *Niles' National Register*, July 3, 1847.

5. Campbell to Wife, April 17, 1847, Campbell Family Papers; *Daily American*, January 12, 1882.

6. *Republican Banner*, June 7, 1847; Tipton Journal, TSLA; McClellan, *Diary*, 116; Hackenburg, *Pennsylvania*, 35.

7. Hughes and Stonesifer, *Pillow*, 70; Johnson, *Gallant Little Army*, 90.

8. Peskin, ed., *Volunteers*, 78; McClellan, *Diary*, 117–18; Robertson, *Reminiscences*, 244–45.

9. McClellan, *Diary*, 117–18.

10. *Republican Banner*, June 7, 1847; Hughes and Stonesifer, *Pillow*, 71.

11. *Memphis Daily Enquirer*, May 18, 1847; McClellan, *Diary*, 118; Robertson, *Reminiscences*, 246; Peskin, ed., *Volunteers*, 78.

12. G. W. Hartman, *A Private's Own Journal* (Greencastle, PA: E. Robinson, 1849), 11.

13. Smith, *War with Mexico*, II: 57; Johnson, *A Gallant Little Army*, pp. 90–91; *Republican Banner*, June 7, 1847; McAdoo quoted in Hughes and Stonesifer, *Pillow*, p. 71.

14. Hackenburg, *Pennsylvania*, 38; Hughes and Stonesifer, *Pillow*, 72; McClellan, *Diary*, 118.

15. *Memphis Daily Enquirer*, May 18, 1847; Peskin, ed., *Volunteers*, 78; N. D. Smith to James Lauderdale, April 23, 1847, Lauderdale Papers; Hughes and Stonesifer, *Pillow*, 72.

16. McClellan, *Diary*, 119; Anonymous, "Tennessee Cavalry Journal"; Johnson, *Gallant Little Army*, 92.

17. Anonymous, "Tennessee Cavalry Journal."

18. McClellan, *Diary*, 119; Smith, *War with Mexico*, II: 57.

19. Hughes and Stonesifer, *Pillow*, 73; Duffy to brother, April 28, 1847, Duffy Papers; William Campbell to David Campbell, April 18, 1847, Sioussat, ed., *Mexican War Letters*, 163–64; McClellan, *Diary*, 126, 136; Hill, *Diary*, 71.

20. Johnson, *Gallant Little Army*, 96. Second Tennessee casualties: Killed— Lieutenant Charles G. Gill (Shelby County), Lieutenant Frederick B. Nelson (Meigs County), Henry Bynum (Shelby County), Sgt. Brown (McMinn County), George W. Keeney (Knox County), William O. Stribling (Madison County), Ephraim Price, (Madison County), Charles A. Sampson (Shelby County), Samuel Floyd (Knox County), Robert Kierman (Madison County), Thomas Griffin (Madison County), Fleming Willis (Madison County), Richard L. Bohannon (Shelby County), John Gunter (Shelby County). Wounded—Gideon Pillow (Maury County), David H. Cummings (Knox County), Henry F. Murray (Carroll County), William Yearwood (McMinn County), Wiley P. Hale (Madison County), Charles Ross (Shelby County), Benjamin Hardin (Shelby County), Josiah Prescott (Shelby County), James M. Woods (McMinn County), John L. Dearman (McMinn County), William England (Knox County), Littleberry W. Fussell (Madison County), James Wittingdon (Madison County), John Burress (Madison County), Charles Johnson (Madison County), George A. Smith (Madison County), Alonzo White (Madison County), Benjamin Francis Bibb (Carroll County), Marion Brewer (Carroll County), James Forrest (McMinn County), George T. Southerland , Andrew Carson (Knox County), Timothy Bradley (Knox County), Ethert H. McAdoo (Knox County), Henry Mowry (Knox County, Aaron Dockry (Knox County), Peter Wheeler (Knox County), Aaron Capps (Knox County), Simon G. Williams (Knox County), Ivory Kent (Carroll County), William Bennett (Knox County), Samuel Davis (Knox County), Isaac Graham (Knox County), Lewis L. Jones (Knox County), Edward Robinson (Shelby County), Benton Plunkett

(Shelby County), John Isler (Shelby County), Abraham Gregory (Shelby County), John Gregory (Shelby County), Joseph Burns (Madison County), J. Withington (Madison County), Jason Cloud (Madison County), Thomas Boyd (Madison County), Nathan Moore (Madison County), James M. Allison (Hamilton County). *Republican Banner*, May 12 and 21, 1847.

21. Robertson, *Reminiscences*, 250; Hughes and Stonesifer, *Pillow*, 73.

22. McClellan, *Dairy*, 120.

23. Claiborne, "Reminiscences," 8; *The Nashville Daily Union*, May 26, 1847; Richard Ewell to mother, April 22, 1847, Ewell Papers.

24. *The Nashville Daily Union*, May 26, 1847; Memphis *Daily Enquirer*, May 14, 1847.

25. Hughes and Stonesifer, *Pillow*, 73.

26. *Republican Banner*, June 7, 1847; *Knoxville Tribune*, June 9, 1847.

27. Williams, *Historic Madison*, 119.

28. John McClanahan to Sarah McClanahan, April 28, 1847, McClanahan and Taylor Papers.

29. Gilley, *Goodspeed's Histories*, 825; Haskell File, TSLA.

30. Robertson, *Reminiscences*, 251–52; Patrick Duffy to brother, April 28, 1847, Duffy Papers. Local Jackson, Tennessee oral tradition suggests that a demoralized and depressed Haskell intentionally caused the explosion in an unsuccessful suicide attempt. However, this cannot be documented.

31. Furber, *Twelve Months*, 601; Robertson, *Reminiscences*, 256.

32. Anonymous Diary, TSLA; Campbell to David Campbell, April 25, 1847, Sioussat, ed., *Campbell Letters*, 165.

33. Claiborne, *Reminiscences*, 25–26.

34. Furber, *Twelve Months*, 613–14; Robertson, *Reminiscences*, 276.

35. Johnson, *Gallant Little Army*, 102; Robertson, *Reminiscences*, 275; *Memphis Daily Enquirer*, May 15, 1847.

36. Campbell to David Campbell, April 25, 1847, Sioussat, ed., *Campbell Letters*, 166; Fakes, "Memphis," 135–36.

37. Pillow to Adjutant General, April 18, 1847, published in *Memphis Daily Enquirer*, June 2, 1847; Pillow's Rebuttal, June 7, 1847, *Niles' National Register*, vol. 72, July 3, 1847.

38. Hughes and Stonesifer, *Pillow*, 75.

39. William Haskell's Reply, *Niles' National Register*, vol. 72, July 17, 1847.

40. *Daily Enquirer*, June 4 and 5, 1847.

41. Hughes and Stonesifer, *Pillow*, p. 76.

42. Ellis, *Moving Appeal*, 64.


CHAPTER EIGHT  *Opposition in the Volunteer State*

1.  Losson, *Tennessee's Forgotten Warriors*, 16; Campbell speech, June 1847, Campbell Collection.

2.  Campbell speech, June 1847, Campbell Collection.

3.  *Memphis Daily Enquirer*, June 9, 1847.

4.  Williams, *Historic Madison*, 119; Fakes, "Memphis," 136–38.

5.  Fakes, "Memphis," 138–39.

6.  Gilley, "Tennessee Whigs," 52; *Nashville Whig*, June 16, 30, July 11; *Eagle*, May 5, June 7.

7.  For these quotations and other perceptive insights into the personality, character, and motivations of James K. Polk, see Haynes, *Polk*.

8.  John C. Pinheiro, *Manifest Ambition: James K. Polk and Civil-Military Relations During the Mexican War* (Westport, CT: Praeger Security International, 2007), 39.

9.  Schroeder, *Mr. Polk's War*, x, xv.

10. *Nashville Daily Union*, April 23, 1847; *Republican Banner*, July 23, 1847; Schroeder, *Mr. Polk's War*, 91.

11. Theodore J. Crackel, *Mr. Jefferson's Army: Political and Social Reform of the Military Establishment, 1801–1809* (New York: New York University Press, 1987), 12–14, 58–62, 71–73, 180–81.

12. Scott's 1844 "Peace and War" essay was reproduced in Winfield Scott, *Memoirs of Lieut.-General Winfield Scott*, ed. Timothy D. Johnson (Knoxville: University of Tennessee Press, 2015), 192–93; Timothy D. Johnson, *Winfield Scott: The Quest for Military Glory* (Lawrence: The University Press of Kansas, 1998), 151.

13. Nevins, ed., *Polk Diary*, 102; quotations are from correspondence between Scott and Secretary of War William Marcy, and are found, along with a more in-depth treatment, in Johnson, *Scott*, 150–59; *The National Union*, April 28, 1847; Winders, *Mr. Polk's Army*, 33.

14. Nevins, ed., *Polk Diary*, 175; Pinheiro, *Manifest Ambition*, 60, 71; Winders, *Mr. Polk's Army*, 37.

15. Pinheiro, *Manifest Ambition*, 51–55; Crittenden quoted on 43.

16. Nevins, ed., *Polk Diary*, 167; Gilley, "Tennessee Whigs," 47–48; Pinheiro, *Manifest Ambition*, 71; Winders, *Mr. Polk's Army*, 36. Chapter three of Winders's study is an exceptional and succinct evaluation of the president's blatant politicization of the war.

17. Schroeder, *Mr. Polk's War*, 44–47.

18. Schroeder, *Mr. Polk's War*, 46–47; Gilley, "Tennessee Whigs," 52, 58; Atkins, *Parties, Politics*, 150.

19. Atkins, *Parties, Politics*, 145; Barrow quoted in John McGlone, "'What Became of General Barrow?' The Forgotten Story of George Washington Barrow," *Tennessee Historical Quarterly* 48 (Spring 1989): 39; Richardson, ed., *Messages and Papers*, IV, 437.

20. *Republican Banner*, April 5, and July 9 and 23, 1847.

21. Ewing quoted in Gilley, "Tennessee Whigs," 63.

22. Walton, "The Elections of Thirtieth Congress," 186–87, 190–92; Tucker, ed., *Encyclopedia of Mexican War*, vol. 1, 164; Holt, *American Whig Party*, p. 244, quotation found on 243.

23. Atkins, *Parties, Politics*, 147; Gilley, "Tennessee Whigs," 51–52.

24. Johannsen, *Halls of the Montezumas*, 114–18; Atkins, *Parties, Politics*, 147; *The National Union*, May 26, 1847.

25. Brother to George Nixon, March 29, 1847, Nixon Papers, Lawrence County Archives.

26. Patrick Duffy to Brother, April 28, 1847, Duffy Papers.

27. W. T. Smart to John Cheatham, May [date illegible], 1847, Cheatham Papers.

28. Schroeder, *Mr. Polk's War*, 92.

29. Coulter, *William G. Brownlow*, 44, n. 12; Queener, "Pre–Civil War Period," 100–101.

30. John C. Pinheiro, *Missionaries of Republicanism: A Religious History of the Mexican-American War* (New York: Oxford University Press, 2014), 135, 146; David Edwin Harrell, "Disciples of Christ Pacifism in Nineteenth-Century Tennessee," in Michael W. Casey and Douglas A. Foster, eds., *The*

*Stone-Campbell Movement: An International Religious Tradition* (Knoxville: The University of Tennessee Press, 2002), 457; *Lebanon Banner*, April 30, 1847.

31. Richard T. Hughes, *Reviving the Ancient Faith: The Story of Churches of Christ in America* (Abilene, TX: Abilene Christian University Press, 1996), 127; quotations found in *The Millenial Harbinger*, vol. III, no. VIII: 473 and no. XI: 641–42. Campbell wrote his most celebrated antiwar essay after the war, which appeared in *The Millenial Harbinger* vol. V, no. VII: 361–85.

32. Mollie Claiborne, "Memoirs," 12, TR.

33. Dorris, "Narrative," Dr. W. D. Norris Narrative of Family History, Nashville Public Library, Nashville, TN, 46–51, 70.

34. Robert E. Hooper, *Crying in the Wilderness: A Biography of David Lipscomb* (Nashville: David Lipscomb College, 1979), 9–10, 21–23; Hughes, *Reviving the Ancient Faith*, 119, 127; Dorris, "Narrative," 74.

35. Pinheiro, *Missionaries of Republicanism*, 131, 135.

36. *The Jackson Republican*, July 30, 1847.

CHAPTER NINE *The Pillow Factor*

1. *Nashville Whig*, March 13, 1847; Burkitt, *Concise History*, 336. William Allen's younger brother, Sam Houston Allen, was in the same Lawrence County company, but he died of disease in Mexico. The brothers are buried beside each other. A local account said that after their death, their mother never smiled again. J. F. Hobbs, "Lawrence County Historical Society Bulletin," May 7, 1953,

2. Fakes, "Memphis," 135, 140.

3. Ellis, *Moving Appeal*, 65.

4. *The Jackson Republican*, July 30, 1847; Hughes and Stonesifer, *Pillow*, 74.

5. Fakes, "Memphis," 139–40; Cox, *Foot Volunteers*, 1.

6. Losson, *Tennessee Forgotten Warriors*, 16–17; *Nashville Tennessean*, June 21, 1908; *The National Union*, April 28, 1847.

7. Johnson, *Gallant Little Army*, p. 273. Scott had also maintained a small garrison at Perote mostly to care for the army's sick and for the Cerro Gordo wounded.

8. Diary, Cheatham Papers; Claiborne, "Reminiscences," 55.

9. Claiborne, "Reminiscences," 11, 32–33.

10. Robert Bruce Wynne to Almira Wynne, n.d., Wynne Family Papers. If Wynne had indeed mended his intemperate ways, his reform was only temporary. In the postwar years, he had a reputation for over indulging. In 1860, at the age of thirty-three, he was shot to death by neighbor Redmond Quinn. Some of the details surrounding his death are in dispute, but what is not disputed is that Wynne's young son had quarreled with Quinn's son, had come home bruised and bleeding, and an armed and drunken Wynne set out for Quinn's house to get answers. He was outside Quinn's house when the owner came to the door and shot Wynne to death with a shotgun. Kevin E. Smith, "Deconstructing and Reconstructing the Death of Robert Bruce Wynne (1827–1860)," unpublished paper written for Bledsoe's Lick Historical Association, 2016.

11. Diary, Cheatham Papers.

12. Cheatham to father, February 14, 1848, Cheatham Papers.

13. Whitfield to George Nixon, April 5, 1848, Nixon Papers.

14. Cheatham to father, February 14, 1848, Cheatham Papers.

15. Heitman, *Historical Register*, I:971; West, *Tennessee Encyclopedia*, 994–95.

16. Johnson, *Gallant Little Army*, pp. 141–42. Pillow's column and that of George Cadwalader mentioned earlier, traveled separately with Pillow's command not arriving at Perote until after a skirmish at Las Vigas Pass had cleared the way. Ten days after Cadwalader reached Perote, Pillow arrived and the two generals combined their forces and marched the rest of the way to Puebla together.

17. George Cadwalader, John Quitman, James Shields, and David Twiggs, along with Pillow, Scott and Trist attended the conference. Johnson, *Gallant Little Army*, pp. 142–44; Hughes & Stonesifer, *Pillow*, p. 80; Ohrt, *Defiant Peacemaker*, 122.

18. Johnson, *A Gallant Little Army*, 149, 283–86.

19. Johnson, *A Gallant Little Army*, 162–90; Hughes & Stonesifer, *Pillow*, 82–92 and nt. 51, 357.

20. Hughes & Stonesifer, *Pillow*, 95–96.

21. Hill, *Diary*, 121, 123.

22. Scott to Marcy, September 18, 1847, and Major John L. Gardner's battle

report, September 20, 1847, Record Group 94, Letters Received, Adjutant General's Office; Daniel Harvey Hill, *Fighter From Way Back,* 125; Johnson, *Gallant Little Army,* 216.

23. Johnson, *Gallant Little Army,* 218–20; Bauer, *Mexican War,* 317; Smith, *War with Mexico,* 2:156; James D. Elderkin, *Biographical Sketches and Anecdotes of a Soldier of Three Wars* (Detroit, MI: James D. Elderkin, 1899), 69.

24. Johnson, *Gallant Little Army,* 227–28; Peskin, ed., *Volunteers,* 179.

25. Pillow to Moses Barnard, September 19, 1847, Barnard Reminiscences; Scott to Pillow, October 2, 1847, and Pillow to Scott, October 3, 1847, and Scott to Pillow, October 4, 1847, House Exec. Doc. 60, 30th Congress, 1st Sess.

26. Hughes and Stonesifer, *Pillow,* 104, 106.

27. James C. Kelly, "Landscape and Genre Painting in Tennessee, 1810–1985," *Tennessee Historical Quarterly* 44 (Summer 1985): 58.

28. Hughes and Stonesifer, *Pillow,* 104–7.

29. "The Letter of 'Leonidas,'" *New Orleans Picayune,* September 17, 1847; Johnson, *Gallant Little Army,* 343, n. 37.

30. A. P. Hill to brother, September 12, 1847, Hill Papers; Ethan Allen Hitchcock to Pillow, November 24, 1847, Hitchcock Papers; John D. Wilkins to mother, November, 1847, Wilkins Papers; Johnson, *Gallant Little Army,* 260; Hughes and Stonesifer, *Pillow,* 107.

31. Hughes and Stonesifer, *Pillow,* 109–10.

32. Scott's General Order No. 349, Senate Doc. No. 65, 30th Congress., 1st Sess.; Johnson, *Gallant Little Army,* 260–62.

33. Hughes and Stonesifer, *Pillow,* 114–15, Pillow letter to wife quoted on 113.

34. R. E. Lee to Mary, March 15, 1848, Lee Family Papers; Laidley to father, February 11, 1848, in Theodore Laidley, *Surrounded by Dangers of All Kinds: The Mexican War Letters of Lieutenant Theodore Laidley,* ed. James M. McCaffrey (Denton: University of North Texas Press, 1997), 145; Hill, *Diary,* 151, 171; Ayres, Mexican War Diary.

35. Johnson, *Gallant Little Army,* 265; Bauer, *Mexican War,* 373–74.

36. Tucker, ed., *Encyclopedia of the Mexican-American War,* I: 279.

CHAPTER TEN  *Mexican War Legacies*

1. The Confederate soldier was Carleton McCarthy, and he was quoted in David W. Blight, *Race and Reunion: The Civil War in American Memory* (Cambridge: Harvard University Press, 2001), 171. William Gardner to brother, October 24, 1847, Gardner Papers; Thomas Williams quoted in Smith and Judah, *Chronicles of the Gringos*, 418.

2. Durham, *Old Sumner*, 364; Bennett quoted on 364; Lauderdale quoted on 373. A check of other states that sent at least 4,500 volunteers to Mexico reveals a similarly high mortality rate due to disease. Missouri lost 338 in the war, 88 percent of them from disease, and disease accounted for 96 percent of Louisiana's 396 deaths, 88 percent of Illinois's 851, and 91 percent of Indiana's 570. A compilation of losses by unit can be found in Executive Document No. 24, 31st Congress, 1st Session, but a more convenient source is Winders, *Mr. Polk's Army*, 147–51.

3. States with counties named for Polk are Arkansas, Florida, Georgia, Iowa, Minnesota, Nebraska, Oregon, and Tennessee. For presidents' ratings see Arthur M. Schlesinger, Sr., "Historians Rate the U.S. Presidents," *Life Magazine* (November 1, 1948), 65; Schlesinger, Jr., "Rating the Presidents," *Political Science Quarterly* 112 (Summer 1997): 181–84.

4. Chaffin, *Met His Every Goal*, 44, 46; Robert D. Kaplan, *The Revenge of Geography* (New York: Random House, 2012), 33.

5. *Lincoln Journal*, November 26, 1846; *The Tennessean*, September 18, 1850; Fitzgibbon to Captain A. E. Magill, Nov. 7, 1863, *OR*, Series I, Vol. 3: 240.

6. Walter T. Durham, *Volunteer Forty-Niners: Tennesseans and the California Gold Rush* (Nashville, TN: Vanderbilt University Press, 1997), 30, 57–60, 252, n. 14.

7. Ibid., 30, 36, 60–61; Spence, *Hickman County*, 77.

8. George H. Tinkham, *Stockton, A History of Stockton* (San Francisco: W. M. Hinton and Company, 1880), 188.; Johnson, "Cheatham," 25–26; Losson, *Tennessee's Forgotten Warriors*, 20–21.

9. Seth Warner, "George Earl Maney: Soldier, Railroader, and Diplomat," *Tennessee Historical Quarterly* 65 (Summer 2006): 132–36, quotation on 145; Warner, *Generals in Gray*, 210; Losson, *Tennessee's Forgotten Warriors*, 190–92.

10. E. G. Eastman to James Buchanan and Gideon Pillow to James Buchanan, both on January 29, 1847, Nixon Papers, and Samuel Rucker, Jr. To George Nixon, January 25, 1848, all in Lawrence County Archives.

11. *Tennesseans in the Civil War*, I: 104–5, 279–80.

12. Walter Stokes, Jr., "Christ Church, Nashville," lecture published in *Seven Early Churches of Nashville* (Nashville, TN: Elder's Book Store, 1972), 44–45; Robert E. May, *Manifest Destiny's Underworld: Filibustering in Antebellum America* (Chapel Hill: University of North Carolina Press, 2002), 36; Joseph E. Chance, *José María de Jesús Carvajal: The Life and Times of a Mexican Revolutionary* (San Antonio, TX: Trinity University Press, 2006), 18–19, 200.

13. May, *Manifest Destiny's Underworld*, 36, 65; Claiborne, "Reminiscences," 34; Stokes, "Christ Church," 44–45.

14. Randy Bishop, *Civil War Generals of Tennessee* (Gretna, LA: Pelican Publishing Co., 2013), 22–25, 58–60, 68–69, 114, 138, 209, 217, 253.

15. John Berrien Lindsley, *Military Annals of Tennessee, Confederate*, 2 vols., Nashville: J. M. Lindsley & Co., Publishers, 1886; reprint ed. Wilmington, NC: Broadfoot Publishing, 1995), 604–5; McGavock, *Pen and Sword*, 589.

16. Benjamin Franklin Cooling, *Forts Henry and Donelson: The Key to the Confederate Heartland* (Knoxville: University of Tennessee Press, 1987), 201–4; Hughes and Stonesifer, *Pillow*, 223–37, Pillow to Floyd quotation found on 237; McGavock, *Pen and Sword*, 603; Grant and Buckner conversation recorded in William S. McFeely, *Grant: A Biography* (New York: W. W. Norton, 1981), 102.

17. Ellis, *Moving Appeal*.

18. Richard C. Locke, Lycurgus G. Stewart, Charles Talley, John Vining, Marshall Watson, Pension Files, National Archives.

19. Hagewood, "Road to Fratricide," 68–69.

20. Bergeron, *Antebellum Politics*, 103–4; Van West, *Tennessee Encyclopedia*, 674, 994.

21. Hagewood, "Road to Fratricide," 72, 77–78; Atkins, *Parties, Politics*, 174–76.

22. Hagewood, "Road to Fratricide," 102–10, 113.

23. Ibid., 113–15, quotation from 117.

24. Peter Maslowski, *Treason Must Be Made Odious: Military Occupation and Wartime Reconstruction in Nashville, Tennessee, 1862–65* (Millwood, NY: KTO Press, 1978) 21, 84, 148; Van West, *Tennessee Encyclopedia*, 121.

25. Wyatt-Brown, *Southern Honor*, 4; quotation found in Young, "Haskell," *Christian Advocate*.

26. Austin and Moore, eds., *Tennessee*, II: 140.

27. Campbell, *Attitude of Tennesseans*, p. 77; Young, "Haskell," *Christian Advocate*.

28. Ellis, *The Moving Appeal*, 65; Young, "Haskell," *Christian Advocate*; Charles Richards, Haskell Collection.

29. Stephen Joseph and Stephen Regal, *Post-Traumatic Stress* (New York: Oxford University Press, 2010), 9–11, 15, 20.

30. McGavock, *Pen and Sword*, 382–83.

31. Foster and Moore, eds., *Tennessee*, 141; Young, "Haskell"; McGavock, *Pen and Sword*, 448; Haskell Notes, Williams Papers.

32. Haskell Notes, Williams Papers.

CHAPTER ELEVEN *The Quest for Recognition and Respect*

1. Davies, "Mexican War Veterans," pp. 221–22.

2. A. M. Kenaday, *Proceedings of the National Convention of the Veterans of the Mexican War* (Washington: John H. Cunningham, Printer, 1874), 5; Ezra Warner, *Generals in Blue: Lives of the Union Commanders* (Baton Rouge: Louisiana State University Press, 1964), 341–42. In the seventy years following the Civil War, Fort Negley was neglected and allowed to deteriorate. In the 1936, the WPA rebuilt an exact replica of the fort on precisely the same footprint as it had occupied in the 1860s. That reproduction had also been allowed to deteriorate over the years until preservationists and city officials took an interest in saving the stone structure in the 1990s.

3. Kenaday, *Proceedings*, 5; Davies, "Mexican War Veterans," 222. Widow and orphan pensions were available for survivors of soldiers who died while in the service, as were disability pensions for the war's survivors, but Congress had made no provision for a service pension.

4. Davies, "Mexican War Veterans," 222; Kenaday, *Proceedings*, 8, 11; Hughes and Stonesifer, *Pillow*, 317–19; Pillow letter quoted in Alys D. Beverton, "We Knew no North, no South": U. S.-Mexican War Veterans and the Construction of Public Memory in the Post Civil War United States, 1874–1897," *American Nineteenth Century History* 17, no. 1 (2016): 6.

5. Davies, "Mexican War Veterans," 222, 225; Negley's speech quoted in Kenaday, "*Proceedings*," p. 13.

6. Michael Scott Van Wagenen, *Remembering the Forgotten War: The Enduring Legacies of the U.S.-Mexican War* (Amherst: University of Massachusetts Press, 2012), 65, 266, n. 22.

7. Kenaday, *Proceedings*, 13; Davies, "Mexican War Veterans," 222; Beverton, "We Knew no North," 7–8.

8. Undated newspaper article in William H. Walton Papers. Signatories to the open letter included Burrill G. Wood, E. P. Turner, John Lellyett, Henry W. Hart, Joseph Weems, and Abram Joseph.

9. Van Wagenen, *Remembering*, 64–65.

10. *The Daily American*, September 6, 1882.

11. *The Nashville Daily World*, September 15, 1882; Robert Rutland, "Captain William B. Walton, Mexican War Volunteer," *Tennessee Historical Quarterly*, vol. XI, no. 2 (June 1952): 177; Beverton, "We Knew no North," 2.

12. An account of the day's events in the following five paragraphs, along with a reproduction of the Claiborne, Caldwell, and Bate speeches that are quoted herein, are found in *The Nashville Daily American*, September 15, 1882.

13. Davies, "Mexican War Veterans," 232.

14. *The Nashville Daily American*, September 15, 1882.

15. West, *Tennessee Encyclopedia*, pp. 60, 407; Davies, "Mexican War Veterans," pp. 224–25.

16. *The Nashville Daily American*, September 16, 1882.

17. Rutland, "Captain Walton," 177; Minute Book, Walton Papers.

18. Minute Book, Walton Papers; Rutland, "Captain Walton," 177–78.

19. Case to Walton, June 6, 1885, Walton Papers.

274   *Notes to Pages 221–229*

20. Minute Book, Walton Papers; Losson, *Tennessee's Forgotten Warriors*, 277–78.

21. *The Nashville Daily American*, September 15, 1882; Minute Book, Walton Papers; Article from unidentified newspaper, "Mexican Veterans: Only Forty-four Known in Davidson County," March 29, 1888, Walton Papers.

22. Minute Book, Walton Papers; Rutland, "Captain Walton," 178.

23. Article from unidentified newspaper, "Mexican Veterans: Only Forty-four Known in Davidson County," March 29, 1888, Walton Papers.

24. Beverton, "We Knew no North," 2–3, 6, 9.

25. *The Nashville American*, July 19, 1897; Campbell Collection, Fort Campbell.

26. Minute Book, Walton Papers; Rutland, "Captain Walton," 177.

27. Moscow Carter to William Walton, May 17, 1906, Walton Papers. Walton lived two more years after this 1906 exchange of letters.

# BIBLIOGRAPHY

UNPUBLISHED

Beinecke Library, Yale University, New Haven, CT
    Moses Barnard Reminiscences
    John Darragh Wilkins Papers
Charles Richards, Personal Collection, Jackson, TN
    William T. Haskell Collection
The Filson Historical Society, Louisville, KY
    Blackburn Family Papers
    Madison Mills Diary
John O'Brien, Personal Collection, Fort Campbell
    William B. Campbell Collection
King Family Papers, Jackson, TN
    Daniel King Letters
Lawrence County Archives, Leoma, TN
    George Henry Nixon Papers
Library of Congress, Washington, DC
    Robert Anderson Papers
    Ethan Allen Hitchcock Papers
    William L. Marcy Papers
Madison County Public Library, Jackson, TN
    Emma I. Williams Papers
Nashville Public Library, Nashville, TN
    Dr. W. D. Norris Narrative of Family History
National Archives, Washington, DC
    Pension Records
    Record Group 94, Letters Received, Adjutant General's Office
Perkins Library, Duke University, Durham, NC
    Campbell Family Papers
Southern Historical Collection, The University of North Carolina,
        Chapel Hill, NC
    Romeyn B. Ayres, Mexican War Diary

McClanahan and Taylor Family Papers

William Montgomery Gardner Papers

William R. Caswell Letters

Tennessee State Library and Archives, Nashville, TN

Anonymous Diary

Benjamin Franklin Cheatham Papers

Albert Gallatin Cooper Papers

Duffy Family Papers

Foster-Woods Papers

Wiley Pope Hale Papers

William T. Haskell File

Adolphus Heiman Letter

Adolphus Heiman's unpublished "Concise Description of the
Services on the First Regiment of Tennessee Volunteers."

Blackstone McDannel Family Papers

Lauderdale Family Papers

George Henry Nixon Letters

Unidentified Soldier Letter

Tennessee Historical Society Misc. Manuscript File

Jonathan Wade H. Tipton Journal

William H. Walton Papers

Wynne Family Papers (George Winchester Wynne)

University of Tennessee Library, Knoxville, TN

William R. Caswell Papers

Second Tennessee Cavalry Regiment Journal

University of Texas–Arlington, Arlington, TX

Henry W. Benham Papers

Israel Uncapher Mexican War Diary

Travellers Rest, Nashville, TN

Mollie M. Claiborne, typescript "Rescued Records and Memoirs"

Thomas Claiborne Mexican War Reminiscences (typescript)

Virginia Historical Society, Richmond, VA

Richard S. Ewell Papers

Ambrose Powell Hill Papers

George Bolling Lee Papers

Lee Family Papers

NEWSPAPERS

*The Academist* (Lawrenceburg)

*The Chattanoogan.com*

*The Jackson Republican*

*Knoxville Tribune*

*Lebanon Banner of Peace and Cumberland and Presbyterian Advocate*

*Lincoln Journal*

*Memphis Daily Enquirer*

*Memphis Eagle*

*Nashville Daily American*

*Nashville Daily Union*

*Nashville Daily World*

*Nashville Republican Banner*

*Nashville Whig*

*National Union*

*New Orleans Picayune*

*New York Times*

*Niles National Register*

*Sumner County News*

*The Tennessean*

*West Tennessee Whig* (Jackson)

*Western Weekly Review* (Franklin)


PUBLISHED SOURCES

Alford, Bobby. "History of Lawrence County Tennessee." Lawrence County
    Archives, Leoma, TN.

Anderson, Robert. *An Artillery Officer in the Mexican War, 1846–7*. New York:
    G. P. Putnam's Sons, 1911.

Armstrong, Zella. *The History of Hamilton County and Chattanooga Tennessee*. 2
    vols. Johnson City, TN: The Overmountain Press, 1931.

Atkins, Jonathan M. *Parties, Politics, and the Sectional Conflict in Tennessee, 1832–1861*. Knoxville: University of Tennessee Press, 1997.

———. "Politicians, Parties, and Slavery: The Second Party System and the Decision for Disunion in Tennessee." In *Tennessee History: The Land, the People, and the Culture*. Edited by Carroll Van West, Knoxville: University of Tennessee Press, 1998.

Bauer, K. Jack. *The Mexican War, 1846–1848*. New York: Macmillan Publishing Co., 1974.

———. *Surfboats and Horse Marines: U.S. Naval Operations in the Mexican War, 1846–48*. Annapolis, MD: U.S. Naval Institution Press, 1969.

———. *Zachary Taylor: Soldier, Planter, Statesman of the Old Southwest*. Baton Rouge: Louisiana State University Press, 1985.

Beall, Jonathan A. "The United States Army and Urban Combat in the Nineteenth Century." *War in History* 16, no. 2 (April 2009): 157–88.

Bergeron, Paul H. *Antebellum Politics in Tennessee*. Lexington: The University Press of Kentucky, 1982.

Bergeron, Paul H., Stephen V Ash, and Jeanette Keith. *Tennesseans and Their History*. Knoxville: University of Tennessee Press, 1999.

Beverton, Alys D. *Biographical and Historical Memoirs of Louisiana*. 2 vols. Chicago: The Goodspeed Publishing Company, 1892.

———. "We Knew no North, no South": U. S.-Mexican War Veterans and the Construction of Public Memory in the Post–Civil War United States, 1874–1897." *American Nineteenth Century History* 17, no. 1 (2016): 1–22.

———. *Biographical and Historical Memoirs of Louisiana*. 2 volumes. Chicago: The Goodspeed Publishing Company, 1892.

Bill, Alfred Hoyt. *Rehearsal for Conflict: The War with Mexico, 1846–1848*. New York: Alfred A. Knopf, 1969. First published 1947 by Cooper Square Publishers (New York).

Bishop, Randy. *Civil War Generals of Tennessee*. Gretna, LA: Pelican Publishing Co., 2013.

Blatti, Jo, ed. *A. C. Pickett's Private Journal of the U. S.-Mexican War*. Little Rock: The Butler Center for Arkansas Studies, 2011.

Blight, David W. *Race and Reunion: The Civil War in American Memory*. Cambridge, MA: Harvard University Press, 2001.

Borneman, Walter R. *Polk: The Man Who Transformed the Presidency and America*. New York: Random House, 2008.

Brands, H. W. *Andrew Jackson: His Life and Times*. New York: Doubleday, 2005.

Burke, James Wakefield. *David Crockett, The Man Behind the Myth*. Austin, TX: Eakin Press, 1984.

Burkitt, Henry L. *A Concise History of the Kehukee Baptist Association*. Philadelphia: Lippincott, Grambo and Co., 1850.

Caldwell, Mary French. *Tennessee: The Dangerous Example*. Nashville, TN: Aurora Publishers, 1974.

Campbell, Mary Emily Robertson. *The Attitude of Tennesseans Toward the Union, 1847–1861*. New York: Vantage Press, 1961.

Cantrell, Gregg. *Stephen F. Austin: Empresario of Texas*. New Haven, CT: Yale University Press, 1999.

Cash, W. J. *The Mind of the South*. New York: Knopf, 1941.

Chaffin, Tom. *Met His Every Goal? James K. Polk and the Legends of Manifest Destiny*. Knoxville: University of Tennessee Press, 2014.

Chance, Joseph E. *Jefferson Davis's Mexican War Regiment*. Jackson: University Press of Mississippi, 1991.

———. *José María de Jesús Carvajal: The Life and Times of a Mexican Revolutionary*. San Antonio, TX: Trinity University Press, 2006.

Cheathem, Mark R. *Andrew Jackson: Southerner*. Baton Rouge: Louisiana State University Press, 2013.

Cisco, Jay Guy. *Historic Sumner County, Tennessee*. Nashville, TN: Jay Guy Cisco, 1909.

Claiborne, Francis Hamtramack. *Life and Correspondence of John A. Quitman*. 2 vols. New York: Harper & Brothers, 1860.

Coe, Carl R. "Politics and Assassination: The Story of General Levin Hudson Coe." *Tennessee Historical Quarterly* 54 (1995): 30–39.

Cooling, Benjamin Franklin. *Forts Henry and Donelson: The Key to the Confederate Heartland*. Knoxville: University of Tennessee Press, 1987.

Cooper, William J. *Jefferson Davis, American*. New York: Vintage Books, 2000.

Corlew, Robert E. *Tennessee: A Short History*. Knoxville: University of Tennessee Press, 1981.

Corlew, Robert E., Folmsbee, Stanley J., Mitchell, Enoch L. *History of Tennessee*. 4 vols. New York: Lewis Historical Publishing Company, Inc., 1960.

Coulter, E. Merton. *William G. Brownlow: The Fighting Parson of the Southern Highlands*. Chapel Hill: University of North Carolina Press, 1937.

Cox, Brent A. *Foot Volunteers: Tennesseans in the Mexican-American War 1845–1848*. Milan, TN: Sons of the South Publications, 1986.

Crackel, Theodore J. *Mr. Jefferson's Army: Political and Social Reform of the Military Establishment, 1801–1809*. New York: New York University Press, 1987.

Cutrer, Thomas W., ed. *The Mexican War Diary and Correspondence of George B. McCellan*. Baton Rouge: Louisiana State University Press, 2009.

Davies, Wallace E. "The Mexican War Veterans as an Organized Group." *The Mississippi Valley Historical Review* 35, no.2 (September 1948): 221–38.

Davis, William C. *Jefferson Davis, The Man and His Hour*. New York: HarperCollins, 1991.

Dishman, Christopher D. *A Perfect Gibraltar: The Battle for Monterrey, Mexico, 1846*. Norman: University of Oklahoma Press, 2010.

Durham, Walter T. *Balie Peyton of Tennessee: Nineteenth Century Politics and Thoroughbreds*. Franklin, TN: Hillsboro Press, 2004.

———."Mexican War Letters to Wynnewood." *Tennessee Historical Quarterly* 33 (Winter 1974): 389–409.

———. *Old Sumner: A History of Sumner County, Tennessee from 1805 to 1861*. Nashville, TN: Parthenon Press, 1972.

———. *Volunteer Forty-Niners: Tennesseans and the California Gold Rush*. Nashville, TN: Vanderbilt University Press, 1997.

Dusinberre, William. *Slavemaster President: The Double Career of James Polk*. New York: Oxford University Press, 2003.

Elderkin, James D. *Biographical Sketches and Anecdotes of a Soldier of Three Wars*. Detroit, MI: James D. Elderkin, 1899.

Ellis, B. G. *The Moving Appeal: Mr. McClanahan, Mrs. Dill, and the Civil War's Great Newspaper Run*. Macon, GA: Mercer University Press, 2003.

Fakes, Turner J. "Memphis and the Mexican War." *West Tennessee Historical Society Papers* 11 (1948): 119–44.

Foster, Austin P., and Moore, John Trotwood, eds. *Tennessee: The Volunteer State, 1769–1923*. 6 vols. Nashville: S. J. Clark Publishing Co., 1923.

Furber, George C. *The Twelve Months Volunteer: Journal of a Private, in the Tennessee Regiment of Cavalry, in the Campaign, in Mexico, 1846–7.* Cincinnati: U. P. James, 1857.

Germany, Kent Barnett. "Patriotism and Protest: Louisiana and General Edmund Pendleton Gaines's Army of Mexican-American War Volunteers, 1845–1847." *Louisiana History: The Journal of the Louisiana Historical Association* 37 (Summer 1996): 325–35.

Gilley, B. H. *The Goodspeed Histories of Madison County, Tennessee.* Columbia, TN: Woodward & Stinson Printing Co., 1972 (reprinted from *Goodspeed's History of Tennessee*).

———. "Tennessee Whigs and the Mexican War." *Tennessee Historical Quarterly* 40 (Spring 1981): 46–67.

Grant, Ulysses S. *Personal Memoirs of U. S. Grant.* Lincoln: University of Nebraska Press, 1996.

Greenberg, Amy S. *Manifest Manhood and the Antebellum American Empire.* New York: Cambridge University Press, 2005.

Greer, James Kimmins. *Texas Ranger: Jack Hays in the Frontier Southwest.* College Station: Texas A&M University Press, 1993.

Groneman III, William. *David Crockett, Hero of the Common Man.* New York: Tom Doherty Associates, 2005.

Hackenburg, Randy W. *Pennsylvania in the War with Mexico.* Shippensburg, PA: White Mane Publishing Company, 1992.

Hagewood, Lowell. "The Road to Fratricide: William Bowen Campbell and the Secessionist Crisis in Tennessee." PhD diss., Middle Tennessee University, 1995.

Harrell Jr., David Edwin. "Disciples of Christ Pacifism in Nineteenth-Century Tennessee." In *The Stone-Campbell Movement: An International Religious Tradition.* Edited by Michael W. Casey and Douglas A. Foster, Knoxville: The University of Tennessee Press, 2002.

Hartman, G. W. *A Private's Own Journal.* Greencastle, PA: E. Robinson, 1849.

Haynes, Sam W. *James K. Polk and the Expansionist Impulse.* New York: Longman, Inc., 2002.

Heitman, Francis B. *Historical Register and Dictionary of the United States Army.* 2 vols. 1903; Baltimore, MD: Genealogical Publishing, 1994.

Henry, Robert Selph. *The Story of the Mexican War*. New York: Da Capo Press, 1950.

Hill, Daniel Harvey. *A Fighter from Way Back: The Mexican War Diary of Lt. Daniel Harvey Hill*. Edited by Nathaniel Cheairs Hughes and Timothy D. Johnson. Kent, OH: Kent State University Press, 2002.

Hobbs, J. F. "Lawrence County Historical Society Bulletin," May 7, 1953.

Holladay, Bob. "Ideas Have Consequences: Whig Party Politics in Williamson County, Tennessee, and the Road to Disunion." *Tennessee Historical Quarterly* 63 (Fall 2004): 155–77.

Holt, Michael F. *The Rise and Fall of the American Whig Party*. New York: Oxford University Press, 1999.

Hooper, Robert E. *Crying in the Wilderness: A Biography of David Lipscomb*. Nashville, TN: David Lipscomb College, 1979.

Hoss, Elijah Embree, and William B. *History of Nashville, Tenn*. Nashville, TN: Publishing House of the Methodist Episcopal Church, 1890.

House Executive Document No. 17 & No. 60, 30th Congress 1st Session.

Howell Jr., H. Grady, ed. *A Southern Lacrimosa: The Mexican War Journal of Dr. Thomas Neely Love, Surgeon, Second Regiment Mississippi Volunteer Infantry, U.S.A.* Jackson, MI: Chickasaw Bayou Press, 1995.

Hughes Jr, Nathaniel Cheairs, and Roy P Stonesifer Jr. *The Life and Wars of Gideon J. Pillow*. Chapel Hill: University of North Carolina Press, 1993.

Hughes, Richard T. *Reviving the Ancient Faith: The Story of Churches of Christ in America*. Abilene, TX: Abilene Christian University Press, 1996.

Jarvis, N. S. "Abstract of Letter Written by U. S. Army Surgeon at Monterrey, October 1846." *New York Journal of Medicine* (March 1847): 151–59.

Johannsen, Robert W. *To the Halls of the Montezumas: The Mexican War in the American Imagination*. New York: Oxford University Press, 1985.

Johnson, Timothy D. *A Gallant Little Army: The Mexico City Campaign*. Lawrence: The University Press of Kansas, 2007.

———. "Benjamin Franklin Cheatham: The Making of a Confederate General." Master's thesis, The University of Alabama, 1982.

———. *Winfield Scott: The Quest for Military Glory*. Lawrence: The University Press of Kansas, 1998.

Joseph, Stephen, and Stephen Regel. *Post-Traumatic Stress*. New York: Oxford University Press, 2010.

Judah, Charles and George Winston Smith. *Chronicles of the Gringos: The U.S. Army in the Mexican War, 1846–1848*. Albuquerque: University of New Mexico Press, 1968.

Kanon, Tom. *Tennesseans at War, 1812–1815: Andrew Jackson, the Creek War, and the Battle of New Orleans*. Tuscaloosa: University of Alabama Press, 2014.

Kaplan, Robert D. *The Revenge of Geography*. New York: Random House, 2012.

Keating, J. M. *History of the City of Memphis and Shelby County Tennessee*. 2 vols. Syracuse, NY: D. Mason & Company, Publishers, 1888.

Kelly, James C. "Landscape and Genre Painting in Tennessee, 1810–1985." *Tennessee Historical Quarterly* 44 (Summer 1985): 7–152.

Kenaday, A. M. *Proceedings of the National Convention of the Veterans of the Mexican War*. Washington: John H. Cunningham, Printer, 1874.

Kohl, Lawrence Frederick. *The Politics of Individualism: Parties and the American Character in the Jacksonian Era*. New York: Oxford University Press, 1989.

Laidley, Theodore. *Surrounded by Dangers of All Kinds: The Mexican War Letters of Lieutenant Theodore Laidley*. Edited by James M. McCaffrey, Denton: University of North Texas Press, 1997.

Langsdon, Phillip, *Tennessee: A Political History*. Franklin, TN: Hillsboro Press, 2000.

LeBaron, J. Hugh. *Perry Volunteers in the Mexican War: First Regiment of Alabama Volunteers, 1846–1847 and the Mexican War Diary of Captain William G. Coleman*. Bowie, MD: Heritage Books, Inc., 2002.

Leonard, Thomas M. *James K. Polk: A Clear and Unquestionable Destiny*. Wilmington, DE: Scholarly Resources, Inc. 2001.

Lewis, Felice Flanery. *Trailing Clouds of Glory: Zachary Taylor's Mexican War Campaign and His Emerging Civil War Leaders*. Tuscaloosa: The University of Alabama Press, 2010.

Lindsley, John Berrien. *Military Annals of Tennessee, Confederate*. 2 vols. Wilmington, NC: Broadfoot Publishing, 1995. First published 1886 by J. M. Lindsley & Co. (Nashville, TN).

Losson, Christopher. *Tennessee's Forgotten Warriors: Frank Cheatham and His Confederate Division*. Knoxville: University of Tennessee Press, 1989.

Marshall, Park. *A Life of William B. Bate: Citizen, Soldier and Statesman*. Nashville, TN: The Cumberland Press, 1908.

Maslowski, Peter. *Treason Must Be Made Odious: Military Occupation and Wartime Reconstruction in Nashville, Tennessee, 1862–65*. Millwood, NY: KTO Press, 1978.

May, Robert E. *John A. Quitman: Old South Crusader*. Baton Rouge: Louisiana State University Press, 1985.

May, Robert E. *Manifest Destiny's Underworld: Filibustering in Antebellum America*. Chapel Hill: University of North Carolina Press, 2002.

McCaffrey, James M. *Army of Manifest Destiny: The American Soldier in the Mexican War 1846–1848*. New York: New York University Press, 2002.

McCaslin, Richard. *Lee in the Shadow of Washington*. Baton Rouge, LA: LSU Press, 2004.

McFeely, William S. *Grant: A Biography*. New York: W. W. Norton, 1981.

McGavock, Randal W. *Pen and Sword: The Life and Journals of Randal W. McGavock*. Edited by Jack Allen and Herschel Gower. Nashville, TN; Tennessee Historical Commission, 1959.

McGee, Gentry R. *A History of Tennessee from 1663 to 1930*. Nashville, TN: Charles Elder, 1930.

McGlone, John. "'What Became of General Barrow?' The Forgotten Story of George Washington Barrow." *Tennessee Historical Quarterly* 48 (Spring 1989): 37–45.

McLean, Malcomb D., ed. *Papers Concerning Robertson's Colony in Texas*. 19 vols. Arlington: University of Texas at Arlington Press, 1974–93.

Merry, Robert W. *A Country of Vast Designs: James K. Polk, the Mexican War, and the Conquest of the American Continent*. New York: Simon & Schuster, Inc., 2009.

*The Millenial Harbinger*. "War and Slavery," vol III, no. VIII: 473; "War," vol. III, no. XI: 638–42; "An Address on War," vol. V, no. VII: 361–85.

Montgomery, Robin. *Transformation of the Miracle City: A History of Conroe and Montgomery County as Told Through Selected Columns of Robin Montgomery, as They Appeared in the The Courier of Montgomery County*. San Antonio, TX: Historical Publishing Network, 2014.

Morgan, Robert. *Lions of the West: Heroes and Villains of the Westward Expansion*. Chapel Hill, NC: Algonquin Books, 2011.

Nevins, Allan, ed. *Polk: The Diary of a President, 1845–1849*. New York: Longmans, Green and Co., 1929.

Ohrt, Wallace. *Defiant Peacemaker: Nicholas Trist in the Mexican War*. College Station: Texas A&M University Press, 1997.

Peskin, Allan, ed. *Volunteers: The Mexican War Journals of Private Richard Coulter and Sergeant Thomas Barclay, Company E. Second Pennsylvania Infantry*. Kent, OH: Kent State University Press, 1991.

Peters, Gerhard. "Presidential Vetoes." *The American Presidency Project*. Edited by John T. Woolley and Gerhard Peters. Santa Barbara: University of California, 1999–2017.

Peterson, Merrill D. *The Great Triumvirate: Webster, Clay, and Calhoun*. New York: Oxford University Press, 1987.

Peterson, Norma Lois. *The Presidencies of William Henry Harrison & John Tyler*. Lawrence: The University Press of Kansas, 1989.

Pinheiro, John C. *Manifest Ambition: James K. Polk and Civil-Military Relations During the Mexican War*. Westport, CT: Praeger Security International, 2007.

———. *Missionaries of Republicanism: A Religious History of the Mexican-American War*. New York: Oxford University Press, 2014.

Pletcher, David M. *The Diplomacy of Annexation: Texas, Oregon, and the Mexican War*. Columbia: University of Missouri Press, 1973.

Queener, Verton Madison. "The Pre-Civil War Period of the Life of William G. Brownlow." Master's thesis, University of Tennessee, 1930.

Ramsey, Albert C., ed. and trans. *The Other Side; or, Notes for the History of the War between Mexico and the United States*. New York: John Wiley, 1850.

Remini, Robert V. *Andrew Jackson and the Course of American Democracy, 1833–1845*. New York: Harper & Row Publishers, 1984.

Richardson, James D., ed., *A Compilation of the Messages and Papers of the Presidents*. 11 vols. New York: Bureau of National Literature and Art, 1911.

Robertson Jr., James I. *Stonewall Jackson: The Man, the Soldier the Legend*. New York: Macmillan Publishing, 1997.

Robertson, John Blount. *Reminiscences of a Campaign in Mexico by a Member of "The Bloody First."* Nashville, TN: John York and Co., Publishers, 1849.

Rowland, Dunbar, ed., *Jefferson Davis, Constitutionalist, His Letters, Papers and Speeches*. 10 vols. Jackson: Mississippi of Archives and History, 1923.

Rowles, W. P. *Life of William Bethel Allen*. Printed by W. P. Rowles, 1850. Copy in Lawrence County Archives.

Rutland, Robert. "Captain William B. Walton, Mexican War Volunteer."
    *Tennessee Historical Quarterly*, vol. XI, no. 2 (June 1952): 171–79.

Santa Anna, Antonio López. *The Eagle: The Autobiography of Santa Anna.*
    Edited by Ann Fears Crawford. Austin, TX: Pemberton Press, 1967.

Sargent, Chauncey Forward. *Gathering Laurels in Mexico: The Diary of an
    American Soldier in the Mexican American War.* Edited by Ann Brown
    Janes. Lincoln, MA: The Cottage Press, 1990.

Schlesinger Jr., Arthur M. "Rating the Presidents." *Political Science Quarterly*
    112 (Summer 1997): 179–90.

Schlesinger Sr., Arthur M. "Historians Rate the U.S. Presidents." *Life Magazine*
    (November 1, 1948): 65–74.

Schroeder, John H. *Mr. Polk's War: American Opposition and Dissent, 1846–
    1848.* Madison, The University of Wisconsin Press, 1973.

Scott, Winfield, *Memoirs of Lieut.-General Winfield Scott.* Edited by Timothy D.
    Johnson. Knoxville: University of Tennessee Press, 2015.

Sellers, Charles Grier. *James K. Polk, Jacksonian 1795–1843.* Princeton, NJ:
    Princeton University Press, 1957.

Senate Document No. 65, 30th Congress., 1st Session.

Silbey, Joel H. *Storm Over Texas: The Annexation Controversy and the Road to*
    *Civil War.* New York: Oxford University Press, 2005.

Sioussat, St. George L., ed. *Mexican War Letters of Col. William Bowen Campbell
    of Tennessee, Written to Governor David Campbell of Virginia, 1846–1847.*
    Granville, PA: Wert Bookbinding, 1989. First print of pamphlet June 1913
    by Tennessee Historical Magazine.

Smith, George Winston, and Charles Judah. *Chronicles of the Gringos.*
    Albuquerque: University of New Mexico Press, 1968.

Smith, Justin H. *The War with Mexico.* 2 vols. New York: Houghton Mifflin,
    1919.

Smith, Kevin E. Anthropologist at Middle Tennessee State University and
    archaeology site director at Wynnewood State Historic Site, interview,
    June 10, 2017.

———. "Deconstructing and Reconstructing the Death of Robert Bruce
    Wynne (1827–1860). Unpublished paper written for Bledsoe's Lick
    Historical Association, 2016.

Spence, W. Jerome D. and David L. Spence. *A History of Hickman County Tennessee*. Nashville, TN: Gospel Advocate Publishing Co., 1900.

Stokes Jr., Walter. "Christ Church, Nashville." Lecture published in *Seven Early Churches of Nashville*. Nashville, TN: Elder's Book Store, 1972.

Tennery, Thomas D. *The Mexican War Diary of Thomas D. Tennery*. Edited by D. E. Livingston-Little. Norman: University of Oklahoma Press, 1970.

*Tennesseans in the Civil War*. 2 vols. Nashville, TN: Civil War Centennial Commission, 1964.

Tinkham, George H. *A History of Stockton*. San Francisco: W. M. Hinton and Company, 1880.

Tucker, Spencer C. *The Encyclopedia of the Mexican-American War: A Political, Social, and Military History*. 3 vols. Santa Barbara: ABC-CLIO, 2013.

Van Wagenen, Michael Scott. *Remembering the Forgotten War: The Enduring Legacies of the U.S.–Mexican War*. Amherst: University of Massachusetts Press, 2012.

Walton, Brian G. "The Elections for the Thirtieth Congress and the Presidential Candidacy of Zachary Taylor." *Journal of Southern History* 35, no. 2 (May 1969): 186–202.

Warner, Ezra J. *Generals in Blue: Lives of the Union Commanders*. Baton Rouge: Louisiana State University Press, 1964.

———. *Generals in Gray: Lives of the Confederate Commanders*. Baton Rouge: Louisiana State University Press, 1959.

Warner, Ezra J., and W. Buck Yearns. *Biographical Register of the Confederate Congress*. Baton Rouge: Louisiana State University Press, 1975.

Warner, Seth. "George Earl Maney: Soldier, Railroader, and Diplomat." *Tennessee Historical Quarterly* 65 (Summer 2006): 130–47.

West, Carroll Van, ed., *The Tennessee Encyclopedia of History and Culture*. Nashville, TN: Rutledge Hill Press, 1998.

Wilcox, Cadmus M. *History of the Mexican War*. Washington: The Church News Publishing Company, 1892.

Williams, Emma Inman. *Historic Madison: The Story of Jackson and Madison County Tennessee*. Jackson, TN: Jackson Service League, 1972.

Williams, John Hoyt. *Sam Houston: A Biography of the Father of Texas*. New York: Simon & Schuster, 1993.

Winders, Richard Bruce. *Crisis in the Southwest: The United States, Mexico, and the Struggle over Texas*. Wilmington, DE: Scholarly Resources, Inc., 2002.

Winders, Richard Bruce. *Mr. Polk's Army: The American Military Experience in the Mexican War*. College Station: Texas A&M University Press, 1997.

Winders, Richard Bruce. *Panting for Glory: The Mississippi Rifles in the Mexican War*. College Station: Texas A&M University Press, 2016.

Wyatt-Brown, Bertram. *Southern Honor: Ethics and Behavior in the Old South*. New York: Oxford University Press, 1982.

Young, R. A. "William T. Haskell." *Christian Advocate*. April 28, 1859.

# INDEX

Cheatham, Benjamin F., 38, 46, 69, 82, 83–84, 85, 88, 92, 95, 102–3, 134–35, 183, 184–85, 186, 187–88, 205–6, 224, 229

Cheatham, John, 135

Cheatham, Leonard Pope, 187

Childress, George, 11

Churchwell, Daniel, 132

Churchwell, Ephriam, 132

Churubusco, 184, 188, 191, 194, 195–96

Citadel (Black Fort), 74, 77, 78, 79–81, 88

Claiborne, Mollie, 177

Claiborne, Thomas Jr., 64–65, 105, 143, 153–54, 157, 177, 185, 207–8, 223, 225, 274n12

Claiborne, Thomas Sr., 64, 105

Claiborne County, 45

Clay, Henry, 15, 26–27, 28, 37, 176

Clay Guards, 37

Cleveland, Grover, 230

Cliff, Daniel B., 251n13

Cloud, Jason, 264n20

Clymer, John, 61

Coe, Levin H., 51–52

Coffee, B. F., 257n41

Coffee, John, 76

Coffee County, 186

Collins, Henry, 257n41

Commercial Hotel, 53

Compromise of 1850, 211–12

Contreras, 184, 190–91, 194, 195–96

Cook, Morgan B., 35, 42

Cooper, A. G., 44

Cooper, James C., 205

Cooper, Joseph, 220

Cooper, William, 96

Corlew, Robert, 2

Cornersville Rifles, 38

Crittenden, John J., 170

Crockett, David, 8, 11, 16–17

Croghan, George, 89

Cummings, David H., 41, 264n20

Dalton, Brooker H., 257n41

Davidson, Henry B., 208

Davidson County, 17, 38, 39, 40, 41, 105, 144, 204, 212, 230, 257n42

Davis, Jefferson, 70, 79, 83–84, 91, 94–96

Davis, Samuel, 264n20

Dean, Jabez, 22

Dearman, John L., 264n20

Dekalb County, 45, 50, 110, 114, 175, 224

Democrat Party, 9, 10, 13, 15, 17, 18–28, 30–31, 37, 39, 51–52, 96, 103, 105, 106–7, 136, 165–75, 182, 187, 188, 189, 198, 205–6, 211–12, 213, 222, 241n4

Dickson County, 38, 257n41

Dishman, Christopher, 2

Dockry, Aaron, 264n20

Dorris, Joseph, 82, 177

Dorris, William, 82, 177–78

Dover Air Force Base, 237

Duane, William, 15

Duffy, Francis, 92

Duffy, Patrick, 71, 83, 85, 90, 92, 103, 151, 174–75

Duffy, Tom, 93

Duncan, James, 197–98

Dusinberre, William, 241n2

Hackenburg, Randy, 2

Hale, Wiley, 49, 58, 65, 98, 99, 109, 131,
    133, 155, 123, 249n39, 264n20

Hamer, Thomas L., 71

Hamilton County, 42, 49, 262n14, 265n20

Hancock, Winfield Scott, 222

Hardin, Benjamin, 264n20

Harding, John, 227

Harney, William S., 134

Harrison, B. F., 231

Harrison, William Henry, 18, 20, 23, 24

Hart, Henry W., 138, 223, 228, 231, 274n8

Haskell, Caroline, 48–49, 98, 155, 249n39

Haskell, Charles, 48, 109

Haskell, Joshua, 43

Haskell, William T., 8, 41, 43, 48–49,
    65, 98, 99, 109, 113, 130, 134–35,
    159–61, 164–65, 182, 189, 196, 211,
    220, 222, 225, 249n39; and Battle
    of Cerro Gordo, 144–45, 147–52,
    154–56, 265n30; post war career,
    178–79, 213–18

Hassell Zebulon, 40

Hawkins, Isaac, 42–43, 145

Haynes, Milton, 45, 50

Hays, general over West Tennessee
    mobilization, 36

Hays, Harmon, 76

Hays, John Coffee (Jack), 76, 88

Hays, Richard J., 220

Hebb, George V., 205

Heiman, Adolphus, 6, 39, 68, 77, 83, 89

Henderson, James P., 71, 91

Herrera, José Joaquín, 29

Hickman County, 38, 40, 204

Hill, A. P., 196

Hill, Calvin, 114

Hill, Daniel Harvey, 89, 101–2, 151,
    191–92, 198

Hill, Jim, 206

Hill, John A., 257n41

Holt, John S., 254n15

Hooker, Joseph, 195

Horseshoe Bend, Battle of, 8

Hotel de Mexico, 205

Houston, Sam, 8, 11, 21, 22, 23

Hughes, Nathaniel, 152


Isler, John, 264n20


Jackson, Andrew, 5, 6, 7, 9, 10, 11, 12,
    13–21, 24, 25, 27, 28, 30, 31, 38, 47,
    49, 76, 82, 93, 177, 188, 229, 230,
    238–39

Jackson, Thomas J., 136, 207

Jackson Greens, 35

Jalapa, 138–39, 153, 156–57, 174, 184,
    185–86, 188, 202

James, Benjamin, 989

James K. Polk Memorial Association,
    238–39

Jarvis, N. S., 78, 91, 254n14, 256n35

Jefferson, Thomas, 167

Johnson, Andrew, 213

Johnson, Bushrod, 208

Johnson, Cave, 6

Johnson, Charles, 264n20

Johnson, James H., 257n41

Jones, James C., 20, 34

Jones, Lewis L., 264n20